DEFENSE, SECURITY AND STRATEGIES

HOMELAND SECURITY

SELECTED CONGRESSIONAL ISSUES AND APPROPRIATIONS

DEFENSE, SECURITY AND STRATEGIES

Additional books in this series can be found on Nova's website under the Series tab.

Additional e-books in this series can be found on Nova's website under the eBooks tab.

DEFENSE, SECURITY AND STRATEGIES

HOMELAND SECURITY

SELECTED CONGRESSIONAL ISSUES AND APPROPRIATIONS

MALCOLM LEONARD MORENO
EDITOR

nova publishers
New York

Library of Congress Cataloging-in-Publication Data

ISBN: 978-1-63484-754-4

Published by Nova Science Publishers, Inc. † New York

CONTENTS

PREFACE

In 2001, in the wake of the terrorist attacks of September 11th, "homeland security" went from being a concept discussed among a relatively small cadre of policymakers and strategic thinkers to a broadly discussed issue in Congress. Debates over how to implement coordinated homeland security policy led to the passage of the Homeland Security Act of 2002 and the establishment of the Department of Homeland Security (DHS). Evolution of America's response to terrorist threats has continued under the leadership of different Administrations, Congresses, and in a shifting environment of public opinion. This book outlines an array of homeland security issues that may come before the 114th Congress. It provides a brief discussion of the definitions of homeland security, the homeland security budget, and the role of homeland security actors in the intelligence community; discusses the FY2016 appropriations for the DHS and provides an overview of the Administration's FY2016 request; and discusses appropriations for the components of DHS included in the second title of the homeland security appropriations bill.

In: Homeland Security
Editor: Malcolm Leonard Moreno
ISBN: 978-1-63484-754-4

Chapter 1

SELECTED ISSUES IN HOMELAND SECURITY POLICY FOR THE 114TH CONGRESS*

William L. Painter

SUMMARY

In 2001, in the wake of the terrorist attacks of September 11th, "homeland security" went from being a concept discussed among a relatively small cadre of policymakers and strategic thinkers to a broadly discussed issue in Congress. Debates over how to implement coordinated homeland security policy led to the passage of the Homeland Security Act of 2002 (P.L. 107-296) and the establishment of the Department of Homeland Security (DHS). Evolution of America's response to terrorist threats has continued under the leadership of different Administrations, Congresses, and in a shifting environment of public opinion.

DHS is currently the third-largest department in the federal government, although it does not incorporate all of the homeland security functions at the federal level, even if one constrains the definition of homeland security to the narrow field of prevention and response to domestic acts of terrorism. In policymaking terms, homeland security is a very broad and complex network of interrelated issues. In its executive summary the Quadrennial Homeland

* This is an edited, reformatted and augmented version of a Congressional Research Service publication R44041, prepared for Members and Committees of Congress dated May 19, 2015.

Security Review issued in 2014 delineates the missions of the homeland security enterprise as follows: prevent terrorism and enhance security; secure and manage the borders; enforce and administer immigration laws; safeguard and secure cyberspace; and strengthen national preparedness and resilience.

This report outlines an array of homeland security issues that may come before the 114th Congress. After a brief discussion of the definitions of homeland security, the homeland security budget, and the role of homeland security actors in the intelligence community, the report divides the specific issues into four broad categories:

- Counterterrorism and Security Management,
- Border Security and Trade,
- Disaster Preparedness, Response, and Recovery, and
- DHS Management Issues.

Each of those areas contains a survey of topics briefly analyzed by Congressional Research Service experts. The information included only scratches the surface of most of these issues.

WHAT IS HOMELAND SECURITY?

There is no statutory definition of homeland security that reflects the breadth of the enterprise as currently understood. Although there is a federal Department of Homeland Security, it is neither solely dedicated to homeland security missions, nor is it the only part of the federal government with significant responsibilities in this arena.

The Department of Homeland Security (DHS) was established by the Homeland Security Act of 2002 (P.L. 107-296), which was signed into law on November 25, 2002. The new department was assembled from components pulled from 22 different government agencies and began official operations on March 1, 2003. Since then, DHS has undergone a series of restructurings and reorganizations to improve its effectiveness and efficiency.

Although DHS does include many of the homeland security functions of the federal government, several of these functions or parts of these functions remain at their original executive branch agencies and departments, including the Departments of Justice, State, Defense, and Transportation. Not all of the missions of DHS are officially "homeland security" missions. Some components have historical missions that do not directly relate to conventional homeland security definitions, such as the Coast Guard's environmental and boater safety missions, and Congress has in the past debated whether FEMA and its disaster relief and recovery missions belong in the department.

Some criminal justice elements could arguably be included in a broad definition of homeland security. Issues such as the role of the military in law enforcement, monitoring and policing transfers of money, human trafficking, explosives and weapons laws, and aspects of foreign policy, trade, and economics have implications for homeland security policy.

Rather than trying to resolve the question of what is and is not homeland security, this report is a survey of issues that have come up in the context of homeland security policy debates. It is neither exhaustive nor exclusive in its scope, but representative of the broad array of issues likely to be taken up in one way or another by Congress in the coming months. After initial discussion of the definitions of homeland security, the homeland security budget, and the role of homeland security actors in the intelligence community, the report groups the issues into four general themes:

- Counterterrorism and Security Management;
- Border Security and Trade;
- Disaster Preparedness, Response, and Recovery; and
- DHS Management Issues

Homeland Security: Missions and Strategy

Prior to 9/11, the United States addressed threats to our homeland through the separate prisms of national defense, law enforcement, and emergency management. Policy discussions about how the government should confront emerging threats were made more urgent by the 9/11 attacks. Despite the reorganization put in motion after the attacks, including the Homeland Security Act of 2002, and concurrent evolution of homeland security policy, over 30 federal departments, agencies, and entities have homeland security responsibilities and receive annual appropriations to execute homeland security missions.

Under the American structure of government, the executive branch is responsible for the development and execution of homeland security strategy, and Congress is charged with providing oversight and approving funding. It can be argued that the White House has the responsibility of coordinating homeland security activities that cut across the federal government, and encouraging state and local governments and the private sector to be willing and active partners in securing the homeland.

Expression of national homeland security strategy predates DHS, and the documents by the executive branch show an evolution in their view of national homeland security priorities. The first homeland security strategy document issued by President George W. Bush's Administration was the 2003 *National Strategy for Homeland Security*, which was revised in 2007. In 2008, the Department of Homeland Security (DHS) issued the *Strategic Plan—One Team, One Mission, Securing Our Homeland.* The 2007 *National Strategy for Homeland Security* primarily focused on terrorism, whereas the 2008 *Strategic Plan* included references to all-hazards and border security. Arguably, the 2003 and 2007 national strategies for homeland security addressed terrorism in response to such incidents as the 9/11 terrorist attacks and the attempted bombing of American Airlines Flight 93 on December 22, 2001, whereas the 2008 Strategic Plan addressed terrorism and all-hazards in response to natural disasters such as Hurricane Katrina, which occurred in 2005. These documents have been superseded by several other documents which are now considered the principal homeland security strategies, but they represent evolutionary steps in the development of the current policy.

Presentation of Homeland Security Priorities

One way the Administration presents its thinking on homeland security to Congress and the public is through the QHSR process. This involves DHS reviewing its homeland security policy and programs, and then reporting to Congress on the results. Arguably, the review process may inform the development of combined national security and homeland security strategy. The 2014 QHSR endorsed the five mission areas spelled out in the 2010 QHSR, noting that the mission areas needed to be "refined in response to reflect the evolving landscape of homeland security threats and hazards."[1] The five mission areas are:

- Prevent Terrorism and Enhance Security;
- Secure and Manage our Borders;
- Enforce and Administer Our Immigration Laws;
- Safeguard and Secure Cyberspace; and
- Strengthen National Preparedness and Resilience.[2]

Another way of looking at the Administration's thinking on homeland security is through the budget process. OMB's annual budget guidance—

Circular A-11—provides federal departments and agencies with information on how to report to Congress on its homeland security expenditures. OMB states in its 2015 version of Circular A-11 that the six critical mission homeland security areas are identified in the 2004 National Strategy for Homeland Security.

These six critical mission areas are:

- Intelligence and Warning;
- Border and Transportation Security;
- Domestic Counterterrorism;
- Protecting Critical Infrastructure and Key Assets;
- Defending Against Catastrophic Threats; and
- Emergency Preparedness and Response.[3]

Arguably, OMB's continued use of 2004 homeland security strategy mission areas in current guidance alongside the homeland security discussions in the 2014 QHSR and *2015 National Security Strategy* indicates that these original missions still contribute to the Administration's analysis of homeland security matters by defining the terms of the budgetary discussion.

Presentation of the Homeland Security Strategy

The current primary national homeland security strategic document is the *2015 National Security Strategy*, which is similar to the *2010 National Security Strategy* that incorporated homeland security into the nation's national security strategy.[4] The *2015 National Security Strategy* identifies guarding against terrorism as the core responsibility of homeland security. The strategy also identifies improved information sharing, aviation and border security, and international cooperation as homeland security priorities. Community-based efforts and local law enforcement programs are identified as ways to counter homegrown violent extremism and protect vulnerable individuals from extremist ideologies that could lead them to join conflicts overseas or carry out attacks in the United States. Finally, the 2015 strategy states the federal government will work with the owners and operators of the nation's critical cyber and physical infrastructure to decrease vulnerabilities and increase resilience.[5] At the national level, the *2015 National Security Strategy* guides not just DHS's activities, but also all federal government homeland security activities.

Considerations for Congress

As noted above, Congress is responsible for providing oversight of and appropriating funds for homeland security activities. For Congress to exercise effective oversight and ensure efficient usage of taxpayer dollars, clear understanding of priorities for homeland security missions, goals and activities needs to exist between the branches. Policymakers could then use a process based on these defined priorities to ensure existing programs are on track and new developments can be addressed in a more strategic fashion. While the dynamic threat environment may not allow strategic priorities to be set in stone, Congress could encourage the use of a consistent broadly- drawn list of homeland security missions in budget and policy discussions, in order to facilitate strategic decisionmaking.

Even though the conventional wisdom since 9/11 has often identified counterterrorism as the core responsibility of homeland security—a mission that is often interpreted as a federal-level national security function—it can be argued that homeland security, at its core, is about the coordination of disparate stakeholders to confront the full range of risks to the country—not just terrorism.[6]

This is the ultimate challenge of strategic homeland security policymaking: arriving at a consensus on what the current risk portfolio is, how that portfolio is evolving, what the appropriate missions are in response, and how to prioritize them—not just once, but constantly. This consensus isn't just "horizontal"—at the federal level—but "vertical"—reaching down to those with homeland security roles at the state, local, tribal and territorial levels, as well as in the private sector.

Consistency in discussion of homeland security missions and strategy could also facilitate debate about the appropriate role of various federal, state, local and private sector stakeholders in ensuring homeland security. Such discussions are important in ensuring each level understands its role and can invest the proper level of resources to carry it out.

The Budget and Security

According to data from the Office of Management and Budget (OMB), the entire U.S. government spent $564 billion (in nominal dollars) on "homeland security" — defined in law as "those activities that detect, deter, protect against, and respond to terrorist attacks occurring within the United States and its territories" — in the 10 years after the 9/11 attacks. Such spending peaked in FY2009 at $73.8 billion. The total budget for homeland security activities for FY2014, the last year for which there is complete data, was $66.2 billion, a reduction of $7.6 billion from its high-water mark in nominal terms.[7]

By comparison, the budget for the Department of Homeland Security has grown from $31.2 billion in FY2003, when it did not have its own appropriations bill, to $59.9 billion in FY2014, the last year for which we have complete budget data. Roughly $35.8 billion of that amount, or 58.6%, was considered "homeland security" spending by OMB's accounting under the above definition. Some argue that the definition in law is too focused on explicit and directly attributable counterterrorism activities compared to broader theories that have been part of the national discussion, which consider immigration and border control or disaster response as a part of homeland security.

DHS Appropriations

The Administration requested $38.3 billion in adjusted net discretionary budget authority for DHS for FY2015, plus over $6.4 billion to pay for the costs of major disasters under the Stafford Act. In the 113th Congress, the House Appropriations Committee reported legislation (H.R. 4903) that would have provided $39.2 billion in adjusted net discretionary budget authority, plus the requested disaster relief, and the Senate Appropriations Committee reported legislation (S. 2534) that would have provided $39.0 billion, plus the requested disaster relief and $0.2 billion in overseas contingency operations funding for the Coast Guard.[8] Neither bill received floor consideration in the 113th Congress, and annual appropriations for DHS were not included in P.L. 113-235, the Consolidated and Further Continuing Appropriations Act, 2015. As no DHS annual appropriation was enacted, DHS continued to operate under a continuing resolution, which was extended by P.L. 113-235 through February 27, 2015.

With the beginning of the 114th Congress, both House- and Senate-reported FY2015 annual homeland security appropriations bills were no longer available for action. H.R. 240, a new FY2015 annual homeland security appropriations bill, was introduced on January 9, 2015, and considered in the House the following week under a structured rule that allowed five immigration policy-related amendments. After adopting these five amendments, the bill passed the House on January 14, 2015. On February 27, the Senate passed an amended H.R. 240 without the legislative text added by the House amendments.

After the House did not pass a three-week extension of the continuing resolution, the Senate and House passed a one week extension of the continuing resolution to avoid a lapse in annual appropriations for DHS. On March 3, 2015, the House voted to approve the Senate version of H.R. 240. The bill was signed into law on March 4, 2015, as P.L. 114-4. As enacted, the bill provided $39.7 billion in adjusted net discretionary budget authority, plus the requested disaster relief, and $0.2 billion in overseas contingency operations funding for the Coast Guard.

For FY2016, the Administration has requested $41.2 billion in adjusted net discretionary budget authority for DHS, plus $6.7 billion to pay for the costs of major disasters under the Stafford Act, as part of an overall budget of almost $64.9 billion.

The current budget environment will likely present challenges to homeland security programs and the department going forward, as the demands of the mission, ongoing capital investment efforts and staffing needs will compete with the budget demands of the rest of the government for limited funds. The potential impact of the changed budget environment is discussed at various points throughout this report.

Homeland Security and the U.S. Intelligence Community

While many think of homeland security only in terms of DHS, it is a primary mission of the entire Intelligence Community (IC). In the years since 9/11, the "wall" between foreign and domestic intelligence has fallen and many efforts have been initiated to better integrate the capabilities residing in intelligence and law enforcement organizations.[9] "National intelligence" has come to mean "all intelligence," not just foreign intelligence.[10]

The many barriers between foreign and domestic intelligence that existed prior to 9/11 were intended to prevent government spying on U.S. persons and focused the IC on foreign intelligence. The tragedy of the 9/11 attacks overcame earlier concerns and led Congress and the executive branch to enact legislation, policies and regulations designed to enhance information- sharing across the U.S. government.

The Homeland Security Act (P.L. 107-296) gave the DHS responsibility for fusing together law enforcement and intelligence information relating to terrorist threats to the homeland. Provisions in the Intelligence Reform and Terrorist Prevention Act (IRTPA) of 2004 (P.L. 108-458) established the National Counterterrorism Center (NCTC) as the coordinator at the federal level for terrorism information and assessment and created the position of Director of National Intelligence (DNI) to provide strategic management across the IC. New legal authorities accompanied these organizational changes.[11] At the state and local level, initiatives to improve collaboration across the federal system, such as the FBI-led Joint Terrorism Task Forces (JTTFs), have expanded—the number of JTTFs across the country grew from 34 to over 100 between 2001 and 2015—and new ones, such as DHS's National Network of Fusion Centers (NNFC), have been put in place.[12]

The "community" of U.S. government entities that perform some kind of intelligence-related activity has gradually evolved into 17 organizations/ agencies that span six separate government departments and one independent agency (the CIA). Two intelligence elements of DHS and one element of the FBI are most closely associated with homeland security.[13]

- DHS's missions include "preventing terrorism and enhancing security; securing and managing our borders; enforcing and administering our immigration laws; strengthening cyberspace and critical infrastructure; and strengthening national preparedness and resilience to disasters."[14] DHS's Intelligence and Analysis (I&A) section provides intelligence support across the full range of DHS missions. It serves as the DHS focal point for all policy issues and activities involving the entire IC. It is the federal government lead for information and intelligence sharing "with state, local, tribal and territorial governments and the private sector."[15] Much of the information sharing is done through the NNFC— with I&A providing personnel, systems and training.[16]
- The U.S. Coast Guard, made part of DHS in 2002, has intelligence elements that deal with information relating to maritime security and homeland defense. The USCG's responsibilities include protecting citizens from the sea (maritime safety), protecting America from threats delivered by the sea (maritime security), and protecting the sea itself (maritime stewardship). Its diverse mission sets and broad legal authorities allow it to fill a unique niche within the IC.[17]
- The FBI's National Security Branch (NSB) serves as the focal point in the department for all policy issues and activities involving the IC. The key intelligence functions of the FBI relate to counterterrorism and counter- intelligence. Law enforcement information is expected to be shared with other intelligence agencies for use in all-source

products. Robert Mueller, then- Director of the FBI when he testified in 2011, stated:

> Protecting the United States against terrorism demanded a new framework for the way the FBI carries out its mission: a threat-based, intelligence-led approach. Rather than collecting information to solve a particular case, the new approach prioritizes the collection and utilization of intelligence to develop a comprehensive threat picture, enabling strategic disruptions of terrorist networks before they act. This focus on the overall threat picture also elevates the need for information sharing, thereby changing the FBI's role in and relationships with both the intelligence and law enforcement communities. Under this new model, intelligence drives how we understand threats, how we prioritize and investigate these threats, and how we target our resources to address these threats.[18]

Selected IC Issues with Homeland Security Implications

Domestic Surveillance

Domestic surveillance issues will likely be a concern for the 114th Congress principally because three amendments to the Foreign Intelligence Surveillance Act (FISA) of 1978 (P.L. 95-511)[19] will expire on June 1, 2015, unless Congress votes to extend them.[20]

FISA provides a statutory framework regulating when government agencies may gather foreign intelligence through electronic surveillance or physical searches, capture the numbers dialed on a telephone line (pen registers) and identify the originating number of a call on a particular phone line (with trap and trace devices), or access specified business records and other tangible things. Authorization for such activities is typically obtained via a court order from the Foreign Intelligence Surveillance Court (FISC), a specialized court created to act as a neutral judicial decisionmaker in the context of FISA.

Shortly after the 9/11 terrorist attacks, Congress amended FISA to enable the government to obtain information in a greater number of circumstances.[21] Three temporary amendments to FISA are known as the "roving" wiretap provision, the "Section 215" provision, and the "lone wolf" provision. The first two of these provisions were part of the USA PATRIOT Act of 2001[22] and the third was passed as part of the IRTPA of 2004.[23] Distinctions between the three temporary amendments include:

- Multipoint, or "roving" wiretaps allow wiretaps to follow an individual even when he or she changes the means of communication (i.e., wiretaps which may follow a target even when he or she changes phones). If it is allowed to expire, FISA provisions require a separate FISA Court authorization to tap each device a target uses.[24]
- "Section 215" broadens the types of records and "other tangible things" that can be made accessible to the government under FISA. If it is allowed to expire, FISA provisions will read as they did prior to passage of the USA PATRIOT Act, and accessible business records will be limited to "common carrier, public accommodation facility, physical storage facility, or vehicle rental facility."[25]
- The "lone wolf" provision allows the government to monitor individuals acting alone and potentially engaged in international terrorism, providing that they are not citizens or permanent residents of the United States. If it is allowed to expire, there is no provision for individuals acting alone.[26]

An extension of these authorities would need to be enacted prior to June 1, 2015, in order for them to be maintained. Otherwise, the amended FISA authorities will revert to the text as it appeared before the enactment of the USA PATRIOT Act and IRTPA. However, foreign intelligence investigations that began prior to the sunset date may continue to use these authorities beyond their expiration.

The National Security Agency (NSA) has been collecting bulk telephone data as "tangible things" since 2001, and doing so using Section 215 authorities as a legal basis for that activity since 2006.[27] As Congress considers extending Section 215, the U.S. Court of Appeals for the Second Circuit recently ruled that Section 215 does not authorize the "bulk collection" of phone records on the scale of the NSA program "[b]ecause we find that the program exceeds the scope of what Congress has authorized."[28] The court ruling appears to suggest that the bulk data collection program needs a separate authorization either within Section 215, or in addition to Section 215.

At this time, three bills have been introduced in the 114th Congress to extend all three provisions. The House and Senate versions (H.R. 2048, S. 1123), popularly known as the "USA FREEDOM Act of 2015,"[29] would not only extend the three amendments until December 15, 2019, but would also propose a number of FISA reforms.[30] A separate Senate bill (S. 1035) extends the three amendments until December 31, 2020. S. 1035 is being called a "clean bill" because it contains no new provisions.[31]

Information-Sharing and Collaboration

The "wall" between domestic and foreign intelligence has come down metaphorically, but barriers to information-sharing and collaboration[32] continue between the IC and law enforcement entities,[33] between IC entities in the various levels of government—federal, state, local, tribal, territorial—and between the public and private sector. DHS has efforts underway to overcome those barriers. For example, in order to meet the DHS's public-private cybersecurity data sharing and analytical collaboration mission, DHS has developed a Critical Infrastructure Information Sharing and Collaboration Program (CISCP) that shares threat, incident and vulnerability information between government and industry across critical infrastructure sectors such as the chemical, energy, dams, and financial services sectors.[34]

Congress may choose to explore how the DHS is measuring progress in efforts such as CISCP, and, based on those metrics, where DHS and the IC as a whole are in terms of information- sharing and collaboration on homeland security-related issues such as cybersecurity, border security, transportation security, disaster response, drug interdiction, critical infrastructure protection, and homegrown violent extremism. As Congress reviews cases of collaboration between multiple agencies, it may examine if it is clear which agency has the lead, and whether any single organization is accountable if a collaborative arrangement fails. Congress may also choose to pass legislation designed to encourage information-sharing and collaboration in specific fields, such as cybersecurity.[35]

Counterterrorism and Security Management

The Transnational Trend of Terrorism

Terrorism remains a transnational threat that entails risks to U.S. global interests emanating from and manifesting in both the international and domestic environment. Central to U.S. efforts to address transnational terrorism are actions taken to detect, deter, and defeat Al Qaeda and the Islamic State. While recognizing that numerous other terrorist groups may wish to harm U.S. global security interests, the Administration primarily focuses on addressing threats from Al Qaeda, its affiliated organizations, and adherents to its violence-based philosophy and the Islamic State. Understanding how Al Qaeda and the Islamic State continue to evolve into global entities with a diverse set of actors and capabilities is central to formulating sound strategic policy and overseeing its effective implementation.

Al Qaeda

The past few years have witnessed an increase in terrorist actions by entities claiming some affiliation with or philosophical connection to Al Qaeda. Many of the past year's global terrorist attacks were conducted by individuals or small terrorist cells that received support ranging from resources and training to having minimal connections, if any, with the terrorist groups to which they claim allegiance. Some argue that recent U.S. counterterrorism successes may be reducing the level of terrorist threats to the nation emanating from core Al Qaeda. U.S. officials suggest that the killing of Osama bin Laden in May 2011 coupled with continuous post-9/11 global military and intelligence counterterrorism actions have significantly degraded Al Qaeda's ability to successfully launch a catastrophic terrorist attack against U.S. global interests. Others suggest that Al Qaeda has changed from an organization to a philosophical movement, making it more difficult to detect and defeat. These security experts suggest that Al Qaeda and associated affiliates will remain viable, due in part to the prospective security implications related to the nation's budgetary situation. Counterterrorism analyst Daveed Gartenstein-Ross argues that "The U.S. will not be (defeated) by Al Qaeda. But one can see that as the national debt increases, we (will) have to make spending cuts and as Al Qaeda gets stronger in multiple countries simultaneously—Somalia, Yemen, Pakistan, maybe Mali—suddenly you're looking at multiple theaters from where catastrophic strikes can be launched."[36]

The Islamic State[37]

The Islamic State (IS, also known as the Islamic State of Iraq and the Levant, ISIL, or ISIS) is a transnational Sunni Islamist insurgent and terrorist group that has expanded its control over areas of parts of Iraq and Syria since 2013. There is debate over the degree to which the Islamic State organization might represent a direct terrorist threat to U.S. facilities and personnel in the region or to the U.S. homeland. The forerunners of the Islamic State were part of the insurgency against coalition forces in Iraq, and the organization has in the years since the 2011 U.S. withdrawal from Iraq expanded its control over significant areas of both Iraq and Syria. The Islamic State has thrived in the disaffected Sunni tribal areas of Iraq and taken control of some eastern provinces of Syria affected by the civil war. In 2014, Islamic State-led forces, supported by groups linked to ousted Iraqi President Saddam Hussein and some Sunni Arabs, advanced along the Tigris and Euphrates rivers in Iraq, taking population centers including Mosul, one of Iraq's largest cities. Since then, IS forces have killed Syrian and Iraqi adversaries, including some civilians, often from ethnic or religious minorities, and killed hostages, including U.S. citizens. Islamic State attempts to make further gains continue. The group's tactics have drawn international ire, and raised U.S. attention to Iraq's political problems and to the war in Syria.

Considerations

The balance between ensuring effective counterterrorism policies and being mindful of the current budget environment is not lost on senior Administration officials. In recent years John Brennan, in his former capacity as the Assistant to the President for Homeland Security, now the Director of the Central Intelligence Agency, has spoken of Osama bin Laden's often stated objective of pursuing global acts of terrorism against the nation's interests with the desire to "bleed [the U.S.] financially by drawing us into long, costly wars that also inflame anti-American sentiment."[38]

The terrorist threat to U.S. global interests will likely remain an important issue for the Administration and the 114th Congress. Over the past few years numerous individuals were arrested in the homeland and abroad for conducting attacks and planning terrorism-related activities directed at U.S. national security interests. All of the attacks—successful and unsuccessful—were of a transnational dimension and ranged from a lone shooter who appears to have become radicalized over the Internet to terrorist organizations wishing to use airliners as platforms for destruction to individuals attempting to detonate large quantities of explosives in symbolic areas frequented by large groups of people.

The 113th Congress undertook efforts, largely through hearings, to better understand the nature of terrorism in various geographic regions and assess the effectiveness of U.S. and partnering nations' counterterrorism efforts. Programs and policies that Congress has reviewed include public diplomacy efforts; imposition of sanctions; terrorism financing rules; the nexus between international crime, narcotics, and terrorism; and the relationship between domestic and international terrorism activities. The 114th Congress may continue to assess the Obama Administration's counterterrorism-related strategies, policies, and programs to ascertain if additional guidance or legislation is required. These assessments will likely entail considerations of how best to balance perceived risks to U.S. global security interests with concerns about the long-term fiscal challenges facing the nation.

The Homegrown Violent Jihadist Threat: Four Key Themes

Homegrown violent jihadist[39] activity since 9/11 defies easy categorization. CRS analysis of homegrown violent jihadist plots and attacks since 9/11 suggests four broad themes:

- **Various Endgames for Plans:** Plots have involved individuals interested in a variety of ways to harm U.S. interests. Some individuals focused on becoming foreign fighters in conflict zones, such as Somalia. Others planned attacks using explosives, incendiary devices, or firearms. Yet others incorporated multiple, unspecific, or unique tactics. Finally, outside of the post-9/11 violent plots, additional individuals intended only to fund or materially support jihadist activities.
- **Little Interest in Martyrdom:** Only a minority of homegrown jihadists clearly exhibited interest in killing themselves while engaged in violent jihad.
- **Success of Lone Wolves:** Individuals acting alone, so-called "lone wolves," conducted all four successful homegrown attacks since 9/11.
- **Divergent Capabilities:** The operational capabilities of participants diverge greatly. Some evinced terrorist tradecraft such as bomb-making skills. Others appeared to be far less experienced.

Congress may wish to keep these four themes in mind as it considers responses to the threat of homegrown terrorism as opposed to foreign plots.

One aspect of the overall threat picture is the potential threat posed by "foreign fighters" from the United States and elsewhere involved in the Syrian civil war.[40] These foreign fighters join terrorist groups such as the Islamic State (IS, also known as ISIS or ISIL). According to Nicholas J. Rasmussen, the Director of the National Counterterrorism Center (NCTC), more than 20,000 foreign fighters from approximately 90 nations have traveled to Syria. Most are from the Middle East and North Africa, with about 3,400 westerners who have joined the influx.[41]

U.S. intelligence officials have pointed out that not all individuals traveling to Syria take on the role of a "foreign fighter." According to James Clapper, the Director of National Intelligence, 180 people from the United States have gone to Syria. Not all have joined the Islamic State, and about 40 have returned.[42]

The federal government's terrorist watchlisting process plays a key role in tracking people suspected of having ties to the Islamic State.[43] When federal law enforcement or intelligence agencies identify someone known or reasonably suspected of terrorism, they are required to share that information to help create a federal consolidated watchlist of known or suspected terrorists. The watchlist supports "the ability of front line screening agencies to positively identify known or suspected terrorists trying to obtain visas, enter the country, board aircraft, or engage in other activity.... "[44]

Preempting and Monitoring Potential Terrorists

Preemption and monitoring of possible IS terrorist activity by U.S. law enforcement can be broadly described in terms of interdiction, investigation, and countering violent extremism in the United States.

Interdiction involves—among other things—stopping a suspected terrorist from entering the United States. For example, within DHS, components such as Customs and Border Protection draw on information from the federal government's consolidated terrorist watchlist as they engage in intelligence-driven screening to mitigate the risk posed by certain travelers destined for the United States.[45] DHS Secretary Jeh C. Johnson has broadly alluded to U.S. coordination with allies on foreign fighters. In an August 29, 2014, press release, he noted:

> This government, in close collaboration with our international partners, has ... taken a series of steps to track foreign fighters who travel in and out of Syria, and we are contemplating additional security measures concerning foreign fighters. Some of the security measures will be visible to the public and some understandably will be unseen.[46]

Johnson has also mentioned enhanced screening at select overseas airports.[47] One of the known efforts targeting foreign fighters pursued by DHS involves enhancements to the Electronic System for Travel Authorization (ESTA) used by Customs and Border Protection to vet prospective travelers from visa waiver countries "to determine if they pose a law enforcement or security risk before they board aircraft destined for the United States."[48]

Investigation largely focuses on Joint Terrorism Task Forces (JTTFs) led by the Federal Bureau of Investigation (FBI) and supported by local, state, and federal agencies—including DHS.[49] The task forces fill the chief role in coordinating federal counterterrorism cases across the United States, bringing together federal, state, and local participants in the process. JTTFs have been involved in stopping individuals trying to leave the United States to fight with the Islamic State as well as investigating people who have returned from the conflict zone. Beyond U.S. borders, the FBI has legal attachés around the world that coordinate with foreign law enforcement partners to fight terrorist activity. Additionally, the Department of Justice (DOJ) has worked to expand its presence in countries that serve as transit points for foreign fighters.[50]

Countering violent extremism (CVE) involves the intricacies of radicalization. It focuses on determining when individuals are in danger of shifting from radical activity involving First Amendment-protected behavior to violent extremism.[51] In part, CVE programs endeavor to prevent this shift without relying on traditional policing techniques such as investigation and prosecution. U.S. CVE programs can help keep people from traveling abroad to join terrorist groups. Additionally, such efforts provide law enforcement with vital links to U.S. communities that may provide tips regarding people who have returned from fighting in Syria and Iraq. Much of the federal work in this area includes outreach to local communities. Regarding the Islamic State, the FBI, DHS, and NCTC are striving to understand the motivations driving people to radicalize and join the group.[52] Also, DHS and NCTC provide information to U.S. community groups about the recruitment efforts of violent extremist groups including those based in Syria and Iraq.[53] Finally, largely in response to the Islamic State, the federal government is pursuing a program "in cities across the country to bring together community representatives, public safety officials and religious leaders to counter violent extremism."[54] DOJ, DHS, and NCTC have chosen Boston, MA; Los Angeles, CA; and Minneapolis-St. Paul, MN, as pilot cities for the program.[55]

Cybersecurity

Cyber threats to the United States are a current and growing concern to policymakers. Technology is ubiquitous and relied upon in almost every facet of modern life, such as supporting government services, corporate business processes, and individual professional and personal pursuits. Many of these technologies are interdependent and the disruption to one piece of equipment may have a negative cascading effect on other devices. A denial of service, theft or manipulation of data, or damage to critical infrastructure through a cyber-based attack could have significant impacts on national security, the economy, and the livelihood of individual citizens. These concerns raise many questions for Congress, among them,

- Who are the aggressors in cyberspace and what are their intentions and capabilities?
- What are the impacts and implications of cyberattacks?
- What legislative and policy actions have the executive branch and Congress taken to respond to threats from cyberspace? What further steps should be taken?

Cyber Threats

Cyber-based technologies[56] are now ubiquitous around the globe. The vast majority of their users pursue lawful professional and personal objectives. However, criminals, terrorists, and spies also rely heavily on cyber-based technologies to support organizational objectives. These malefactors may access cyber-based technologies in order to deny service, steal or manipulate data, or use a device to launch an attack. Entities using cyber-based technologies for illegal purposes take many forms and pursue a variety of actions counter to U.S. global security and economic interests.

The threats posed by these cyber-aggressors and the examples of types of attacks they can pursue are not mutually exclusive. For example, a hacker targeting the intellectual property of a corporation may be categorized as both a cyberthief and a cyberspy. A cyberterrorist and cyberwarrior may be employing different technological capabilities in support of a nation's security and political objectives. Commonly recognized cyber-aggressors and representative examples of the harm they can inflict include the following:

Cyberterrorists are state-sponsored and non-state actors who engage in cyberattacks as a form of terrorism. Transnational terrorist organizations, insurgents, and jihadists have used the Internet as a tool for planning attacks, radicalization and recruitment, a method of propaganda distribution, and a means of communication.[57] While no unclassified reports have been published regarding a cyberattack on a critical component of the nation's infrastructure, the vulnerability of critical life- sustaining control systems being accessed and destroyed via the Internet has been demonstrated. In 2009, the Department of Homeland Security (DHS) conducted an experiment that revealed some of the vulnerabilities to the nation's control systems that manage power generators and grids. The experiment, known as the Aurora Project, entailed a computer-based attack on a power generator's control system that caused operations to cease and the equipment to be destroyed.[58]

Cyberspies are individuals who steal classified or proprietary information used by governments or private corporations to gain a competitive strategic, security, financial, or political advantage. These individuals often work at the behest of, and take direction from, foreign government entities. For example, a 2011 FBI report noted, "a company was the victim of an intrusion and had lost 10 years' worth of research and development data—valued at $1 billion—virtually overnight."[59] Likewise, in 2008 the Department of Defense's (DOD's) classified computer network system was unlawfully accessed and "the computer code, placed there by a foreign intelligence agency, uploaded itself undetected onto both classified and unclassified systems from which data could be transferred to servers under foreign control."[60] 2013 was the last time the intelligence community reportedly produced a classified National Intelligence Estimate (NIE) focused on cyberspying against U.S. targets from abroad. The NIE reportedly addressed activities relating to the "Chinese government's broad policy of encouraging theft of intellectual property through cyberattacks."[61] Around the time the classified report was due to be issued then-DOD Secretary Leon Panetta stated, "it's no secret that Russia and China have advanced cyber capabilities."[62]

Cyberthieves are individuals who engage in illegal cyberattacks for monetary gain.[63] Examples include an organization or individual who illegally accesses a technology system to steal and use or sell credit card numbers and someone who deceives a victim into providing access to a financial account. One estimate has placed the annual cost of cybercrime to individuals in 24 countries at $388 billion.[64] However, given the complex and sometimes ambiguous nature of the costs associated with cybercrime, and the reluctance in many cases of victims to admit to being attacked, there does not appear to be any publicly available, comprehensive, reliable assessment of the overall costs of cyberattacks.

Cyberwarriors are agents or quasi-agents of nation-states who develop capabilities and undertake cyberattacks in support of a country's strategic objectives.[65] These entities may or may not be acting on behalf of the government with respect to target selection, timing of the attack, and type(s) of cyberattack and are often blamed by the host country when accusations are levied by the nation that has been attacked. Often, when a foreign government is provided evidence that a cyberattack is emanating from its country, the nation that has been attacked is informed that the perpetrators acted of their own volition and not at the behest of the government. In August 2012 a series of cyberattacks were directed against Saudi Aramco, the world's largest oil and gas producer and most valuable company, according to the *New York Times*. The attacks compromised 30,000 of the company's computers and the code was apparently designed to disrupt or halt the production of oil. Some security officials have suggested that Iran may have supported this attack. However, numerous cyberwarrior groups, some with linkages to nations with objectives counter to those of Saudi Arabia, have claimed credit for this incident.[66]

Cyberactivists are individuals who perform cyberattacks for pleasure, philosophical, or other nonmonetary reasons. Examples include someone who attacks a technology system as a personal challenge (who might be termed a "classic" hacker), and a "hacktivist" such as a member of a group who undertakes an attack for political reasons. The activities of these groups can range from simple nuisance-related denial of service attacks to disrupting government and private corporation business processes.

Ascertaining information about the aggressor and their capabilities and intentions is very difficult.[67] The threats posed by these aggressors coupled with the United States' proclivity to be an early adopter of emerging technologies,[68] which are often interdependent and contain vulnerabilities, make for a complex environment when considering operational responses, policies, and legislation designed to safeguard the nation's strategic economic and security interests.

Legislative Branch Efforts to Address Cyber Threats69

More than 50 federal statutes address various aspects of cybersecurity either directly or indirectly, but there is no overarching cybersecurity framework legislation in place.

Since the 111th Congress, many bills have been introduced that would address specific cybersecurity issues. The main topics addressed by the bills include:

- **Information Sharing**—easing access of the private sector to classified threat information and removing barriers to sharing within the private sector and with the federal government. *Issues:* Roles of DHS and the Intelligence Community (IC), impacts on privacy and civil liberties, and risks of misuse by the federal government or the private sector.
- **Federal Information Security Management Act (FISMA) Reform**—updating the 2002 law to reflect changes in information and

communications technology and the threat landscape. *Issues:* Role of DHS, OMB, and Commerce, and flexibility of requirements.

- **Research and Development (R&D)**—updating agency authorizations and strategic planning requirements. *Issues:* Agency roles, topics for R&D, and levels of funding.
- **Workforce**—improving the size, skills, and preparation of the federal and private-sector cybersecurity workforce. *Issues:* Hiring and retention authorities, occupational classification, recruitment priorities, and roles of DHS, NSA, the National Science Foundation (NSF), and NIST.
- **Privately Held Communications Infrastructure (CI)**—improving protection of private-sector CI from attacks with major impacts. *Issues:* Roles of DHS and other federal agencies, and regulatory vs. voluntary approach.
- **Data-Breach Notification**—requiring notification to victims and other responses after data breaches involving personal or financial information of individuals. *Issues:* Federal vs. state roles and what responses should be required.
- **Cybercrime Laws**—updating criminal statutes and law-enforcement authorities relating to cybersecurity. *Issues:* Adequacy of current penalties and authorities, impacts on privacy and civil liberties.

Although comprehensive cybersecurity legislation was not enacted by the 113th Congress, five bills that contained cybersecurity provisions were passed and signed into law in December, 2014:

- **Federal Information Security Modernization Act of 2014** (S. 2521; P.L. 113- 283)—amended FISMA to clarify the cybersecurity authorities for the Office of Management and Budget and DHS.
- **Cybersecurity Workforce Assessment Act** (H.R. 2952; P.L. 113-324)— provided for an annual review of the DHS cybersecurity workforce and required the development of a DHS cybersecurity workforce strategy.
- Sections 3 and 4 of the **Border Agency Pay Reform Act of 2014** (S. 1691; P.L. 113-277)—mandated an assessment of the DHS cybersecurity workforce and authorized special recruitment and retention measures for cybersecurity personnel.

- **National Cybersecurity Protection Act of 2014** (S. 2519; P.L. 113-240)— authorized establishment of a national cybersecurity and communications integration center within DHS;
- **Cybersecurity Enhancement Act of 2014** (S. 1353, P.L. 113-274)— addressed a broad range of themes, including NSF and NIST activities in cybersecurity research and development, standards, workforce development, the NIST Framework, and cybersecurity awareness and education programs.

Many observers believe that enactment of comprehensive cybersecurity legislation will be attempted again in the 114th Congress.

Executive Branch Actions to Address Cyber Threats[70]

In 2008, the George W. Bush Administration established the Comprehensive National Cybersecurity Initiative (CNCI) through National Security Presidential Directive 54/Homeland Security Presidential Directive 23 (NSPD-54/HSPD-23). Those documents are classified, but the Obama Administration released a description of them in March 2010.[71] Goals of the 12 initiatives in that description include consolidating external access points to federal systems; deploying intrusion detection and prevention systems across those systems; improving research coordination and prioritization and developing "next-generation" technology, information sharing, and cybersecurity education and awareness; mitigating risks from the global supply chain for information technology; and clarifying the federal role in protecting critical infrastructure.

In December 2009, the Obama Administration created the position of White House Cybersecurity Coordinator. The responsibilities for this position include government-wide coordination of cybersecurity-related issues, including overseeing the implementation of the CNCI. The Coordinator works with both the National Security and Economic Councils in the White House. However, the Coordinator does not have direct control over agency budgets, and some observers argue that operational entities such as the DOD's National Security Agency (NSA) have far greater influence over federal cybersecurity issues.[72] Reportedly, in October 2012 President Obama signed a classified Presidential Decision Directive that "enables the military to act more aggressively to thwart cyberattacks on the Nation's web of government and private computer networks."[73]

The complex federal role in cybersecurity involves securing federal systems, assisting in protecting nonfederal systems, and pursuing military, intelligence, and law enforcement community detection, surveillance, defensive, and offensive initiatives. Under current law, all federal agencies have cybersecurity responsibilities relating to their own systems and dozens of agencies have government-wide aggressor, issue, and critical infrastructure sector-specific responsibilities and legislative authorities. The cybersecurity roles and responsibilities of these agencies are often complementary but at times are overlapping or competing. In the absence of enactment of overarching cybersecurity legislation, during the past two years the White House has issued a number of executive orders and presidential directives addressing intelligence issues, critical infrastructure protection, and safeguarding of classified materials.[74]

Continuity of Government Operations

Continuity of government operations refers to programs and initiatives to ensure that governing entities are able to recover from a wide range of potential operational interruptions. Government continuity planning may be viewed as a process that incorporates preparedness capacities, including agency response plans, employee training, recovery plans, and the resumption of normal operations. These activities are established in part to ensure the maintenance of civil authority, provision of support for those affected by an incident, infrastructure repair, and other actions in support of recovery. Arguably, any emergency response presumes the existence of an ongoing, functional government to fund, support, and oversee recovery efforts. Interruptions for which contingency plans might be activated include localized acts of nature, accidents, technological emergencies, and military or terrorist attack-related incidents.

Current authority for executive branch continuity programs is provided in the 2007 National Security Presidential Directive (NSPD) on National Continuity Policy, NSPD-51.[75] To support the provision of essential government activities, NSPD-51 sets out a policy "to maintain a comprehensive and effective continuity capability composed of continuity of operations[76] and continuity of government[77] programs in order to ensure the preservation of our form of government[78] under the Constitution and the continuing performance of national essential functions (NEF) under all conditions."

Executive Order (E.O.) 12656, Assignment of Emergency Preparedness Responsibilities, was issued in 1988,[79] and assigns national security emergency preparedness responsibilities to federal executive departments and agencies. E.O. 12656 requires the head of each federal department and agency to "ensure the continuity of essential functions in any national security emergency by providing for: succession to office and emergency delegation of authority in accordance with applicable law; safekeeping of essential resources, facilities, and records; and establishment of emergency operating capabilities." Subsequent sections require each department to carry out specific contingency planning activities in its areas of policy responsibility.

Although contingency planning authorities are chiefly based on presidential directives, Congress could consider whether current authorities accurately reflect current government organization and goals, the costs of these programs, potential conflicts that might result from departments and agencies complying with different authorities, and the extent to which government contingency planning ensures that the federal executive branch will be able to carry out its responsibilities under challenging circumstances.

Medical Countermeasures to Chemical, Biological, Radiological, and Nuclear Terrorism

The 2014 Ebola outbreak highlighted the lack of available medical countermeasures against many of the highest risk chemical, biological, radiological, and nuclear (CBRN) threats. Following the 2001 anthrax attacks, the federal government created several programs to develop, procure, and distribute CBRN medical countermeasures. Despite these efforts, many of the CBRN threats that the government deems likely to pose the highest risk lack available countermeasures, and some experts question the government's ability to distribute countermeasures quickly. The 114th Congress may consider the effectiveness of federal efforts and whether current programs should be continued, modified, or ended.

Federal efforts to support the research, development, and procurement of CBRN medical countermeasures include components from the Departments of Defense, Homeland Security, and Health and Human Services (HHS). In light of the current fiscal environment and demonstrated gaps in available countermeasures, Congress may increase its scrutiny of the planning, coordination, and accountability of this complicated multiagency enterprise. Policymakers may be aided in their evaluation of these programs by the first iterations of the annual countermeasure strategy and implementation plan and coordinated multiyear budget mandated by the Pandemic and All-Hazards Preparedness Reauthorization Act of 2013 (P.L. 113-5).

To help HHS procure new medical countermeasures, Congress passed the Project BioShield Act (P.L. 108-276) in 2004. Through Project BioShield, HHS can encourage the private sector to develop CBRN medical countermeasures by creating a guaranteed federal market. Project BioShield allows the government to agree to buy a countermeasure up to 10 years before the product is likely to finish development. The federal government used this program to acquire medical countermeasures against anthrax, smallpox, botulinum toxin, some nerve agents, and some radiological and nuclear threats. However, many threats, including Ebola, continue to lack effective medical countermeasures. Congress funded Project BioShield through a $5.6 billion advance appropriation for FY2004-FY2013. Since FY2014, Congress has provided annual appropriations for this program. Some countermeasure developers assert that another multiyear advance appropriation would increase their ability to develop countermeasures.[80] The 114th Congress may consider whether modifying the funding amount or providing an advance appropriation would improve the program's efficiency or performance.

Distribution of existing medical countermeasures during a CBRN emergency remains a challenge for the federal government and its partners. The federal government maintains programs, including the Centers for Disease Control and Prevention's Strategic National Stockpile, that stockpile and distribute stores of medical countermeasures. Some experts question the sufficiency of these federal programs, and whether state governments have the capacity to receive and effectively disseminate federal stockpiles.[81] Congress may continue evaluating the effectiveness of federal programs and may consider additional stockpiling and distribution methods. Such methods may include stockpiling countermeasures in homes or businesses or using the U.S. Postal Service to distribute countermeasures. These proposals may raise concerns regarding program costs, unintended use of countermeasures, and local implementation.

BioWatch: Detection of Aerosol Release of Biological Agents

The BioWatch program—begun in 2003—deploys pathogen sensors in more than 30 large U.S. cities to detect the possible aerosol release of a bioterrorism pathogen, in order that medications can be distributed before exposed individuals become ill.[82] The DHS Office of Health Affairs (OHA) manages the system. The Centers for Disease Control and Prevention (CDC) oversees some aspects of laboratory testing. Local jurisdictions would manage the public health response to a bioterrorism incident.

BioWatch has not detected a bioterrorism incident since its inception, although it has detected pathogens of interest; scientists believe that natural airborne "background" levels of these or related pathogens exist in certain regions. In July 2012, the *Los Angeles Times* published the first in a series of investigative articles criticizing the performance of BioWatch, claiming that the system is prone to false alarms and is also insufficiently sensitive to detect an actual incident.[83] DHS disputed these claims.[84] In addition, some state and local health officials defended the program, saying, among other things, that it has fostered collaboration among federal, state, and local officials, who would be called upon to work together in response to an actual incident.[85]

Timely treatment can reduce casualties during a bioterrorism incident. Federal officials have sought to improve the responsiveness of the BioWatch system by replacing daily sensor filter collection and analysis with so-called autonomous sensors, which would transmit pathogen detection findings in near-real time. Beginning in 2007, OHA pursued procurement of this type of sensor, which it termed Generation 3, or Gen-3. However, after a critical GAO review,[86] several procurement delays, and growing skepticism among some Members of Congress,[87] DHS announced the termination of further Gen-3 procurement activities in April 2014.[88]

Congressional appropriators have at times sought to limit funding for BioWatch program expansion and called for program reviews.[89] Authorizing committees in each Congress since the 108th have held hearings on the program. In addition, Members of the House Committee on Energy and Commerce began an investigation of the program in the 112th Congress.[90] The Administration requested FY2015 and FY2016 funding solely to maintain current BioWatch operations without upgrade. Congress provided funding for FY2015 slightly above the request to replace aging system components. Both House and Senate Appropriations Committees urged OHA to continue its efforts to improve the program's detection capability.[91]

Food Defense

Foods may be intentionally contaminated for purposes of terrorism, fraud (e.g., the dilution of a valuable commodity), or other harmful intent. Food safety efforts have long focused on protecting against unintentional contaminants, such as infectious pathogens or pesticide residues. Since the 2001 terrorist attacks, regulators and others have added a focus on *food defense*, the protection of the food supply from deliberate or intentional acts of contamination or tampering.[92] Large-scale foodborne outbreaks can sicken hundreds of people. Sales of affected commodities—as well as unaffected commodities that the consuming public perceives to be involved—can suffer. An intentional incident of food contamination, especially if it were an act of terrorism, could have serious economic consequences, in addition to any illnesses it caused.

Federal food safety responsibility rests primarily with the U.S. Department of Agriculture (USDA) and the Food and Drug Administration (FDA). USDA's Food Safety and Inspection Service (FSIS) regulates most meat and poultry and some egg products; FDA is responsible for the safety of most other foods.[93] State and local authorities assist with inspection, outbreak response, and other food safety functions, and regulate retail establishments. DHS notes

> The Food and Agriculture Sector is almost entirely under private ownership and is composed of an estimated 2.2 million farms, 900,000 restaurants, and more than 400,000 registered food manufacturing, processing, and storage facilities. This sector accounts for roughly one-fifth of the nation's economic activity.[94]

The 111th Congress enacted a comprehensive food safety law, the Food Safety Modernization Act (FSMA, P.L. 111-353), focused mainly on foods regulated by FDA.[95] FSMA attempts to prevent both intentional and unintentional contamination of foods through a variety of production and processing strategies and through enhanced regulatory authorities. However, FDA has not yet implemented some of the law's provisions.[96] Among other things, FSMA requires the Secretaries of Health and Human Services and Agriculture to develop a National Agriculture and Food Defense Strategy, implementation plan, and research agenda. This strategy and the accompanying documents have not yet been published.[97] FDA has published a proposed rule that would require food facilities to address vulnerabilities to intentional contamination,[98] and is under a court order to finalize this rule by May 2016.[99]

GAO has named food safety as a high-risk issue, citing the fragmentation of federal oversight, among other concerns.[100] GAO specifically noted delays in the implementation of the nation's food and agriculture defense policy, Homeland Security Presidential Directive 9 (HSPD-9). This directive, issued by the George W. Bush Administration in 2004, assigns various emergency response and recovery responsibilities to USDA, FDA, DHS, and other agencies. GAO found that there is no centralized coordination of HSPD-9 implementation efforts, and recommended that DHS take on this role to assure that the nation's food and agriculture defense policy is fully in place. In addition, GAO recommended that the executive branch develop a government-wide performance plan for all of its food safety activities. These and several other GAO recommendations regarding food defense have not been implemented as of March 2015.[101]

Electric Grid Physical Security

The electric utility industry operates as an integrated system of generation, transmission, and distribution facilities to deliver electric power to consumers. In the United States, this system consists of over 9,000 electric generating units connected to over 200,000 miles of high-voltage transmission lines strung between large towers and rated at 230 kilovolts (kV)[102] or greater.[103] This network is interspersed with hundreds of large electric power transformers whose function is to adjust electric voltage as needed to move power across the network. High voltage (HV) transformer units make up less than 3% of transformers in U.S. power substations, but they carry 60%-70% of the nation's electricity.[104] Because they serve as vital transmission network nodes and carry bulk volumes of electricity, HV transformers are critical elements of the nation's electric power grid.

The various parts of the electric power system are all vulnerable to failure due to natural or manmade events. However, HV transformers are considered by many experts to be the most vulnerable to intentional damage from malicious acts. Security analysts have long asserted that a coordinated and simultaneous attack on multiple HV transformers could have severe implications for reliable electric service over a large geographic area, crippling its electricity network and causing widespread, extended blackouts. Such an event could have severe electric reliability consequences, demonstrated in recent grid security exercise, as well as serious economic and social consequences.[105] A handful of recent physical attacks on individual transformer substations—most notably a 2013 attack on an HV transformer substation in Metcalf, CA—did not cause widespread blackouts, but did highlight the physical vulnerability of HV transformer substations and drew the attention of both the media and federal officials to the utility industry's substation security efforts.[106]

Over the last decade or so the electric utility industry and government agencies have engaged in a number of initiatives to secure HV transformers from physical attack and to improve recovery in the event of a successful attack. These initiatives include coordination and information sharing, spare equipment programs, security standards, grid security exercises, and other measures. Several grid security guidelines or standards have been developed or proposed to address the physical security of the grid, including HV transformers. These standards have been promulgated by the North American Electric Reliability Corporation as voluntary best practices since at least 2002, with subsequent revisions. However, in late 2014, following the Metcalf attack, the Federal Energy Regulatory Commission ordered the imposition of mandatory physical security standards for HV transformer substations.[107]

There is widespread agreement among state and federal government officials, utilities, and manufacturers that HV transformers in the United States are vulnerable to terrorist attack, and that such an attack potentially could have catastrophic consequences. But the most serious, multi- transformer attacks would require acquiring operational information and a certain level of sophistication on the part of potential attackers. Consequently, despite the technical arguments, without more specific information about potential targets and attacker capabilities, the true vulnerability of the grid to a multi-HV transformer attack remains an open question. Incomplete or ambiguous threat information may lead to inconsistency in physical security among HV transformer owners, inefficient spending of limited security resources at facilities that may not really be under threat, or deployment of security measures against the wrong threat.

Congress has long been concerned about grid security in general, but the recent security exercises, together with the Metcalf attack have focused congressional interest on the physical security of HV transformers, among other specific aspects of the grid.[108] Legislative proposals in the 113th Congress, especially the Grid Reliability and Infrastructure Defense Act (H.R. 4298 and S. 2158), sought to strengthen federal authority to secure the U.S. grid. As the electric utility industry and federal agencies continue their efforts to improve the physical security of critical HV transformer substations, the 114th Congress may consider several key issues as part of its oversight of the sector: identifying critical transformers, confidentiality of critical transformer information, adequacy of HV transformer protection, quality of federal threat information, and recovery from HV transformer attacks.

Security of Chemical Facilities

The 113th Congress authorized DHS to regulate security at chemical facilities through P.L. 113- 254, the Protecting and Securing Chemical Facilities from Terrorist Attacks Act of 2014. This act repealed the prior statutory authority that had been granted in the Homeland Security Appropriations Act, 2007 (P.L. 109-295, §550). The new authority expires in January 2019. As Congress has recently enacted chemical facility security legislation, the focus of many congressional policymakers in the 114th Congress will likely shift from enacting new legislation to increasing oversight. Even before the 2013 explosion of the West Fertilizer Company in West, TX, various stakeholders had criticized the content of DHS chemical facility security regulation, known as the Chemical Facility Anti-Terrorism Standards (CFATS), and the effectiveness and pace of its implementation. With the new authority granted by the 113th Congress, DHS may move forward with regulations implementing this authority.

P.L.113-254 maintained aspects of the existing regulatory scheme identified by experts as potentially containing security or implementation challenges. The Obama Administration and other stakeholders have determined that existing regulatory exemptions, such as for community water systems and wastewater treatment facilities, pose potential risks. Environmental and "right- to-know" groups additionally advocate that Congress include requirements for facilities to adopt or identify "inherently safer technologies" and widely disseminate security-related information to first responders and employees. The regulated industry generally opposes granting DHS the ability to require implementation of inherently safer technologies or other specific security measures. They question the maturity and applicability of the inherently safer technology concept as a security measure and cite the need to tailor security approaches for each facility. The Obama Administration has identified potential security concerns if chemical security-related information is more broadly disseminated. However, the discovery that information about the chemical inventory of the West Fertilizer Company was not effectively shared between federal agencies has led to reconsideration of existing information-sharing policies. Starting with Executive Order 13650, "Improving Chemical Facility Safety and Security," the Obama Administration is engaged in a multiagency effort to coordinate federal chemical safety and security activities.

Policymakers performing oversight of the CFATS program face critical decisions regarding DHS program changes. The DHS regulatory program is still in its early stages. Historically, it has experienced implementation challenges and delays. Many regulated entities have not yet received approval of their security plans. The current rate of facility security plan approval indicates that it will be still two or more years before DHS has completed its review and approval of information submitted by regulated facilities.

Transit Security

Bombings of passenger trains in Europe and Asia have illustrated the vulnerability of passenger rail systems to terrorist attacks. Passenger rail systems—primarily subway systems—in the United States carry about five times as many passengers each day as do airlines, over many thousands of miles of track, serving stations that are designed primarily for easy access. The increased security efforts around air travel have led to concerns that terrorists may turn their attention to "softer" targets, such as transit or passenger rail. A key challenge Congress faces is balancing the desire for increased rail passenger security with the efficient functioning of transit systems, with the potential costs and damages of an attack, and with other federal priorities.

The volume of ridership and number of access points make it impractical to subject all rail passengers to the type of screening all airline passengers undergo. Consequently, transit security measures tend to emphasize managing the consequences of an attack. Nevertheless, steps have been taken to try to reduce the risks, as well as the consequences, of an attack. These include vulnerability assessments; emergency planning; emergency response training and drilling of transit personnel (ideally in coordination with police, fire, and emergency medical personnel); increasing the number of transit security personnel; installing video surveillance equipment in vehicles and stations; and conducting random inspections of bags, platforms, and trains.

The challenges of securing rail passengers are dwarfed by the challenge of securing bus passengers. There are some 76,000 buses carrying 19 million passengers each weekday in the United States. Some transit systems have installed video cameras on their buses, but the number and operation characteristics of transit buses make them all but impossible to secure.

The Implementing Recommendations of the 9/11 Commission Act of 2007 (P.L. 110-53), passed by Congress on July 27, 2007, included provisions on passenger rail and transit security and authorized $3.5 billion for FY2008-FY2011 for grants for public transportation security. The act required public transportation agencies and railroads considered to be high-risk targets by

DHS to have security plans approved by DHS (§1405 and §1512). Other provisions required DHS to conduct a name-based security background check and an immigration status check on all public transportation and railroad frontline employees (§1414 and §1522), and gave DHS the authority to regulate rail and transit employee security training standards (§1408 and §1517).

In 2010 TSA completed a national threat assessment for transit and passenger rail, and in 2011 completed an updated transportation systems sector-specific plan, which established goals and objectives for a secure transportation system. The three primary objectives for reducing risk in transit are

- increase system resilience by protecting high-risk/high-consequence assets (i.e., critical tunnels, stations, and bridges);
- expand visible deterrence activities (i.e., canine teams, passenger screening teams, and anti-terrorism teams); and
- engage the public and transit operators in the counterterrorism mission.[109]

TSA surface transportation security inspectors conduct assessments of transit systems (and other surface modes) through the agency's Baseline Assessment for Security Enhancement (BASE) program. The agency has also developed a security training and security exercise program for transit (I-STEP), and its Visible Intermodal Prevention and Response (VIPR) teams conduct operations with local law enforcement officials, including periodic patrols of transit and passenger rail systems, to create "unpredictable visual deterrents."

In the most recent Congressional action prior to the 114th Congress, the House Committee on Homeland Security's Subcommittee on Transportation Security held a hearing in May 2012 to examine the surface transportation security inspector program. The number of inspectors had increased from 175 in FY2008 to 404 in FY2011 (full-time equivalents). Issues considered at the hearing included the lack of surface transportation expertise among the inspectors, many of whom were promoted from screening passengers at airports; the administrative challenge of having the surface inspectors managed by federal security directors who are located at airports, and who themselves typically have no surface transportation experience; and the security value of the tasks performed by surface inspectors.[110] The number of surface inspectors decreased to 300 (full-time equivalent positions) in FY2014, as a result of a reduction in the number of VIPR surface inspectors.[111]

DHS provides grants for security improvements for public transit, passenger rail, and occasionally other surface transportation modes under the Transit Security Grant Program. The vast majority of the funding goes to public transit providers (see Table 1).

In the past, the Government Accountability Office has found opportunity for duplication among four DHS state and local security grant programs with similar goals, one of which was the public transportation security grant program.[112] The Obama Administration has repeatedly proposed consolidating several of these programs in annual budget requests. This proposal has not been supported by Congress in the appropriations process to date, though appropriators have expressed concerns that grant programs have not focused on areas of highest risk and that significant amounts of previously appropriated funds have not yet been awarded to recipients.

BORDER SECURITY AND TRADE

Southwest Border Issues

Drug Trafficking and the Southwest Border

The United States is the world's largest marketplace for illegal drugs and sustains a multi-billion dollar market in illegal drugs.[113] An estimated 24.6 million Americans (9.4% of the 12 and older population) were current users of illicit drugs in 2013.[114] The most recent National Drug Threat Assessment Summary indicates that Mexican drug trafficking organizations continue to dominate the U.S. drug market.[115] Indeed, U.S. officials have outlined this threat:

> Mexican transnational criminal organizations pose the greatest criminal drug threat to the United States; no other group is currently positioned to challenge them. These Mexican poly- drug organizations traffic heroin, methamphetamine, cocaine, and marijuana throughout the United States, using established transportation routes and distribution networks. They control virtually all drug trafficking across the Southwest Border and are moving to expand their share, particularly in heroin and methamphetamine markets.[116]

Table 1. Congressional Funding for Transit Security Grants, FY2002-FY2015

(millions of dollars)		
Fiscal Year	**Appropriation (nominal $)**	**Appropriation (constant 2015 $)**
2002	$63	$82
2003	65	83
2004	50	62
2005	108	131
2006	131	154
2007	251	287
2008	356	394
2009	498[a]	549
2010	253	275
2011	200	213
2012	88[b]	92
2013	84	86
2014	90	91
2015	87[c]	87

Source: FY2002: Department of Defense FY2002 Appropriations Act, P.L. 107-117; FY2003: FY2003 Emergency Wartime Supplemental Appropriations Act, P.L. 108-11; FY2004: Department of Homeland Security FY2004 Appropriations Act, P.L. 108-90; FY2005-FY2011: United States Government Accountability Office, *Homeland Security: DHS Needs Better Project Information and Coordination among Four Overlapping Grant Programs*, GAO-12- 303, February 2012, Table 1; FY2012-2014: DHS, Transit Security Grant Program annual funding opportunity announcements; FY2015: P.L. 114-4.

Notes: FY2002 funding represents post -9/11 appropriations through the Defense Appropriations Act to Washington Metropolitan Area Transit Authority and the Federal Transit Administration. In FY2003-FY2004, grants were made through the Urban Areas Security Initiative. The Transit Security Grant Program was formally established in FY2005. Does not include funding provided for security grants for intercity passenger rail (Amtrak), intercity bus service, and commercial trucking. Nominal dollar amounts adjusted to constant 2015 dollars using the Total Non-defense column from "Table 10: Gross Domestic Product and Deflators Used in the Historical Tables: 1940-2020," published in the *Historical Tables volume of the Budget of the United States Government, Fiscal Year 2016* (http://www.whitehouse.gov/omb/budget/Historicals).

a. Includes $150 million provided in the American Recovery and Reinvestment Act.

b. Congress did not specify an amount for transit security grants, but provided a lump sum for state and local grant programs, leaving funding allocations to the discretion of DHS.

c. Estimated by CRS; Congress provided $100 million for Public Transportation, Amtrak, and Over-the-Road Bus Security grants, and specified that no less than $10 million was for Amtrak and no less than $3 million was for bus grants (P.L. 114-4).

Mexican criminal networks either (1) transport or (2) produce and transport drugs north across the United States-Mexico border. After being smuggled across the border by criminal networks, the drugs are distributed and sold within the United States. The illicit proceeds may then be laundered or smuggled south across the border. The proceeds may also be used to purchase weapons in the United States that are then smuggled into Mexico. While drugs are the primary goods trafficked by the criminal networks, those networks also generate income from other illegal activities, such as the smuggling of humans and weapons, counterfeiting and piracy, kidnapping for ransom, and extortion.

One of the current domestic drug threats fueled, in part, by Mexican traffickers is heroin. Not only has there been an increase in heroin use in the United States over the past several years, but there has been a simultaneous increase in its availability. This availability is driven by a number of factors, including increased production and trafficking of heroin by Mexican criminal networks.[117] Some Mexican farmers have reported abandoning marijuana cultivation in favor of growing opium poppies; the switch may be partly due to the decline in wholesale prices of marijuana in Mexico—which some claim is linked to increased marijuana legalization in the United States—and an increase in U.S. heroin demand.[118] Increases in Mexican heroin production and its availability in the United States have been coupled with increased heroin seizures at the Southwest border. Reportedly, these seizures increased by over 320% between 2008 and 2013.[119]

The 114th Congress may consider a number of supply-reduction and demand-reduction options in attempting to reduce drug trafficking from Mexico to the United States. For instance, policymakers may be interested in examining the implementation of the 2013 National Southwest Border Counternarcotics Strategy, of which the overarching strategic goal is to "[s]ubstantially reduce the flow of illicit drugs, drug proceeds, and associated instruments of violence across the Southwest border."[120] To accomplish this, the strategy aims to enhance intelligence and information sharing; interdict drugs, money, and weapons both at and between the ports of entry as well as through air and marine operations; disrupt and dismantle drug trafficking organizations; stem the trans-border flow of illicit proceeds and weapons; bolster border communities; and increase bilateral U.S.-Mexico cooperation.[121]

Illicit Proceeds and the Southwest Border

The flow of money outside legal channels not only presents challenges to law enforcement, but it also has a significant nexus with homeland security policy. Proceeds from illegal enterprises are sometimes used to fund broader destabilizing activities, such as smuggling, illegal border crossings, or more violent activities, such as terrorist operations—including those controlled by the FARC (Revolutionary Armed Forces of Colombia) in Colombia.[122] While this is an issue with a global scope, this section focuses specifically on the policies affected by movement of illicit funds across the Southwest border.

As noted in the State Department's 2014 International Narcotics Control Strategy Report, "drug trafficking organizations send between $19 and $29 billion annually to Mexico from the United States."[123] Money from the traffickers' illegal sale of drugs in the United States is moved across the border into Mexico, and these funds fuel the drug traffickers' criminal activities. This money is not directly deposited into the U.S. financial system, but rather is illegally laundered through mechanisms such as bulk cash smuggling and the Black Market Peso Exchange,[124] or placed in financial institutions, cash-intensive front businesses, prepaid or stored value cards, or money services businesses.[125]

New technologies have provided additional outlets through which drug trafficking organizations may conceal their illicit proceeds. The use of stored value cards,[126] mobile banking systems, and other technologies allows traffickers to move profits more quickly and stealthily. In addition, profits that the Mexican drug traffickers generate from the sale of Colombian cocaine can be moved directly from the United States to the source country without traversing through middlemen.[127] There has been debate, however, as to the extent that these technologies may be used relative to other laundering techniques.[128]

Various departments and agencies—including the Drug Enforcement Administration, Federal Bureau of Investigation, U.S. Immigration and Customs Enforcement, U.S. Customs and Border Protection, and the Financial Crimes Enforcement Network (FinCEN)—share responsibility for combating drug-related activity and the flow of illicit proceeds both along the Southwest border and throughout the United States. Many of these agencies are also represented in Mexico, increasing U.S.-Mexican bilateral cooperation. Further, while some efforts explicitly target money laundering and bulk cash smuggling, other efforts are more tangentially related. For instance, operations targeting southbound firearms smuggling may intercept individuals smuggling not only weapons, but cash proceeds from illicit drug sales as well. As such, the 114th Congress may examine interagency coordination to reduce the flow of illicit money (and other goods) across the Southwest border.

Cross-Border Smuggling Tunnels

Mexican traffickers rely on cross-border tunnels to smuggle persons and drugs, as well as other contraband, from Mexico into the United States. The use of smuggling tunnels has increased not only in frequency but in the sophistication of the tunnels themselves.[129] More than 150 tunnels have been discovered along the Southwest border since the 1990s;[130] notably, there has been an 80% uptick in tunnels detected since 2008.[131] Early tunnels were rudimentary "gopher hole" tunnels dug on the Mexican side of the border, traveling just below the surface, and popping out on the U.S. side as close as 100 feet from the border. Slightly more advanced tunnels relied on existing infrastructure, which may be shared by neighboring border cities such as Nogales, AZ, in the United States and Nogales, Sonora, in Mexico. These interconnecting tunnels may tap into storm drains or sewage systems, allowing smugglers to move drugs further and more easily than in tunnels they dug themselves. The most sophisticated tunnels can have rail, ventilation, and electrical systems. One of the most elaborate and sophisticated of such tunnels discovered to date was found in November 2011 in San Diego, CA. It stretched 612 yards in length, boasted electric rail cars, lighting, reinforced walls, and wooden floors, and its discovery resulted in the seizure of 32 tons of marijuana.[132] In April 2014, two sophisticated drug smuggling tunnels were uncovered in the San Diego area of the Southwest border in less than a week.[133]

U.S. law enforcement uses various tactics to detect these cross-border tunnels. Law enforcement may use sonic equipment to detect the sounds of digging and tunnel construction and seismic technology to detect blasts that may be linked to tunnel excavation. Another tool for tunnel detection is ground penetrating radar.[134] However, factors including soil conditions, tunnel diameter, and tunnel depth can limit the effectiveness of this technology.

Despite these tools, U.S. officials have acknowledged that law enforcement currently does not have technology that is reliably able to detect sophisticated tunnels.[135] Rather, tunnels are more effectively discovered as a result of human intelligence and tips. U.S. officials have noted the value of U.S.-Mexican law enforcement cooperation in detecting, investigating, and prosecuting the criminals who create and use the cross-border tunnels.[136] As a result, the 114th Congress may not only consider how to best help U.S. law enforcement develop technologies that can keep pace with tunneling organizations, but also examine whether existing bi-national law enforcement partnerships are effective and whether they may be improved to enhance investigations of transnational criminals. Policymakers may also question how prominently the issue of combating cross-border smuggling tunnels may play within the larger border security framework.

Cargo Security

U.S. Customs and Border Protection (CBP), within DHS, is America's primary trade enforcement agency, and CBP seeks to balance the benefits of efficient trade flows against the demand for cargo security and the enforcement of U.S. trade laws. Thus, the overarching policy question with respect to incoming cargo is how to minimize the risk that weapons of mass destruction, illegal drugs, and other contraband will enter through a U.S. port of entry (POE), while limiting the costs and delays associated with such enforcement.

CBP's current trade strategy emphasizes "risk management" and a "multi-layered" approach to enforcement.[137] With respect to cargo security, risk management means that CBP segments importers into higher and lower risk pools and focuses security procedures on higher-risk flows, while expediting lower-risk flows. CBP's "multi-layered approach" means that enforcement occurs at multiple points in the import process, beginning before goods are loaded in foreign ports and continuing after the goods have been admitted into the United States. In recent years, congressional attention to cargo security has focused on one of CBP's primary tools for risk management, the Customs-Trade Partnership Against Terrorism (C-TPAT) trusted trader program, and on the statutory requirement that 100% of incoming maritime cargo containers be scanned abroad prior to being loaded on U.S.-bound ships. Congress also faces perennial questions about spending levels for POE infrastructure and personnel.

Customs-Trade Partnership against Terrorism (C-TPAT)

The Customs-Trade Partnership Against Terrorism (C-TPAT) is a voluntary public-private and international partnership that permits certain import-related businesses to register with CBP and perform security tasks prescribed by the agency. In return C-TPAT members are recognized as low-risk actors and are eligible for expedited import processing and other benefits.[138] CBP established C-TPAT in November 2001 following the September 11, 2001 (9/11) terrorist attacks, and the program was authorized as part of the Security and Accountability for Every Port Act of 2006 (SAFE Port Act, P.L. 109-347).

Proponents of C-TPAT favor increased participation in the program as a way to facilitate legal trade flows.[139] Some businesses, however, have criticized the program for providing inadequate membership benefits, especially in light of the time and financial investments required to become certified as C-TPAT members.[140]

Yet there may be no easy way to substantially expand C-TPAT benefits. In the case of land ports, the primary trusted trader benefit is access to dedicated lanes where wait times may be shorter and more predictable. But adding lanes at land ports is difficult because many of them are located in urban areas with limited space for expansion and with limited ingress and egress infrastructure.[141] In the case of maritime imports, the primary trusted trader benefit is a reduced likelihood of secondary inspection.[142] But only about 6% of all maritime containers are selected for such an inspection,[143] so C-TPAT membership may offer little practical advantage in this regard.

100% Scanning Requirement

Section 231 of the SAFE Port Act directed DHS, in coordination with the Department of Energy (DOE), the private sector, and foreign governments, to pilot an integrated system in three foreign ports to scan 100% of cargo containers destined for the United States from those ports.[144] Section 232 of the law required that 100% of cargo containers imported into the United States be *screened* by DHS to identify high-risk containers, and that 100% of containers identified as high risk also be *scanned* through non-intrusive inspection (NII) and radiation detection equipment before arriving in the United States.[145] In 2007, Section 1701 of the Implementing Recommendations of the 9/11 Commission Act of 2007 (9/11 Act; P.L. 110-53) amended the SAFE Port Act to require that by July 1, 2012, 100% of maritime containers imported to the United States—that is, from all ports, whether or not they are identified as high-risk—be scanned by NII and radiation detection equipment before being loaded onto a U.S.-bound vessel in a foreign port.

On May 2, 2012, however, then-DHS Secretary Janet Napolitano notified Members of Congress that she would exercise her authority under the 9/11 Act to extend the deadline for 100% scanning.[146] The decision to delay implementation of the 100% scanning program partly reflects the department's findings from its evaluation of the pilot program. In its final report to Congress on the program, CBP identified three main obstacles to implementing 100% scanning at all foreign ports.[147] First, 100% scanning requires significant host state and private sector cooperation, but some foreign governments and business groups do not support 100% scanning. Second, 100% scanning would be logistically difficult. Initial pilots were deployed in relatively low-volume ports with natural chokepoints, but many cargo containers pass through large volume ports with more varied port architectures. Third, 100% scanning would be costly. In February 2012, the Congressional Budget Office (CBO) estimated that 100% scanning at foreign ports would cost an average of $8 million per shipping lane to implement, or a total of about $16.8 billion for all 2,100 shipping lanes.[148] Port operators and foreign partners also absorb additional costs associated with fuel and utilities, staffing, and related expenses. In a May 2014 letter to Members of Congress, the current Secretary of Homeland Security, Jeh Johnson, reaffirmed the conditions cited by his predecessor in support of another two-year extension of the deadline.[149]

Some Members of Congress have expressed frustration that DHS has made little progress toward implementing 100% scanning.[150] Congress may continue to monitor the 100% scanning requirement and encourage DHS to scan a higher proportion of inbound cargo. On the other hand, in light of the difficulties DHS has identified, Congress may consider changes to the 100% scanning requirement, potentially including provisions to allow DHS to scan less than 100% of U.S.-bound cargo or to allow certain scanning to occur within U.S. ports rather than abroad. In its report to accompany the Department of Homeland Security Appropriations Bill, 2015 (H.R. 4903), the House Appropriations Committee directed DHS, in light of the Secretary of Homeland Security extending the 100% scanning deadline by an additional two years and the "unlikeli[ness] that the ... requirement will be met ... ," to submit an alternative strategy for cargo scanning to Congress that could be realistically achieved within the next two years.[151]

Port of Entry (POE) Infrastructure and Personnel

In light of the substantial flow of cargo and travelers at ports of entry (also see "Immigration Inspections at Ports of Entry"), one perennial issue for Congress is how to allocate additional resources for CBP Office of Field Operations (OFO) personnel and for port infrastructure. Some in Congress have argued that inadequate personnel and infrastructure have contributed to costly delays and unpredictable wait times at ports of entry, particularly at land ports on the U.S.- Mexico border.[152] In general, Congress has invested more heavily since 2004 in enforcement personnel between ports of entry (i.e., U.S. Border Patrol agents) than in OFO officers (also see "Enforcement Between Ports of Entry").[153]

Recent fiscal pressures have been a barrier to POE personnel increases. During the FY2014 budget process, the Administration proposed to hire 3,477 additional CBP officers (about half through increased appropriations and half through fee increases), but Congress approved a slower personnel growth, with half the proposed funding.[154] Congress also authorized a pilot program in the FY2013 appropriations bill that permitted CBP to enter into public-private partnerships (PPPs) with certain localities and permitted the private sector to fund improvements in border facilities and port services, including by funding additional CBP officers and underwriting overtime hours.[155] In its FY2014 budget, the Administration proposed expanding the pilot program by permitting CBP to accept donations to expand port operations. Approving the Administration's request, Congress extended the pilot program in the FY2014 DHS appropriations bill.[156] The current pilot program permits CBP to accept donations to expand port operations, among other things.[157]

Immigration Inspections at Ports of Entry

At ports of entry, CBP's Office of Field Operations (OFO) is responsible for conducting immigration, customs, and agricultural inspections of travelers seeking admission to the United States. The vast majority of people entering through U.S. ports are U.S. citizens, U.S. legal permanent residents (LPRs),[158] and legitimate visitors. Thus, as with cargo security (see "Cargo Security"), CBP officers' goals are to identify and intercept dangerous or unwanted (high-risk) people, while facilitating access for legitimate (low-risk) travelers. CBP seeks to accomplish these tasks without excessive infringement on privacy or civil liberties while controlling enforcement costs.

Travelers seeking admission at ports of entry are required to present a travel document, typically a passport or its equivalent and (for non-U.S. citizens) either a visa authorizing permanent or temporary admission to the United States or proof of eligibility for admission through the Visa Waiver Program (VWP; see "Visa Waiver Program").[159] Foreign nationals are subject to security- related and other background checks prior to being issued a visa or to receiving travel authorization through the VWP. CBP officers at U.S. ports of entry verify the authenticity of travelers' documents and that each document belongs to the person seeking admission (i.e., confirm the traveler's identity). Identity confirmation relies in part on biometric checks against DHS's Automated Biometric Identification System (IDENT) database (see "Entry-Exit System"). Database interoperability allows CBP officers to check travelers' records against other biographic and biometric databases managed by the Departments of Justice, State, and Defense.

The concentration of inspection activity at the border—for travelers and imports—means that sufficient resources must be present in order to minimize congestion and ensure efficient operations. CBP faces pressure to provide for the rapid processing of individuals crossing the border, but expedited processing can lead to missed opportunities for interdicting threats. Moreover, investment in ports of entry arguably has not kept pace with rapid growth in international travel and trade, and there may be inadequate infrastructure to manage flows at some ports of entry (also see "Port of Entry (POE) Infrastructure and Personnel").

In an effort to streamline admissions without compromising security, CBP has implemented several trusted traveler programs. Trusted traveler programs require applicants to clear criminal and national security background checks prior to enrollment, to participate in an in-person interview, and to submit fingerprints and other biometric data.[160] In return, trusted travelers—like trusted traders (see "Customs-Trade Partnership Against Terrorism (C-TPAT)")—are eligible for expedited processing at ports of entry. CBP currently operates three main trusted traveler programs: Global Entry, which allows expedited screening of passengers arriving at 34 major U.S. airports and 10 preclearance airports;[161] NEXUS, which is a joint U.S.-Canadian program for land, sea, and air crossings between the United States and Canada, including through dedicated vehicle lanes at 19 land ports;[162] and the Secure Electronic Network for Travelers Rapid Inspection (SENTRI), which allows expedited screening at land POEs on the U.S.-Mexican border, including through dedicated vehicle lanes at 11 land ports.[163]

Visa Waiver Program

The 2015 terrorist attacks in Paris and Brussels, and the possible threats posed by European citizens fighting abroad for terrorist groups such as the Islamic State,[164] has increased congressional focus on the possible security risk posed by the visa waiver program (VWP).[165] The visa waiver program (VWP) allows nationals from 38 countries,[166] most of which are in Europe, to enter the United States as temporary visitors (nonimmigrants) for business or pleasure without first obtaining a visa from a U.S. consulate abroad. Temporary visitors for business or pleasure from non-VWP countries must obtain a visa from Department of State (DOS) officers at a consular post abroad before coming to the United States. While a foreign national from a VWP country does not need a visa to enter the United States, before embarking to the United States he or she must submit biographical information through the U.S. government's web-based Electronic System for Travel Authorization (ESTA), which determines the eligibility of the foreign national to travel to the United States under the VWP.[167]

While there tends to be agreement that the VWP benefits the U.S. economy by facilitating legitimate travel,[168] there is disagreement on the VWP's effect on national security. Travelers under the VWP do not undergo the screening traditionally required to receive a visa. While the ESTA system has increased the security of the VWP, it is a name-based system and cannot be used to run checks against databases that use biometrics such as DHS's Automated Biometric Identification System (IDENT) and FBI's Integrated Automated Fingerprint Identification System (IAFIS).[169] (Travelers are checked against these systems through US-VISIT when they enter the United States.)[170] In addition, some contend that the relaxed documentary requirements of the VWP increase immigration fraud and decrease border security.[171]

Nonetheless, others argue that the VWP enhances security by setting standards for travel documents, requiring information sharing between the member countries and the United States on criminals and security concerns, mandating reporting of lost and stolen travel documents, and promoting economic growth and cultural ties.[172] For example, travelers under the VWP have to present machine-readable passports or e-passports, and eventually, all travelers entering under the VWP will present e-passports, which tend to be more difficult to alter than other types of passports.[173] In addition, many short-term tourist visas are valid for 10 years,[174] and it is possible that a person's circumstances or allegiances could change during that time.

Entry-Exit System

Section 110 of the Illegal Immigration Reform and Immigrant Responsibility Act of 1996 (IIRIRA, P.L. 104-208, Div. C) required the Attorney General, to develop an automated entry and exit control system within two years of enactment that would collect records of alien arrivals and departures and allow the Attorney General to match such arrivals and departures through online searches and thereby identify nonimmigrant aliens who remain in the United States beyond the periods of their visas. Congress amended the system's requirements and deadlines on several occasions since then, including by adding an entry-exit requirement to legislation authorizing the Visa Waiver Program and by requiring the entry-exit system to include biometric technology and to be fully interoperable with the Departments of

Justice and State databases. The entry-exit system, however, remains incompletely implemented.

The completion of the exit component of the system has been a persistent subject of congressional concern. No exit data are collected from persons leaving through southern border land ports; and data collection at other ports is limited to biographic data, is not always based on machine-readable data, and relies on information sharing with Canada and with air and sea carriers. DHS reportedly believes that the biographic information sharing generally meets its needs for purposes of exit tracking at an acceptable cost,[175] and CBP has indicated, for purposes of immigration screening, that "[w]hile biometric information is growing in importance, the vast majority of data available for use at the POEs is biographical."[176] At the same time, DHS has also argued that strengthening biographic data collection is a necessary precursor to biometric data collection, and views a biographic system as a desirable long-term goal for the entry-exit system.[177]

Enforcement between Ports of Entry

Between ports of entry, CBP's U.S. Border Patrol is responsible for enforcing U.S. immigration law and other federal laws along the border and for preventing all unlawful entries into the United States, including entries of terrorists, unauthorized aliens, instruments of terrorism, narcotics, and other contraband. In the course of discharging its duties, the Border Patrol patrols 7,494 miles of U.S. international borders with Mexico and Canada and the coastal waters around Florida and Puerto Rico.

With support from Congress, CBP—and its predecessor agency the Immigration and Naturalization Service (INS)—have invested in border security personnel, fencing and infrastructure, and surveillance technology since the 1980s, with CBP's budget totaling $10.7 billion in FY2014.[178] Some Members of Congress have raised questions about whether DHS's investments at the border have been effective, and some have argued that enforcement has been compromised by the fact that DHS does not have a single, overarching strategy for border security.[179] Congress also has raised questions about how to measure border security. The Border Patrol traditionally has used border apprehensions as its primary measure of border security, and these apprehensions have fallen since 2006.[180] Yet falling apprehensions may reflect the downturn in U.S. labor market that occurred in recent years or a change in tactics by unauthorized migrants, among other variables, in addition to enforcement. Thus, apprehensions are an imprecise indicator of the effectiveness of border enforcement.

Congress may also question the relative priority attached to the southern and northern borders. While the Southwest border has experienced more unauthorized immigration, some security experts have warned that the northern border may represent a more important point of vulnerability when it comes to terrorism and related threats to homeland security—especially in light of the more limited enforcement resources deployed there.[181]

Domestic Nuclear Detection

Congress has emphasized the need to detect and interdict smuggled nuclear and radiological material before it enters the United States, by funding investment in nuclear detection domestically and abroad. DHS has adopted a strategy of securing the border through emplacement of radiation portal monitors and non-intrusive imaging equipment. Some experts have criticized this combined system as insufficient to detect all smuggled special nuclear material. DHS has spent several years developing, testing, and evaluating next-generation detection equipment. Two of these next-generation systems, the Advanced Spectroscopic Portal and the Cargo Advanced Automated Radiography System, did not meet testing and evaluation milestones, lagged performance and timeline expectations, and ultimately were not procured.[182] Other smaller systems have been successfully developed and deployed.

DHS has deployed radiation portal monitors and other nuclear and radiological material detection equipment since its establishment. In 2005, DHS established a new office, the Domestic Nuclear Detection Office (DNDO), to research, develop, and procure detection equipment and coordinate DHS nuclear detection activities. Such activities are located mainly in Customs and Border Protection, the U.S. Coast Guard, and the Transportation Security Administration. The Government Accountability Office (GAO) and other groups have questioned the efficacy of DNDO's efforts to develop a next-generation radiation detection system.

Congress also has required DHS to scan all containerized cargo entering the United States for nuclear and radiological material. DHS has not yet met this requirement, and stakeholders question whether the DHS approach will meet this requirement in the future. In addition, a shortfall of a key neutron detection material, helium-3, has forced a reconsideration of the current nuclear detection approach.[183] DHS has invested in testing new neutron-detection materials and refitting deployed systems with alternative neutron-detection capabilities. As currently deployed systems approach their design lifetimes, DHS and congressional decisionmakers face questions about whether to recapitalize these systems or invest further in next-generation technology.

DHS activities to detect smuggled radiological and nuclear materials at the U.S. border are part of a large interagency effort to develop a global nuclear detection architecture (GNDA). Congress made DHS, through DNDO, responsible for coordinating federal efforts within the GNDA and implementing this architecture domestically.

The 114th Congress may continue its oversight over the development, testing, and procurement of current and next-generation nuclear detection equipment, interagency coordination in nuclear detection, the sufficiency of the global nuclear detection architecture that links this equipment together, and DHS's approach to the helium-3 shortage.

Transportation Worker Identification Credential (TWIC)

In January 2007, TSA and the Coast Guard issued a final rule implementing the TWIC at U.S. ports.[184] Longshoremen, port truck drivers, railroad workers, merchant mariners, and other workers at a port must apply for a TWIC card to obtain unescorted access to secure areas of port facilities or vessels. The card was authorized under the Maritime Transportation Security Act of 2002 (MTSA, §102 of P.L. 107-295). Since October 2007, when TSA began issuing TWICs, about 2.9 million maritime workers have obtained a card. The card must be renewed every five years.

TSA conducts a security threat assessment of each worker before issuing a card. The security threat assessment uses the same procedures and standards established by TSA for truck drivers carrying hazardous materials, including examination of the applicant's criminal history, immigration status, and possible links to terrorist activity to determine whether a worker poses a security threat. A worker pays a fee of about $130 that is intended to cover the cost of administering the cards. The card uses biometric technology for positive identification. Terminal operators were to deploy card readers at the gates to their facilities, so that a worker's fingerprint template would be scanned each time he enters the port area and matched to the data on the card. Finding a card reader that worked reliably in a harsh marine environment proved difficult. In March 2013, the Coast Guard issued a notice of proposed rulemaking (NPRM)[185] in which it proposed requiring card readers only for facilities or vessels handling dangerous bulk commodities (including barge fleeting areas) or facilities handling more than 1,000 passengers at a time—maritime sectors the Coast Guard considers to be of higher risk. The Coast Guard estimated that 38 U.S.-flag vessels and 352 facilities would be required to have card readers, which equates to about 0.3% of the vessels and 16% of the facilities it regulates under MTSA. Other vessels and facilities, including those handling containerized cargo, would continue to use the TWIC as a "flash pass" (i.e., the biometric data on the card would not be used to positively identify the worker). The comment period for the NPRM closed on June 20, 2013, and a final rule has not yet been issued.[186] Currently, the Coast Guard performs spot checks with hand-held biometric readers while conducting port security inspections.

GAO audits have been highly critical of how TWIC has been implemented. A 2013 audit found that the results of a pilot test of card readers should not be relied upon for developing regulations on card reader requirements because they were incomplete, inaccurate, and unreliable.[187] This audit was discussed at a hearing by the House Subcommittee on Government Operations on May 9, 2013,[188] and by the House Subcommittee on Border and Maritime Security on June 18, 2013.[189] Another 2013 GAO audit examined TSA's Adjudication Center (which performs security threat assessments on TWIC applicants and other transportation workers) and recommended steps the agency could take to better measure the Center's performance.[190] A 2011 audit found internal control weaknesses in the enrollment, background checking, and use of the TWIC card at ports, which were said to undermine the effectiveness of the credential in screening out unqualified individuals from obtaining access to port facilities.[191]

In July 2014, the House passed a bill (H.R. 3202, 113th Congress) requiring DHS to conduct a comprehensive assessment of the benefits and costs of the TWIC card. While no further action was taken on the bill in the 113th Congress, a bill similar to the House-passed version has been reintroduced in the 114th Congress.

Aviation Security

Following the 9/11 terrorist attacks, Congress took swift action to create the Transportation Security Administration (TSA), federalizing all airline passenger and baggage screening functions and deploying significantly increased numbers of armed air marshals on commercial passenger flights. To this day, the federalization of airport screening remains controversial. For example, Representative Bill Shuster, chairman of the House Transportation and Infrastructure Committee, contended that, in hindsight, the decision to create TSA as a federal agency functionally responsible for passenger and baggage screening was a "big mistake." and that frontline screening responsibilities should have been left in the hands of private security companies.[192] While airports have the option of opting out of federal screening, alternative private screening under TSA contracts has been limited to 21 airports out of approximately 450 commercial passenger airports where passenger screening is required.[193] While Congress has sought to ensure that optional private screening remains available for those airports that want to pursue this option, proposals seeking more extensive reforms of passenger screening have not been extensively debated. Rather the aviation security legislation in the aftermath of the 9/11 attacks has largely focused on specific mandates to comprehensively screen for explosives and carry out background checks and threat assessments.

Despite the extensive focus on aviation security for more than a decade, a number of challenges remain, including

- effectively screening passengers, baggage, and cargo for explosive threats;
- developing effective risk-based methods for screening passengers and others with access to aircraft and sensitive areas;
- exploiting available intelligence information and watchlists to identify individuals who pose potential threats to civil aviation;
- effectively responding to security threats at airports and screening checkpoints;
- developing effective strategies for addressing aircraft vulnerabilities to shoulder- fired missiles and other standoff weapons; and
- addressing the potential security implications of unmanned aircraft operations in domestic airspace.

Explosives Screening Strategy for the Aviation Domain

Prior to the 9/11 attacks, explosives screening in the aviation domain was limited in scope and focused on selective screening of checked baggage placed on international passenger flights. Immediately following the 9/11 attacks, the Aviation and Transportation Security Act (ATSA; P.L. 107-71) mandated

100% screening of all checked baggage placed on domestic passenger flights and on international passenger flights to and from the United States.

In addition, the Implementing the 9/11 Commission Recommendations Act of 2007 (P.L. 110-53) mandated the physical screening of all cargo placed on passenger flights. Unlike passenger and checked baggage screening, TSA does not routinely perform physical inspections of air cargo. Rather, TSA satisfies this mandate through the Certified Cargo Screening Program. Under the program, manufacturers, warehouses, distributors, freight forwarders, and shippers carry out screening inspections using TSA-approved technologies and procedures both at airports and at off-airport facilities in concert with certified supply-chain security measures and chain of custody standards. Internationally, TSA works with other governments, international trade organizations, and industry to assure that all U.S.-bound and domestic cargo carried aboard passenger aircraft meet the requirements of the mandate.

Additionally, TSA works closely with Customs and Border Protection (CBP) to carry out risk- based targeting of cargo shipments including use of the CBP Advance Targeting System-Cargo (ATS-C) which assigns risk-based scores to inbound air cargo shipments to identify shipments of elevated risk. Originally designed to combat drug smuggling, ATS-C has evolved and adapted over the years, particularly in response to the October 2010 cargo aircraft bomb plot that originated in Yemen, to assess shipments for explosives threats or other terrorism-related activities.

Given the focus on the threats to aviation posed by explosives, a significant focus of TSA acquisition efforts has been on explosives screening technologies. However, in 2014, Congress found that TSA has continued to face numerous challenges in meeting key performance requirements set for explosives detection, has only recently developed a technology investment plan, and has not consistently implemented DHS policy and best practices for procurement.[194] The Transportation Security Acquisition Reform Act (P.L. 113-245) seeks to address these concerns by requiring a five-year technology investment plan, and to increase accountability for acquisitions through formal justifications and certifications that technology investments are cost beneficial. The act also requires tighter inventory controls and processes to ensure efficient use of procured technologies as well as improvements in setting and attaining goals for small business contracting opportunities.

A major thrust of TSA's acquisition and technology deployment strategy is improving the capability to detect concealed explosives and bomb-making components carried by airline passengers. On December 25, 2009, a passenger attempted to detonate an explosive device concealed in his underwear aboard

Northwest Airlines flight 253 during its approach to Detroit, MI. Al Qaeda in the Arabian Peninsula claimed responsibility. Al Qaeda and its various factions have maintained a particular interest in attacking U.S.-bound airliners. Since 9/11, Al Qaeda has also been linked to the Richard Reid shoe bombing incident aboard American Airlines flight 63 en route from Paris to Miami on December 22, 2001; a plot to bomb several trans-Atlantic flights departing the United Kingdom for North America in 2006; and the October 2010 plot to detonate explosives concealed in air cargo shipments bound for the United States.

In response to the Northwest Airlines flight 253 incident, the Obama Administration accelerated deployment of Advanced Imaging Technology (AIT) whole body imaging (WBI) screening devices and other technologies at passenger screening checkpoints. This deployment responds to the 9/11 Commission recommendation to improve the detection of explosives on passengers.[195] In addition to AIT, next generation screening technologies for airport screening checkpoints include advanced technology X-ray systems for screening carry-on baggage, bottled liquids scanners, cast and prosthesis imagers, shoe scanning devices, and portable explosives trace detection equipment.

The use of AIT has raised a number of policy questions. Privacy advocates have objected to the intrusiveness of AIT, particularly if used for primary screening.[196] To allay privacy concerns, TSA eliminated the use of human analysis of AIT images and does not store imagery. In place of human image analysts, TSA has deployed automated threat detection capabilities using automated targeting recognition (ATR) software. Another concern raised about AIT centered on the potential medical risks posed by backscatter X-ray systems, but those systems are no longer in use for airport screening and current millimeter wave systems emit nonionizing millimeter waves not considered harmful.

Some have advocated for risk-based use of AIT, in coordination with the risk-based approaches to passenger screening discussed below. Past legislative proposals have specifically sought to prohibit the use of WBI technology for primary screening (see, e.g., Sec. 215, H.R. 2200, 111th Congress), although primary screening using AIT is now commonplace, at least at larger airports. Checkpoints at many smaller airports, however, have not been furnished with AIT equipment and other advanced checkpoint detection technologies. This raises questions about TSA's long-range plans to expand AIT to ensure more uniform approaches to explosives screening across all categories of airports. Through FY2014, TSA had deployed about 750 AIT units, roughly 86%, of its projected full operating capability of 870 units. Full operating capability, once achieved, will still leave many smaller airports without this capability. TSA plans to manage this risk to a large extent through risk-based passenger screening measures, primarily through increased use of voluntary passenger background checks under the PreCheck trusted traveler program. However, this program, likewise, has not been rolled out at many smaller airports: currently the program's incentive of expedited screening is offered at less than one-third of all commercial passenger airports.

Risk-Based Passenger Screening

TSA has initiated a number of risk-based screening initiatives to focus its resources and apply directed measures based on intelligence-driven assessments of security risk. These include a trusted traveler program called PreCheck, modified screening procedures for children 12 and under, and a program for expedited screening of known flight crew and cabin crew members. Programs have also been developed for modified screening of elderly passengers similar to those procedures put in place for children.

A cornerstone of TSA's risk-based initiatives is the PreCheck program. PreCheck is TSA's latest version of a trusted traveler program that has been modeled after CBP programs such as Global Entry, SENTRI, and NEXUS. Under the PreCheck program, participants vetted through a background check process as well as other passengers randomly selected and deemed to be low risk under a process known as "managed inclusion" are processed through expedited screening lanes where they can keep shoes on and keep liquids and laptops inside carry-on bags. As of March 2015, PreCheck expedited screening lanes were available at more than 130 airports. The cost of background checks under the PreCheck program is recovered through application fees of $85 per passenger for a five-year membership. TSA's goal is to process 50% of passengers through PreCheck expedited screening lanes, thus reducing the need for standard security screening lanes.

A predecessor test program, called the Registered Traveler program, which involved private vendors that issued and scanned participants' biometric credentials, was scrapped by TSA in 2009 because it failed to show a demonstrable security benefit. Although initial evaluations and consumer response have suggested that PreCheck offers an effective, streamlined screening process, some questions remain regarding whether PreCheck is fully effective in directing security resources to unknown or elevated-risk travelers. While questions remain regarding the security effectiveness of risk-based screening measures like PreCheck, these approaches have demonstrated improved screening efficiency resulting in cost savings for TSA. TSA estimates annual savings in screener workforce costs totaling $110 million as a result of risk-based screening efficiencies.[197]

One concern raised over PreCheck, and the passenger screening process in general, is the public dissemination of instructions, posted on Internet sites, detailing how to decipher boarding passes to determine whether a passenger has been selected for expedited screening, standard screening, or more thorough secondary screening. The lack of encryption and the limited capability TSA has to authenticate boarding passes and travel documents could be exploited to attempt to avoid detection of threat items by more extensive security measures. Other concerns raised over the PreCheck program include the lack of biometric identity authentication and the extensive use of managed inclusion to route travelers not enrolled in or vetted through the PreCheck program through designated PreCheck expedited screening lanes based on random selection or observations by Behavior Detection Officers, canine explosives detection teams, or explosives trace detection equipment. GAO found that TSA had not fully tested its managed inclusion practices and recommended that TSA take steps to ensure and document that testing of the program adheres to established evaluation design practices.[198]

In addition to passenger screening, TSA, in coordination with participating airlines and labor organizations representing airline pilots, has developed a known crewmember program to expedite security screening of airline flight crews.[199] In July 2012, TSA expanded the program to include flight attendants.[200]

TSA has also developed a passenger behavior detection program to identify potential threats based on observed behavioral characteristics. TSA initiated early tests of its Screening Passengers by Observational Techniques (SPOT) program in 2003. By FY2012, the program deployed almost 3,000 BDOs at 176 airports, at an annual cost of about $200 million. Despite its significant expansion, questions remain regarding the effectiveness of the behavioral detection program, and privacy advocates have cautioned that it could devolve into racial or ethnic profiling of passengers despite concerted efforts to focus solely on behaviors rather than individual passenger traits or characteristics. While some Members of Congress have sought to shutter the program, Congress has not moved to do so. For example, H.Amdt. 127 (113th Congress), an amendment to the FY2014 DHS appropriations measure which sought to eliminate funding for the program, failed to pass a floor vote.[36] Congress also has not taken specific action to revamp the program, despite the concerns raised by GAO and the DHS Office of Inspector General.[201]

In the broad context of risk-based passenger screening, TSA policies and procedures regarding prohibited items, including current limitations on the carriage of carry-on liquids, may also be issues of particular interest for congressional oversight for the 114th Congress. In November 2014, outgoing TSA Administrator John Pistole suggested that restrictions on liquids and gels should be relaxed for PreCheck participants.[202]

The Use of Terrorist Watchlists in the Aviation Domain

The failed bombing attempt of Northwest Airlines flight 253 on December 25, 2009, raised policy questions regarding the effective use of terrorist watchlists and intelligence information to identify individuals who may pose a threat to aviation. Specific failings to include the bomber on either the no-fly or selectee list, despite intelligence information suggesting that he posed a security threat, prompted reviews of the intelligence analysis and terrorist watchlisting processes. Adding to these concerns, on the evening of May 3, 2010, Faisal Shazad, a suspect in an attempted car bombing in New York's Times Square, was permitted to board an Emirates Airline flight to Dubai at the John F. Kennedy International airport, even though his name had been added to the no-fly list earlier in the day. He was subsequently identified, removed from the aircraft, and arrested after the airline forwarded the final passenger manifest to CBP's National Targeting Center just prior to departure.[203] Subsequently, TSA modified security directives to require airlines to check passenger names against the no-fly list within two hours of being electronically notified of an urgent update, instead of allowing 24 hours to recheck the list. The event also accelerated the transfer of watchlist checks from the airlines to TSA under the Secure Flight program.

By the end of November 2010, the Department of Homeland Security announced that 100% of passengers flying to or from U.S. airports are being vetted using the Secure Flight system.[204] Secure Flight continues the no-fly and selectee list practices of vetting passenger name records against a subset of the Terrorist Screening Database (TSDB). On international flights, Secure Flight operates in coordination with the use of watchlists by CBP's National Targeting Center— Passenger, which relies on the Advance Passenger Information System (APIS) and other tools to vet both inbound and outbound passenger manifests. In addition to these systems, TSA also relies on risk-based analysis of passenger data carried out by the airlines through use of the Computer- Assisted Passenger Prescreening System (CAPPS). In January 2015, TSA gave notification that it would start incorporating the results of CAPPS assessments, but not the underlying data used to make such assessments, into Secure Flight, along with each passenger's full name, date of birth and PreCheck traveler number (if applicable). These data are used within the Secure Flight system to perform risk-based analyses to determine whether passengers receive expedited, standard, or enhanced screening at airport checkpoints.[205]

Central issues surrounding the use of terrorist watchlists in the aviation domain that may be considered during the 114th Congress include the speed with which watchlists are updated as new intelligence information becomes available; the extent to which all information available to the federal government is exploited to assess possible threats among passengers and airline and airport workers; the ability to detect identity fraud or other attempts to circumvent terrorist watchlist checks; the adequacy of established protocols for providing redress to individuals improperly identified as potential threats; and the adequacy of coordination with international partners.[206]

Security Issues Regarding the Operation of Unmanned Aircraft

Provisions in FAA Modernization and Reform Act of 2012 (P.L. 112-95) require that the Federal Aviation Administration (FAA) take steps by the end of FY2015 to accommodate routine operation of unmanned aircraft systems (UAS, widely referred to as "drones") in domestic airspace. The operation of civilian UAS in domestic airspace raises potential security risks, including the possibility that terrorists could use a drone to carry out an attack against a ground target. It is also possible that drones themselves could be targeted by terrorists or cybercriminals seeking to tap into sensor data transmissions or to cause mayhem by hacking or jamming command and control signals.

Terrorists could potentially use drones to carry out small-scale attacks using explosives, or as platforms for chemical, biological, or radiological attacks. In September 2011, the Federal Bureau of Investigation disrupted a homegrown terrorist plot to attack the Pentagon and the Capitol with large model aircraft packed with high explosives. The incident heightened concern about potential terrorist attacks using unmanned aircraft. Widely publicized drone incidents, including an unauthorized flight at a political rally in Dresden, Germany, in September 2013 that came in close proximity to German Chancellor Angela Merkel; a January 2015 crash of a small drone on the White House lawn in Washington, DC; and a series of unidentified drone flights over landmarks and sensitive locations in Paris, France, in 2015, have raised additional concerns about security threats posed by small unmanned aircraft. Domestically, there have been numerous reports of drones flying in close proximity to airports and manned aircraft, in restricted airspace, and over stadiums and outdoor events. The payload capacities of small unmanned aircraft would limit the damage a terrorist attack using conventional explosives could inflict, but drone attacks using chemical, biological, or radiological weapons could be more serious.

A recent FAA proposal for regulating small unmanned aircraft used for commercial purposes would require TSA to carry out threat assessments of certificated operators as it does for civilian pilots.[207] However, this requirement would not apply to recreational users, who are already permitted to operate small drones at low altitudes. Moreover, while FAA has issued general guidance to law enforcement regarding unlawful UAS operations,[208] it is not clear that law enforcement agencies have sufficient training to respond to this emerging threat.[209]

Technology may help manage security threats posed by unmanned aircraft. Integrating tracking mechanisms as well as incorporating "geo-fencing" capabilities, designed to prevent flights over sensitive locations or in excess of certain altitude limits, into unmanned aircraft systems may help curtail unauthorized flights.[210]

Routine operations of unmanned aircraft by homeland security and law enforcement agencies and others may be vulnerable to jamming or hacking that could result in a crash or hostile takeover, as command and control systems typically use unsecured radio frequencies. Some have recommended that that unmanned aircraft systems be required to have spoof-resistant navigation systems and not be solely reliant on signals from global positioning systems, which can be easily jammed.[211] While TSA has broad statutory authority to address a number of aviation security issues, it has not formally addressed the potential security concerns arising from unmanned aircraft operations in domestic airspace.

While unmanned aircraft may pose security risks, they are also a potential asset for homeland security operations, particularly for CBP border surveillance. CBP currently employs a fleet of 10 modified Predator UASs, and has plans to acquire another 14, to augment its border-patrol capabilities. Operating within specially designated airspace, these unarmed UASs patrol the northern and southern land borders and the Gulf of Mexico to detect potential border violations and monitor suspected drug trafficking, with UAS operators cuing manned responses when appropriate. State and local governments have expressed interest in operating UASs for missions as diverse as traffic patrol, surveillance, and event security. A small but growing number of state and local agencies have acquired drones, some through federal grant programs, and have been issued special authorizations by FAA to fly them. However, many federal, state, and local agencies involved in law enforcement and homeland security appear to be awaiting more specific guidance from FAA regarding the routine operation of public use unmanned aircraft in domestic airspace.

The introduction of drones into domestic surveillance operations presents a host of novel legal issues related to an individual's fundamental privacy interest protected under the Fourth Amendment.[212] To determine if certain government conduct constitutes a search or seizure under that amendment, courts apply an array of tests (depending on the nature of the government action), including the widely used reasonable expectation of privacy test. When applying these tests to drone surveillance, a reviewing court will likely examine the location of the search, the sophistication of the technology used, and society's conception of privacy. For instance, while individuals are accorded substantial protections against warrantless government intrusions into their homes,[213] the Fourth Amendment offers fewer restrictions upon government surveillance occurring in public places,[214] and even fewer at national borders.[215] Likewise, drone surveillance conducted with relatively unsophisticated technology might be subjected to a lower level of judicial scrutiny than investigations conducted with advanced technologies such as thermal imaging or facial recognition. Several measures introduced in Congress would require government agents to obtain warrants before using drones for domestic surveillance, but would create exceptions for patrols of the national borders used to prevent or deter illegal entry and for investigations of credible terrorist threats.[216]

Security Response to Incidents at Screening Checkpoints

On November 1, 2013, a lone gunman targeting TSA employees fired several shots at a screening checkpoint at Los Angeles International Airport (LAX), killing one TSA screener and injuring two other screeners and one airline passenger. The incident raised concerns about the ability of TSA and airport security officials to mitigate and respond to such threats. In a detailed post- incident action report, TSA identified several proposed actions to improve checkpoint security including enhanced active shooter incident training for screeners; better coordination and dissemination of information regarding incidents; expansion and routine testing of alert notification capabilities; and expanded law enforcement presence at checkpoints during peak times. TSA did not recommend mandatory law enforcement presence at checkpoints and did not support proposals to arm certain TSA employees or provide screeners with bulletproof vests.

The Gerardo Hernandez Airport Security Act of 2015 (H.R. 720), named in honor of the TSA screener killed in the LAX incident, addresses security incident response at airports. It would mandate airports to put in place working plans for responding to security incidents including terrorist attacks, active shooters, and incidents targeting passenger checkpoints. Such plans would be required to include details on evacuation, unified incident command, testing and evaluation of communications, timeframes for law enforcement response, and joint exercises and training at airports. Additionally, the bill would require TSA to create a mechanism for sharing information among airports regarding best practices for airport security incident planning, management, and training. The bill also would require TSA to identify ways to expand the availability of funding for checkpoint screening law enforcement support through cost savings from improved efficiencies.

Mitigating the Threat of Shoulder-Fired Missiles to Civilian Aircraft

The threat to civilian aircraft posed by shoulder-fired missiles or other standoff weapons capable of downing an airliner remains a vexing concern for aviation security specialists and policymakers. The State Department has estimated that, since the 1970s, over 40 civilian aircraft have been hit by shoulder-fired missiles, causing 25 crashes and more than 600 deaths. Most of these incidents involved small aircraft operated at low altitudes in areas of ongoing armed conflicts, although some larger jets have also been destroyed. Notably, on April 6, 1994, an executive jet carrying the Presidents of Rwanda and Burundi was shot down while on approach to Kigali, Rwanda, and on October 10, 1998, a Boeing 727 was destroyed by rebels in the Democratic Republic of Congo. The dangers of operating civil aircraft in and near regions of armed conflict has recently been a topic of particular concern following the July 17, 2014, downing of Malaysia Airlines Flight 17, a Boeing 777, over eastern Ukraine after being struck by a much larger surface-to-air missile.

The terrorist threat posed by small man-portable shoulder-fired missiles was brought into the spotlight soon after the 9/11 terrorist attacks by the November 2002 attempted downing of a chartered Israeli airliner in Mombasa, Kenya, the first time such an event took place outside of a conflict zone. In 2003, then-Secretary of State Colin Powell remarked that there was "no threat more serious to aviation."[217] Since then, Department of State and military initiatives seeking bilateral cooperation and voluntary reductions of man-portable air defense systems (MANPADS) stockpiles have reduced worldwide inventories by at least 32,500 missiles.[218] Despite this progress, such weapons may still be in the hands of potential terrorists. This threat, combined with the limited capability to improve security beyond airport perimeters and to modify flight paths, leaves civil aircraft vulnerable to missile attacks.

The most visible DHS initiative to address the threat was the multiyear Counter-MANPADS program carried out by the DHS Science and Technology Directorate. The program concluded in 2009 with extensive operational and live-fire testing along with FAA certification of two systems capable of protecting airliners against heat-seeking missiles. The systems have not been operationally deployed on commercial airliners, however, due largely to high acquisition and life- cycle costs. Some critics have also pointed out that the units do not protect against the full range of potential weapons that pose a potential threat to civil airliners. Proponents, however, argue that the systems do appear to provide effective protection against what is likely the most menacing standoff threat to civil airliners: heat-seeking MANPADS. Nonetheless, the airlines have not voluntarily invested in these systems for operational use, and argue that the costs for such systems should be borne, at least in part, by the federal government. Policy discussions have focused mostly on whether to fund the acquisition of limited numbers of the units for use by the Civil Reserve Aviation Fleet, civilian airliners that can be called up to transport troops and supplies for the military. Other approaches to protecting aircraft, including ground-based missile countermeasures and escort planes or drones equipped with antimissile technology, have been considered on a more limited basis, but these options face operational challenges that may limit their effectiveness.

While MANPADS are mainly seen as a security threat to civil aviation overseas, a MANPADS attack in the United States could have a considerable, long-lasting impact on the airline industry. At the airport level, improving security and reducing the vulnerability of flight paths to potential MANPADS attacks continues to pose unique challenges. While major U.S. airports have conducted vulnerability studies, and many have partnered with federal, state, and local law enforcement agencies to reduce vulnerabilities to some degree, these efforts face significant challenges because of limited resources and large geographic areas where aircraft are vulnerable to attack. While considerable attention has been given to this issue in years past, considerable vulnerabilities remain, and any terrorist attempts to exploit those vulnerabilities could quickly escalate the threat of shoulder-fired missiles to a major national security priority.

DISASTER PREPAREDNESS, RESPONSE, AND RECOVERY

Disaster Assistance Funding

The majority of disaster assistance provided by the Federal Emergency Management Agency (FEMA) to states and localities after a declared emergency or major disaster is funded with monies from the Disaster Relief Fund (DRF).[219]

In general, Congress annually appropriates budget authority to the DRF to ensure that funding is available for recovery projects from previous incidents (some of these projects take several years to complete) and to create a reserve to pay for emergencies and major disasters that might occur that fiscal year. Any remaining balance in the DRF at the end of the fiscal year is carried over to the next fiscal year (see Table 2).

From FY2005 to FY2014 Congress provided additional budget authority for the DRF through a combination of supplemental and continuing appropriations twelve times.[220] The reliance on emergency supplemental appropriations has been of particular congressional concern. Supplemental appropriations for disasters are often designated as an emergency expenditure, which under congressional budgetary procedures can exceed discretionary spending limits. In addition, the number of disasters being declared over the last two decades has risen, as have their costs.[221] These upward trends have led some to discuss how to reduce or offset federal spending on major disasters.

Partly in response to these discussions, Congress included provisions on disaster relief spending when it passed P.L. 112-25, the Budget Control Act (BCA).[222] The BCA sets overall discretionary spending caps and provides two types of adjustments that could be applied to make room for disaster assistance—a limited adjustment specifically for the costs of major disasters under the Stafford Act, and an unlimited adjustment for more broadly defined emergency spending.

The adjustment limitation is not a restriction on disaster assistance—it is a restriction on how much the discretionary budget cap can be adjusted upward by that particular mechanism to accommodate the assistance.

FY2013 represented the first fiscal year in which the DRF received all of the funding available under the BCA's allowable adjustment for disaster relief, and the first time that disaster relief in excess of the allowable adjustment was covered by an emergency designation. The DRF had roughly $7.3 billion available for initial disaster needs when Hurricane Sandy made landfall in the northeastern United States in October 2012. While the $7.3 billion helped address the initial needs of the disaster, it was insufficient to fund the entire recovery. When there is a shortfall in the DRF, additional budget authority has typically been provided through a continuing resolution or supplemental appropriation. In the case of Hurricane Sandy, Congress passed a $50.5 billion package of disaster relief largely focused on responding to Hurricane Sandy, including $11.5 billion for the DRF.[223]

One noteworthy aspect of the supplemental funding for Hurricane Sandy was the amount of time Congress took to pass a supplemental funding measure. Prior to FY2013, when a catastrophic disaster occurred (such as Hurricane Katrina or the terrorist attacks of 9/11) Congress generally had to act expeditiously to provide supplemental funding within days to weeks after an incident. In contrast, supplemental funding for Hurricane Sandy was enacted 91 days after the incident was declared a major disaster.[224] The $7.3 billion in available funds in the DRF at the time of the hurricane may have allowed Congress time to debate supplemental funding as well as target specific areas in need of assistance.

It could be argued that while the BCA included an accommodation to provide dedicated additional funding for many disasters, catastrophic events such as Hurricane Sandy still represent a challenge to those who wish to reduce or eliminate emergency designations for disaster relief funding.

Table 2. Disaster Relief Fund Total Appropriations and Carried-over Balances, FY2012-FY2015

FY2012 through FY2015 (in millions of dollars)		
Fiscal Year	**Total Appropriation**	**Carried over Balance from Prior Fiscal Year**
FY2012	$13,500	$93
FY2013	$18,492	$1,020
FY2014	$6,220	$8,492
FY2015	$6,221	$6,978

Source: Figures include annual and supplemental appropriations; These figures do not include prior-year deobligations. Carryover data derived from the *Disaster Relief Fund: Congressional Monthly Report* for March of 2012, February 2013, and October 2014.

Another potential challenge concerns how the allowable adjustment is calculated. The Office of Management and Budget (OMB) manages the sequestration process and the limits on adjustments available to raise the spending cap. The BCA requires OMB to annually calculate the adjusted 10-year rolling average of disaster relief spending that sets the allowable cap adjustment for disaster relief. The highest and the lowest years in terms of disaster relief costs are eliminated from the calculation. The sizeable initial disaster relief expenditures for Hurricane Katrina and the other 2005 storms will begin to drop out of the 10-year range and start to lose relevance in calculating the allowable adjustment for disaster assistance for FY2016. Disaster relief funding in post-BCA years is defined by congressional designation, so only a fraction of the cost of the Hurricane Sandy supplemental would be counted toward the 10-year rolling average. The absence of significant spending in some years would also lower the allowable adjustment. This reduction could increase the likelihood that the cap will be breached if a large-scale disaster needs funding in excess of the allowable adjustment.

Congress could choose to continue to use emergency funding to meet unbudgeted disaster relief needs, or explore options that might increase the allowable adjustment. For example, emergency declarations and Fire Management Assistance Grants are also funded through the DRF. Congress could require that OMB combine the costs associated with these declarations with major disasters when calculating the allowable adjustment in order to increase the cap on disaster spending.

Another potential issue is the amount of money the federal government is providing for disaster relief. While some might argue the expenditures are justified because they provide important assistance to states and localities, others may be interested in finding ways to reduce federal costs. For example, Congress could change emergency and major disaster declaration criteria to limit the number of events eligible for federal assistance, and reduce the standard 75% federal to state cost-share for recovery to a lower percentage, or convert some (or all) assistance grants to low interest loans.

Firefighter Assistance Programs

Although firefighting activities are traditionally the responsibility of states and local communities, Congress has established federal firefighter assistance grant programs within DHS to provide additional support for local fire departments. In 2000, the 106th Congress established the Assistance to Firefighters Grant Program (AFG), which provides grants to local fire departments for firefighting equipment and training. In the wake of the 9/11 attacks, the scope and funding for AFG were subsequently expanded.

Additionally in 2003, the 108th Congress established the Staffing for Adequate Fire and Emergency Response (SAFER) program, which provides grants to support firefighter staffing.

In the 114th Congress, debate over firefighter assistance programs is likely to take place within the appropriations process. Arriving at funding levels for AFG and SAFER is subject to two countervailing considerations. On the one hand, inadequate state and local public safety budgets have led many to argue for the necessity of maintaining, if not increasing, federal grant support for fire departments. On the other hand, concerns over reducing overall federal discretionary spending have led others to question whether continued or reduced federal support for AFG and SAFER is warranted.

Congress reauthorized AFG and SAFER in the FY2013 National Defense Authorization Act (P.L. 112-239). The reauthorized statute makes changes in AFG grant caps and distribution formulas, and removes or changes certain SAFER grant restrictions and limitations. The 114th Congress will likely continue to oversee the impact of AFG and SAFER grant changes mandated by the reauthorization. The continuing issue is how effectively grants are being distributed and used to protect the health and safety of the public and firefighting personnel against fire and fire-related hazards.

Emergency Communications

Emergency communications systems support first responders and other emergency personnel, disseminate alerts and warnings to residents in endangered areas, and relay calls for help through 911 call networks. Their networks support day-to-day needs to protect the safety of the public and deliver critical information before, during, and after disasters.

The technologies that support emergency communications are converging toward a common platform using the Internet Protocol (IP). Federal, state, and local agencies are investing in IP- enabled communications infrastructure that can be shared to support all forms of emergency communications. Notable examples of new investment are

- Interoperable public safety communications networks;
- Digital alerts and warnings; and
- Next-Generation 9-1-1 (NG 9-1-1) networks.

The transition to IP-enabled networks and devices places additional emphasis on cybersecurity policies. Additionally, adapting these new technologies to existing systems and processes poses additional challenges and requirements for change, such as in governance models, operating procedures, standards development, training and planning for sustainable investments.

Notable federal programs, in addition to grant programs, are the First Responder Network Authority (FirstNet);[225] the Integrated Public Alert and Warning System (IPAWS);[226] and the 9-1-1 Implementation Coordination Office (ICO),[227] which is expected to be re-established in 2015. FirstNet is an independent authority established within the National Telecommunications and Information Administration (NTIA), to develop a nationwide broadband network for emergency communications. IPAWS alert and warning capabilities are coordinated through the Federal Emergency Management Agency with the participation of the Federal Communications Commission. The functions of ICO, which focus on providing a base for improving 9-1-1 infrastructure, are to be shared by the NTIA and the National Highway Traffic Safety Administration. Coordination of these discrete programs is assisted through federal programs and guidance described in the *National Emergency Communications Plan* of the Department of Homeland Security (DHS).[228] The Homeland Security Act of 2002 (P.L. 107-296), Title XVIII, as amended, directs the DHS Office of Emergency Communications to develop and periodically update a plan in consultation with federal, state, local, tribal, territorial, and private sector stakeholders.

The 2014 *National Emergency Communications Plan* recognizes the advantages of converging emergency communications platforms and coordinating across federal, state, local, and tribal agencies. The plan identifies four categories of emergency response that in time should converge. These are: communications for incidence response and coordination; notifications and alerts and warnings; public information exchange; and requests for assistance and reporting. The top three priorities for the plan over the three to five years following publication are: identifying and prioritizing areas for improvement in emergency responders' narrowband networks (Land Mobile Radio, LMR); facilitating the adoption, integration, and use of broadband technologies, notably the broadband network to be deployed by FirstNet; and enhancing coordination among stakeholders across the emergency response community.

Development of the National Preparedness System

The United States is threatened by a wide array of hazards, including natural disasters, acts of terrorism, viral pandemics, and manmade disasters such as the *Deepwater Horizon* oil spill. The way the nation strategically prioritizes and allocates resources to prepare for disasters can significantly influence the ultimate cost to society, both in the number of human casualties and the scope of economic damage. As required by Subtitle C of the Post-Katrina Emergency Reform Act of 2006 (P.L. 109-295, 6 U.S.C. §741-764), the federal government has developed a National Preparedness System (NPS) to guide how the nation, to include the "whole community,"[229] can "prevent, protect against, mitigate the effects of, respond to, and recover from those threats that pose the greatest risk to the security of the Nation."[230]

The NPS is supported by numerous strategic policies, national planning frameworks, and federal interagency operational plans, all as mandated by Presidential Policy Directive 8, National Preparedness (PPD-8).[231] In brief, the NPS and its many component policies embody the strategic vision and planning of the federal government, with input from the whole community, as it relates to preparing the nation for disasters. The NPS also establishes methods for achieving that level of preparedness for both federal and non-federal partners. Furthermore, the NPS includes annual National Preparedness Reports that are the "report cards" of progress made toward achieving national preparedness objectives. The Reports rely heavily on a self-assessment process, called the Threat and Hazard Identification and Risk Assessment (THIRA),[232] to incorporate the perceived risks and goals of the whole community into the national preparedness system. In this respect, the NPS's influence may extend to budgetary decisions, the assignment of duties and responsibilities across the nation, and the creation of long-term policy objectives for disaster preparedness.

The 114th Congress may wish to continue its oversight of how the NPS is developing on a variety of factors, such as whether:

- the NPS conforms to the objectives of the PKEMRA statute;
- federal roles and responsibilities have been properly assigned and resourced to execute the core capabilities needed to prevent, protect against, mitigate the effects of, respond to, and recover from the greatest risks;
- non-federal resources and stakeholders are efficiently incorporated into NPS policies;

- federal, state, and local government officials are allocating sufficient resources to the preparedness mission relative to other homeland security missions.

Hurricane Sandy Recovery

On the evening of October 29, 2012, Hurricane Sandy, the second-largest Atlantic storm on record, made landfall in southern New Jersey. The consequences of the storm were considered to be immense: at least 159 people died, over 23,000 people required temporary shelters, 8.5 million customers were left without power, approximately $65 billion in damages were incurred, and 650,000 homes were damaged or destroyed.[233] In recognition of the scale and complexity of Hurricane Sandy, the Administration initiated a coordinated effort across multiple federal agencies to support the region in responding to and recovering from the disaster. On December 7, 2013, President Barack Obama issued Executive Order (E.O.) 13632, *Establishing the Hurricane Sandy Rebuilding Task Force*.[234]

The key deliverable of the established Task Force, as mandated by Section 5 of E.O. 13632, is the Hurricane Sandy Rebuilding Strategy (HSRS). The HSRS is a wide-ranging, lengthy policy document providing 69 different recommendations for a long-term recovery plan for the impacted region. In their totality, the recommendations of HSRS presented the Administration's strategic vision for the Hurricane Sandy recovery process, including how federal funds should be expended, how federal agencies should synchronize their efforts, and how the region could leverage the recovery process from Sandy to prepare for future disasters. As of a Fall 2014 Progress Report of the HSRS, 50 of the 69 recommendations were reported as completed by the Administration.[235]

There are numerous issues that may arise in the 114th Congress in relation to the Hurricane Sandy recovery process. Congressional oversight may be required for many more years to ensure the appropriate use of billions of dollars in federal assistance to support the completion of major infrastructure projects in the region. Further legislative and executive branch action is also needed to implement many of the HSRS recommendations if they are to apply to future disaster recovery efforts. The 114th Congress may also evaluate whether an entity in the mode of the Hurricane Sandy Task Force is necessary to achieve rebuilding success following future disasters of the magnitude of Hurricane Sandy.

Implementation of the Sandy Recovery Improvement Act

On January 29, 2013, the Disaster Relief Appropriations Act, 2013, a $50.5 billion package of disaster assistance largely focused on responding to Hurricane Sandy, was enacted as P.L. 113-2. In addition to evaluating the need for supplemental appropriations in response to Hurricane Sandy, the 112th and 113th Congresses considered reforming provisions of the Stafford Act. Generally, concerns were raised that the recovery from Hurricane Sandy would be plagued by perceived delays and bureaucratic burdens that inhibited the recovery following Hurricane Katrina. The Sandy Recovery Improvement Act of 2013 (SRIA)[236] revised the Robert T. Stafford Disaster Relief and Emergency Assistance Act (the Stafford Act, P.L. 93-288, as amended), which is the primary source of authorities for disaster assistance programs for the Federal Emergency Management Agency (FEMA).

SRIA amended the Stafford Act with a stated goal of improving the efficiency and quality of disaster assistance provided by FEMA. Briefly, SRIA required FEMA to (among other activities):

- Establish a new set of alternative procedures for administering the Public Assistance Program, which provides assistance for debris removal and the repair and restoration of eligible facilities;
- Revise the administration of the Hazard Mitigation Grant Program, to include a possible advancement of 25% of grant funds;
- Create an alternative dispute resolution procedure (including binding arbitration), building on FEMA's current appeals process, to resolve federal and state disagreements on costs and eligibility questions;
- Update the regulatory factors considered when assessing the need for Individual Assistance in the disaster declaration process; and
- Implement a process for the chief executive of a tribal government to directly request major disaster or emergency declarations from the President, much as a governor can for a state.

The 114th Congress may oversee the continued implementation of these reforms to the Stafford Act and FEMA's disaster assistance programs and policies. Varying levels of progress have been made implementing each of the reforms, though some of the provisions have not been implemented within the timeframe required by SRIA.[237] In addition, the 114th Congress may consider legislation to:

- further address any perceived problems that have arisen in implementing SRIA reforms;
- codify certain policies and regulations FEMA has established to implement SRIA, especially with regards to the Public Assistance Alternative Procedures; or
- direct additional audits and reviews of the reforms.[238]

Public Health and Medical Services

The nation's public health emergency management laws expanded considerably following the terrorist attacks in 2001 and Hurricane Katrina in 2005, in particular. Since then a varied slate of public health incidents—including natural and man-made disasters and outbreaks of infectious disease—show both improvements in the nation's readiness for public health and medical emergencies, and persistent gaps. For example, response plans may not sufficiently anticipate situations that arise. The technology needed to assess threats (such as radiation or chemical exposure) may be limited. Medical countermeasures (i.e., vaccines, antidotes, or treatments for harmful exposures) may not be available in adequate amounts, if at all. The means to distribute existing countermeasures in a timely manner may be limited. The medical system may lack adequate capacity to respond to mass casualty incidents. Funding for response costs may not be available immediately, or at all. Given the robust roles of the private sector and state and local governments in preparedness and response efforts, the federal government's ability to address these gaps through funding and other policies may also be limited.[239]

The 113th Congress reauthorized the body of law that directs most public health and medical preparedness and response activities in the Department of Health and Human Services (HHS) through the Pandemic and All-Hazards Preparedness Reauthorization Act of 2013 (PAHPRA, P.L. 113-5). The reauthorization focused in particular on improving federal programs to assure the availability of medical countermeasures in an emergency.[240] (See also "Medical Countermeasures to Chemical, Biological, Radiological, and Nuclear Terrorism".) PAHPRA also reauthorized grants to states for public health and health system preparedness, as well as funding for a number of other specific programs. In general, the appropriations amounts that are authorized for programs under PAHPRA are lower than the amounts authorized for these programs in the 2006 reauthorization.[241]

Assistance under the Stafford Act[242] can help federal, state, and local agencies with the costs of public health emergency activities such as assuring food and water safety, and monitoring illness rates in affected communities.[243] However, there is no federal assistance program designed specifically to cover the uninsured or uncompensated costs of individual health care—including mental health care—that may be needed as a consequence of a disaster. There is no consensus that this should be a federal responsibility. Nonetheless, when faced with mass casualty incidents, hospitals, physicians, and other providers may face considerable pressure to deliver care without a clear source of reimbursement. On several occasions, Congress has provided special assistance to address uncompensated disaster-related health care costs after an incident.[244] Depending upon its implementation, the Patient Protection and Affordable Care Act (ACA, P.L. 111-148, as amended) may mitigate concerns about disaster-related health care costs by decreasing the ranks of the uninsured.[245]

Funding for the response to a public health incident is a challenge when the incident does not lead to a declaration under the Stafford Act. The HHS Secretary has authority for a no-year Public Health Emergency Fund (PHEF), but this fund does not have a balance, and Congress has not appropriated monies to it for many years.[246] Stating that "The lack of dedicated and flexible funding impeded [HHS's] ability to respond more quickly to control the spread of Ebola at its source in West Africa" in 2014, the Obama administration seeks $110 million for the PHEF in its FY2016 budget request.[247]

DHS Management Issues

The Management Budget

Title I of the Homeland Security Appropriations bill contains the funding for the primary management functions of DHS. Originally envisioned as a skeleton staff, the headquarters and management functions have grown in response to criticism of the department's ability to effectively oversee its own activities. In debates over departmental funding, questioning the size and effectiveness of the department's management cadre is a common theme.

In FY2003, the first year of DHS operations, $195 million was provided for management accounts. In FY2015, those accounts were funded at $743 million. This growth is due to several factors, including increases in staff size required to perform oversight functions, rising personnel costs, technology investments, and increasing real estate expenses for the department's headquarters offices. In recent years, these accounts have been requested at higher levels than might otherwise be expected due to the inclusion of significant capital initiatives, such as headquarters consolidation and data center migration in these accounts, and personnel initiatives aimed at boosting the department's cadre of acquisition oversight staff and reducing the number of contractors in sensitive positions.

Unity of Effort

One of the unresolved debates from the development of DHS was how extensive the involvement would be of departmental management in the functioning of departmental components. Some policy experts supported a strong management function, which would replace the leadership of the components, while others supported a smaller management function that allowed components to function freely in their areas of expertise much as they had before.

Once the department was established, it became clear that a small management cadre could not provide adequate coordination of policy or oversight of the department. The benefits of coordinated action by a large organization, including setting operational and budgetary priorities, were being lost due to the lack of strong leadership. As its components continued to perform their missions, the department undertook efforts to establish a unified identity and way of doing business. The term "One DHS" was used to describe these initiatives under Tom Ridge, the first secretary of the department, and the efforts continued through secretaries Michael Chertoff and Janet Napolitano.

On April 22, 2014, months into his tenure as the fourth secretary of DHS, Jeh Johnson issued a memorandum to DHS leadership, entitled "Strengthening Departmental Unity of Effort." This now-widely circulated memorandum set out an agenda to reform the Department of Homeland Security way of doing business by implementing new analytical and decisionmaking processes to develop strategy, plan, and identify joint requirements. These would bring component leadership together above the component level to ensure unity of effort across the department.

Secretary Johnson described it this way in a Federal Times interview:

> We've embarked on a unity of effort initiative that promotes greater coordination among department, greater centralized decision-making at headquarters, a more strategic approach to our budget building process, a more strategic departmentwide approach to our acquisition strategy. It is clearly a balance. Within the Department of Homeland Security there are components that long predated the Department of Homeland Security. And so what we are not asking components to do is to all act and behave together. They are distinct cultures.... But what we are asking and expecting our component leadership to do is participate with us in a more strategic approach to promote greater efficiency in how we operate, how we conduct ourselves, particularly in our budget process and in our acquisitions.[248]

The memorandum laid out four areas of initial focus. The first was to bring together senior leaders of the department in two groups: a Senior Leaders Council to discuss "overall policy, strategy, operations and Departmental guidance," and a Deputies Management Action Group (DMAG) to "advance joint requirements development, program and budget review, acquisition reform, operational planning, and joint operations." The second area was to make improvements to the departmental management processes for investments. Specifically, incorporating strategic analysis and joint requirements planning into the annual budget development process, directing the DMAG to develop and facilitate a component-driven joint requirements process, and reviewing and updating the DHS acquisition oversight framework. The third was developing a stronger strategy, planning, and analytic capability within the Office of Policy. The fourth was to improve coordination of cross-component operations.

Bipartisan support for these reforms was shown in several hearings in the 113th Congress, and the FY2015 Homeland Security Appropriations Act included funding requested for this initiative. Both House and Senate Appropriations Committee reports included language supportive of the department's managerial reorganization.[249]

Several of the action items included in the memorandum were completed in 2014, such as the establishment of a Cost Analysis Division in the Office of the Chief Financial Officer in May 2014. The role of this division is to ensure life-cycle cost estimates are part of major acquisition plans. DHS also completed development of a Southern Border and Approaches Campaign

Plan— a four-year strategic framework for joint operations securing the southern border of the United States.

The department is continuing to seek legislation to authorize certain aspects of the proposed reforms, and to help make permanent other changes. Congress may wish to consider these requests, potentially debating the appropriate role of departmental level management at DHS, and monitor the progress of management reforms to see how they are proceeding and whether they are having the desired effect.

DHS Financial Management Reforms

From its inception, DHS has faced financial management challenges. Transferring components and their budgets between agencies is a complex process in the best of situations, but doing it in the process of establishing a new department that is performing important national security missions from its first day of operations adds additional complexity. This was further compounded by inherited financial management problems that existed at several major legacy components, including the Coast Guard, FEMA, and elements that formed ICE.[250]

The department tried to develop its own financial management system in-house through a project known as "eMerge2," but failed. A second attempt was made to implement a department-wide system through contracting with outside developers under the Transformation and Systems Consolidation initiative, or TASC. After GAO ruled that DHS had improperly awarded the initial $450 million contract—the latest result from a series of protests and legal challenges that had delayed the project—the award was cancelled and the project shelved.[251]

Although the department has been on the GAO High Risk List since it was created, progress has been made on reducing the number of material weaknesses in the department's financial controls. FY2012 was the first year since its establishment that DHS was able to complete a qualified audit of all its financial statements.

The independent auditor noted five deficiencies in internal controls[252] that were significant enough to be considered material weaknesses:

- Financial Reporting;
- Information Technology Controls and Financial System Functionality;
- Property, Plant and Equipment;

- Environmental and Other Liabilities; and
- Budgetary Accounting.

In FY2013, DHS was able to complete another qualified audit, and the number of material weaknesses dropped to four with the resolution of "Environmental and Other Liabilities." [253] In FY2014 DHS sustained that progress and obtained a clean opinion on all its financial statements for the first time in its history. The DHS Office of Inspector General termed it "a significant achievement that built on previous years' successes,"[254] but noted the four deficiencies in internal control remained. The OIG noted that:

> In FY2015 and beyond, DHS' continuing challenge will be to sustain its progress in achieving an unmodified opinion on its financial statements and avoid slipping backward. To sustain its clean opinion on financial statements and obtain an unqualified (clean) opinion on its internal control over financial reporting, the Department must continue its remediation efforts and stay focused. [255]

The 114th Congress will likely continue its interest in DHS's efforts to improve its internal financial systems, given the relative size of the department's budget, the interest expressed in this issue by authorizing committee leadership, and the current drive for stricter budgetary oversight.

These issues could be examined at the department, component, or program level. Oversight might include a review of the internal financial and administrative controls in the administration of specific grant programs, and improper payments made under the programs. Consideration of the internal financial and management controls might include the extent to which DHS is complying with existing control standards, penalties for noncompliance, and whether the standards should be adjusted to account for any unique elements in the DHS programs.

Headquarters Consolidation

The Department of Homeland Security's headquarters footprint occupies more than 7 million square feet of office space in about 50 separate locations in the greater Washington, DC, area. This is largely a legacy of how the department was assembled in a short period of time from 22 separate federal agencies which were themselves spread across the National Capital region. The fragmentation of headquarters is cited by the department as a major contributor to inefficiencies, including time lost shuttling staff between headquarters elements; additional security, real estate, and administrative costs; and reduced cohesion among the components that make up the department.

To unify the department's headquarters functions, the department approved a $3.4 billion master plan to create a new DHS headquarters on the grounds of St. Elizabeths in Anacostia. According to GSA, this is the largest federal office construction since the Pentagon was built during World War II. $1.4 billion of this project was to be funded through the DHS budget, and $2 billion through the GSA.[256] Thus far a total of over $1.75 billion has been appropriated for the project—$543 million for DHS and $1,207 million to GSA through FY2015. Phase 1A of the project—a new Coast Guard headquarters facility—has been completed with the funding already provided by Congress and is now in use.

In 2013, a revised construction schedule was developed, projecting lower levels of appropriations and a longer timeline for the project. Under the new projection, the project would be completed in FY2026 at a cost of $4.5 billion.[257] The project was criticized by GAO in September 2014 for not conforming to certain leading practices for capital decisionmaking processes. DHS and GSA revised its plans as a result of similar observations by GAO and other critics, announcing a new plan that would be completed in FY2021, and cost $3.7 billion.

According to GSA, even with the cost increases from delaying funding, the project would still result in over $430 million in projected savings compared to leasing over the next 30 years. This estimate does not take into account the costs GSA would have to incur to stabilize and maintain the St. Elizabeths campus if the project were halted, or the efficiencies for DHS that a consolidated headquarters would generate.[258]

With the Coast Guard now operating from St. Elizabeths, the discussion in Congress becomes less about whether to proceed with consolidation at St. Elizabeths, but how. Whether the new headquarters consolidation plan conforms to best practices identified by GAO and the realities of the budget situation are topics that the 114th Congress may explore.

Department of Homeland Security Personnel Issues

An essential consideration underlying the mission and performance of the Department of Homeland Security (DHS) is human resource management

(HRM). Responsibility for HRM is vested in the Office of the Chief Human Capital Officer (OCHCO), an entity organizationally and for appropriations purposes located within the Under Secretary for Management. The OCHCO plays a critical role in supporting and executing the department's "Strategic Plan for Fiscal Years 2012-2016."[259] The current chief human capital officer assumed the position on August 4, 2011, and with the change in the appointment from political to career status, is the first career member of the Senior Executive Service to hold the office.

During the 114th Congress, the House of Representatives and the Senate may conduct oversight of personnel issues at DHS. Among the matters that may be considered are those related to succession management; employee morale; the loaned executive program; the use of digital technology to train, and recruit and retain employees; and veteran employment policies. Each of these issues is briefly discussed below. Hearings conducted by the House of Representatives and the Senate related to DHS appropriations or management matters could include review of these issues.

Each May, during Public Service Recognition Week, the value of public service is discussed and the work of public servants, including federal employees, is highlighted and honored. This observance would provide an occasion for Congress to annually review human resources management at the department, either through meetings with DHS officials and the CHCO or an oversight hearing. Such activities could supplement congressional review and oversight of the OCHCO and current and developing HRM policies at DHS, throughout the year.

Succession Management

Over the last several years, some attention has focused on the Department of Homeland Security's difficulties in retaining rank and file and senior employees[260] and vacancies in its executive positions.[261] This discussion, coupled with the circumstance of the upcoming November 2016 presidential election, may prompt DHS to review its policies and procedures for succession planning.

According to the Office of Personnel Management (OPM), a strategic succession planning system involves "planning, designing, implementing, and evaluating succession management programs" to strengthen the "current and future organizational leadership capacity" of an agency.[262] OPM defines succession management as

> a systematic approach for: Shaping the leadership culture. Building a leadership pipeline/talent pool to ensure leadership continuity. Developing potential successors whose strengths will best fit with the agency's needs. Identifying the best candidates for categories of positions. Concentrating resources on the talent development process, yielding a greater return on investment.[263]

Congress has conducted review and oversight of policies and procedures for succession planning at DHS before, as part of the presidential transition process. For example, the Senate Subcommittee on Oversight of Government Management, the Federal Workforce, and the District of Columbia of the Committee on Homeland Security and Governmental Affairs conducted a hearing on September 18, 2008, prior to the 2008 presidential election, related to presidential transition. DHS Under Secretary for Management Elaine Duke testified about the department's succession planning activities. She told the committee that the DHS transition efforts began in Spring 2007, and involved "identifying critical positions that support component priorities and using our own Critical Position Succession Planning template to ensure a pipeline of successors to critical positions, which are viewed as corporate assets and monitored on a regular basis." She also noted that, "components identified senior career civil servants who will assume responsibility for political positions during the time of transition" and "identified key competencies needed for success in these positions, assessed successor pools, prepared development plans, assessed our ability to recruit externally, and identified critical positions that are vacant or have high succession risk."[264]

A September 24, 2008, hearing conducted by the House Subcommittee on Government Management, Organization, and Procurement of the Committee on Oversight and Government Reform included discussions of transition planning at DHS, aspects of which relate to succession management.[265] The subcommittee received testimony from Doris Hausser who represented a panel of the National Academy of Public Administration (NAPA) and highlighted recommendations for a comprehensive transition program that were discussed in the NAPA report entitled "Addressing the 2009 Presidential Transition at the Department of Homeland Security."[266] Among those recommendations were actions to occur during the period preceding the national party conventions, including that all critical non-career executive positions be identified; a transition training plan with objectives, time frames, participants and resources be developed; and training for career executives to service in new roles during transition be implemented.[267]

However, the department's "Strategic Plan Fiscal Years 2012-2016" and the DHS congressional submission that accompanied the FY2016 budget proposal do not specifically mention succession planning. A search of the DHS website did not reveal a publicly available succession plan or the Critical Position Succession Planning template mentioned during the 2008 Senate hearing.[268]

Congress may be interested in re-examining policies on succession management (both outside of and during a presidential transition) within DHS, including the department's plans to review and update its succession plans, transition plans for executive positions, transition training programs for career executives, and the operation of the rotation program. The House of Representatives and the Senate could include a provision in the annual DHS appropriations bill directing that certain HRM policy documents, such as those related to succession management, be easily accessible on the OCHCO webpage.[269]

Morale of DHS Employees

Concerns about the morale of DHS employees have persisted since the department was created. The responses provided by department employees to the annual Employee Viewpoint Survey conducted by the Office of Personnel Management are regularly examined as evidence of that dissatisfaction. In particular, nine questions in the survey solicit employee views on "My Satisfaction."[270] The 2014 survey results (the most recent available) reveal a continuing decline in DHS employee satisfaction. Responses on two of the questions illustrate this.

The question on how satisfied employees were with their jobs solicited these views from some 40,110 employees:

- "Very satisfied" or "Satisfied" (53.1%),
- "Neither Satisfied nor Dissatisfied" (20.9%), or
- "Dissatisfied" or "Very Dissatisfied" (26%).[271]

The question on how satisfied those employees were with their organization solicited these views from some 40,203 employees:

- "Very satisfied" or "Satisfied" (41.7%),
- "Neither Satisfied nor Dissatisfied" (23.1%), or
- "Dissatisfied" or "Very Dissatisfied" (35.1%).[272]

"to provide individual advice to ... FEMA Region VIII on supporting the restoration of lifeline functions immediately following a catastrophic earthquake along the Wasatch Fault in Utah."[285]

Congress may wish to examine the operation of the Loaned Executive Program, including results expected and achieved to date, the working relationships between the loaned executives and senior executives and career employees in the department, and plans for the use of additional loaned executives by DHS components.

Digital Technology for Training, Recruitment, and Retention

The use of digital technology to facilitate training, and recruitment and retention, and support the management and development of the federal workforce continues to be of interest to federal executives. For example, in January 2015, the National Academy of Public Administration and ICF International reported on the views of randomly selected senior federal civil servants,[286] referred to as "Federal Leaders," who were surveyed on issues related to digital technology and the federal government. The survey defined digital technology as "Technology that systemically connects people with each other and with information (data or content). This includes transactional services (online forms, benefits applications, e-commerce) across a variety of devices (mobile, tablet, desktop), and delivery mechanisms (websites, mobile applications, and social media)."[287]

The views of the Federal Leaders were obtained through an online survey that included approximately 50 questions, some of which solicited "open-ended responses." A total of 510 respondents completed the survey for a response rate of 5.7% and an overall margin of error of +/-4.2 percentage points.[288] A part of the survey included questions related to workforce training, recruiting, and retention and revealed the following views:

- 76% of Federal Leaders responded that "they are adequately trained to take advantage of digital technologies in the workplace"; 36% believed that "their agency's employees are adequately trained." The lack of skilled employees was considered "to be one of the top 5 barriers ... to better implementing digital technology in the workplace."
- 43% of Federal Leaders responded that their agency had created offices or positions[289] to assist in implementing new digital technology; 58% of respondents who have a role in procuring digital

technology reported that such offices or positions had been established.

- 33% of Federal Leaders responded that the use of digital technology in their agency "had a positive impact on recruiting and retention"; less than 25% of respondents viewed the use of digital technology "as a recruiting and retention competitive advantage."[290]

The report recommended that agencies "invest in, develop, and implement training" both on new technology and "to reinforce the use of existing technologies"; use a "a blended approach" for the training "that mixes classroom with online courses, mobile-learning, and on-the-job-training"; and jointly convene interagency groups of the Chief Human Capital Officers Council and the Chief Information Officers Council "to discuss lessons learned and share best practices" as training programs are developed and new positions and offices are established.[291]

A search of the DHS website and the Google and ProQuest databases did not reveal publicly available information on the department's specific use of digital technology for training, and recruitment and retention. The annual Federal Employee Viewpoint survey conducted by the Office of Personnel Management includes a question on how satisfied federal employees are with the training that they receive for their present jobs. Some 40,136 DHS employees responded to this question on the 2014 survey and expressed the views that they were either "Very satisfied" or "Satisfied" (43.6%), "Neither Satisfied nor Dissatisfied" (23.6%), and "Dissatisfied" or "Very Dissatisfied" (32.9%) with the training provided to them.[292]

Congress may examine the use of digital technology for training, and recruitment and retention, at the department, including specific examples of its current use, plans for future applications of technology for these purposes, and human resources information technology implementation and activities at DHS.

Employment of Veterans

Assisting veterans, who are transitioning from military to civilian life, in applying their skills and experiences in the federal workplace is a priority for the Obama Administration. On November 9, 2009, the President issued Executive Order 13518 on "Employment of Veterans in the Federal Government." The Executive Order established an Interagency Council on Veterans Employment to, among other duties, "advise and assist the President and the Director of OPM in establishing a coordinated Government-wide effort to increase the number of veterans employed by the Federal Government by enhancing recruitment and training" and participate in a Veterans Employment Initiative to promote employment opportunities.[293] The Executive Order prescribed specific responsibilities for OPM and several departments, including the Department of Homeland Security. It directed DHS, joined by the Departments of Defense, Labor, and Veterans Affairs, and in consultation with OPM, to "develop and implement counseling and training programs to align veterans' and transitioning service members' skills and career aspirations to Federal employment opportunities, targeting Federal occupations that are projected to have heavy recruitment needs."[294]

The department's website has a page on "Veterans and Homeland Security" and states that veterans comprise 25% (50,000 employees) of the civilian workforce at DHS.[295] The DHS congressional justification that accompanied the FY2016 budget proposal includes the hiring of veterans as a management measure and continues the performance goal of 25% of DHS total new hires being veterans, which has been in place since FY2013. The congressional justification states that the target was exceeded in FY2014, when 27.6% of the department's new hires were veterans.[296]

Congress may be interested in examining the department's existing policies and planned initiatives on the hiring of veterans, including the types of positions for which veterans are being recruited, the targets for hiring of veterans by DHS components, and the results, realized and expected, by the department in carrying out the responsibilities assigned to it by the Executive Order.

Homeland Security Research and Development

Many stakeholders have identified advances in research and development (R&D) as key to creating new or improved technologies that defend against homeland security threats. R&D is generally a multi-year endeavor with significant risk of failure. Additionally, it may take years to realize any benefits from R&D investments. Some congressional and stakeholder expectations regarding the effectiveness and efficiency of agency performance have not been met. The 114th Congress may continue to focus attention on whether investments in homeland security research and development net appropriate rewards, how the distribution of investments among homeland security topics and between R&D activities leads to a balanced portfolio, and what the appropriate funding level for DHS R&D is during a time of fiscal constraint.

The DHS homeland security R&D activities have substantial scope, as these activities must attempt to meet the needs both of DHS component agencies and of other customers outside the agency, such as first responders. Many stakeholders continue to debate the optimal approach to maximizing DHS R&D effectiveness. Some advocates call for substantial increases in particular areas of research and development, asserting that a dedicated research effort with significant investments is more likely to yield technology breakthroughs. Some stakeholders call for a rebalancing of the investment portfolio with an increased focus on technology development, arguing that many prototypes under development in the private sector need only a small boost to convert them to procurable technologies. Still other stakeholders call for a rebalancing of the investment portfolio towards long-term research activities, warning that DHS will lack research outcomes to develop into prototypes if long-term research languishes. Finally, portions of the stakeholder community suggest using a high-risk, high-reward investment strategy similar to that undertaken by the Defense Advanced Research Projects Agency (DARPA) so as to make "leap- ahead" advances relative to terrorist capabilities.

DHS is not the sole provider of federal funds for homeland security R&D, but the DHS Under Secretary for Science and Technology (S&T) is responsible for coordinating homeland security R&D activities within DHS and across the federal government. The Under Secretary for S&T has experienced challenges in attempting to coordinate these activities and has not issued a federal homeland security R&D strategy. A key barrier to coordination of R&D investment within DHS and across the broader federal effort is difficulty in identifying R&D activities across DHS. Congress has historically been interested in identifying and overcoming the barriers to such coordination. The 114th Congress may conduct oversight of how any new strategic approaches taken by DHS address these long-standing concerns, set milestones for future performance, and meet the needs of DHS components and the first-responder community.

Both the Administration and Congress have previously contemplated reorganizing DHS R&D activities. R&D reprioritization efforts and consolidation might change the productivity of DHS R&D activities, which have been criticized by some stakeholders as having little to show for the federal investment. Other stakeholders, including some representatives of DHS operational components, indicate that R&D efforts undertaken by the S&T

Directorate have yielded value. Congressional appropriations for the S&T Directorate have fluctuated in recent years. This may indicate that some congressional policymakers find the slow rate of return shown by S&T Directorate R&D investments unacceptable.

End Notes

[1] Department of Homeland Security, *2014 Quadrennial Homeland Security Review*, Washington, DC, June 2014, p. 5. Available at http://www.dhs.gov/publication/2014-quadrennial-homeland-security-review-qhsr.

[2] Ibid., pp. 6-8.

[3] Office of Management and Budget, *Circular A-11: Instructions for Homeland Security Data Collection*, pp. 7-8, https://www.whitehouse.gov/sites/default/files/omb/assets/a11_current_year/homeland.pdf.

[4] Upon taking office, President Obama combined the National and Homeland Security staffs and this may have affected the decision to combine national and homeland security strategies into a single document.

[5] Office of the President, *National Security Strategy*, Washington, DC, February 2015, pp. 8-9, https://www.whitehouse.gov/sites/default/files/docs/2015_national_security_strategy_2.pdf.

[6] Donald F. Kettl, *System Under Stress: Homeland Security and American Politics*, 2nd ed, Washington, DC, *CQPress*, 2007, p. 82.

[7] Office of Management and Budget, *Fiscal Year 2016 Analytical Perspective of the U.S. Government* (Washington, DC, 2015), p. 344.

[8] The overseas contingency operations (also known as OCO/GWOT) funding request of $0.2 billion, was made on June 26, 2014, after the House Appropriations Committee had reported its measure, but before the Senate Appropriations Committee had reported its measure.

[9] See, for example, National Commission on Terrorist Attacks Upon the United States, *The 9/11 Commission Report* (Washington, DC: GPO, 2004), pp. 78-80, under "Legal Constraints on the FBI and 'the Wall.'" See also, Jerry Berman and Lara Flint, "Guiding Lights: Intelligence Oversight and Control for the Challenge of Terrorism," *Criminal Justice Ethics*, Winter/Spring 2003, at https://www.cdt.org/files/030300guidinglights_3.pdf. They suggest that there were many walls: "There were really many walls, built between and within agencies.... Some walls were meant to protect individual rights. Others were meant to protect national security interests."

[10] P.L. 108-458, §1012.

[11] See for example, the section below examining the three amendments to the Foreign Intelligence Surveillance Act of 1978 which broadened the ability of federal government organizations to collect and share intelligence information domestically.

[12] Federal Bureau of Investigation, "Protecting America From Terrorist Attack: Our Joint Terrorism Task Forces," at http://www.fbi.gov/about-us/investigate/terrorism/terrorism_jttfs; and U.S. Department of Homeland Security, *Fusion Centers and Joint Terrorism Task Forces*, at http://www.dhs.gov/fusion-centers-and-joint-terrorism-task-forces.

[13] For details on all 17 components of the IC see Office of the Director of National Intelligence, *U.S. National Intelligence: An Overview*, at http://www.dni.gov/files/documents/USNI%202013%20Overview_web.pdf.

[14] U.S. Department of Homeland Security, "Homeland Security Roles and Responsibilities," Appendix A in *2014 Quadrennial Homeland Security Review*, June 18, 2014, p. 83, at http://www.dhs.gov/sites/default/files/publications/2014-qhsr-final-508.pdf.

[15] U.S. Department of Homeland Security, "More About the Office of Intelligence and Analysis," March 28, 2014, at http://www.dhs.gov/more-about-office-intelligence-and-analysis-mission.

[16] Ibid.; see also Office of the Director of National Intelligence, *U.S. National Intelligence: An Overview*, pp. 19-20, athttp://www.dni.gov/files/documents/USNI%202013%20 Overview_web.pdf.

[17] U.S. Coast Guard, *Intelligence*, Coast Guard Publication 2-0, May 2010, at https://www.uscg.mil/doctrine/CGPub/CG_Pub_2_0.pdf.

[18] U.S. Congress, House Permanent Select Committee on Intelligence, *Statement of Robert S. Mueller, III; Director FBI*, Federal Bureau of Investigations, Hearing, 112th Cong., 1st sess., October 6, 2011, at http://www.fbi.gov/news/testimony/the-state-of-intelligence-reform-10-years-after-911.

[19] The original FISA legislation, P.L. 95-511 is available at http://www.gpo.gov/fdsys/pkg/STATUTE-92/pdf/STATUTE-92-Pg1783.pdf.

[20] These provisions were last extended in 2011. See P.L. 112-14, "PATRIOT Sunsets Extension Act of 2011." §2. "SUNSET EXTENSIONS: (a) USA PATRIOT Improvement and Reauthorization Act of 2005.—Section 102(b)(1) of the USA PATRIOT Improvement and Reauthorization Act of 2005 (P.L. 109-177; 50 U.S.C. 1805 note, 50 U.S.C. 1861 note, and 50 U.S.C. 1862 note) is amended by striking 'May 27, 2011' and inserting 'June 1, 2015'. (b) Intelligence Reform and Terrorism Prevention Act of 2004.—Section 6001(b)(1) of the Intelligence Reform and Terrorism Prevention Act of 2004 (P.L. 108-458; 50 U.S.C. 1801 note) is amended by striking 'May 27, 2011' and inserting 'June 1, 2015'."

[21] CRS Report R40138, *Amendments to the Foreign Intelligence Surveillance Act (FISA) Extended Until June 1, 2015*, by Edward C. Liu.

[22] P.L. 107-56.

[23] P.L. 108-458.

[24] CRS Report R40138, *Amendments to the Foreign Intelligence Surveillance Act (FISA) Extended Until June 1, 2015*, by Edward C. Liu.

[25] Ibid.

[26] Ibid.

[27] U.S. Congress, House, House Judiciary Committee, "Uniting and Strengthening America by Fulfilling Rights and Ensuring Effective Discipline over Monitoring Act of 2015," Report to Accompany H.R. 2048, H.Rept. 114-109, 114th Cong., 1st sess., May 8, 2015, p. 8.

[28] ACLU v. Clapper, Doc. No. 14-42-cv, (2nd Cir., 2015), p. 5. The ruling did not comment on the program's constitutionality.

[29] U.S. Congress, House, "Uniting and Strengthening America by Fulfilling Rights and Ensuring Effective Discipline Over Monitoring Act of 2015," H.R. 2048, 114th Cong., 1st sess., introduced April 29, 2015; and U.S. Congress, Senate, "Uniting and Strengthening America by Fulfilling Rights and Ensuring Effective Discipline Over Monitoring Act of 2015,"S. 1123,114th Cong., 1st sess., introduced May 11, 2015.

[30] Reforms include: "Pen Register and Trap and Trace Reform," "FISA Acquisitions Targeting Persons Outside the United States Reforms," "Foreign Intelligence Surveillance Court Reforms," and "National Security Letter Reform." These and other suggested changes are not discussed in this report.

[31] U.S. Congress, Senate, "A bill to extend authority relating to roving surveillance, access to business records, and individual terrorists as agents of foreign powers under the Foreign Intelligence Surveillance Act of 1978 and for other purposes," S. 1035, 114th Cong., 1st sess., introduced April 22, 2015.

[32] Barriers to information-sharing and collaboration include different uses of information collected by various organizations (e.g., data gathered for intelligence purposes vs. evidence gathered to prosecute a criminal), access to classified materials, complications associated with information technology, differing organizational cultures, and concerns over the damage caused by leaked information. Various types of DHS, IC, and law enforcement

centers exist to "fuse" or bridge the gaps between organizations at all levels of but the system for integrating intelligence-related information is far from perfect.

[33] A large part of the statutory basis for the 'wall' between law enforcement and intelligence information was removed with passage of the USA PATRIOT Act, which made it possible to share law enforcement information with analysts in intelligence agencies, but many obstacles remain.

[34] U.S. Department of Homeland Security, *CIKR Cyber Information and Collaboration Program*, at http://csrc.nist.gov/groups/SMA/ispab/documents/minutes/2013-06/ispab_june2013 _ menna_ciscp_one_pager.pdf. See also DHS, "Critical Infrastructure and Key Resources Cyber Information Sharing and Collaboration Program," at https://www.us-cert.gov/sites/default/files/c3vp/CISCP_20140523.pdf; and DHS, "Critical Infrastructure Sectors," at http://www.dhs.gov/critical-infrastructure-sectors.

[35] For additional information, see the "Cybersecurity" section, below.

[36] Spencer Ackerman, "Even Dead, Osama Has a Winning Strategy," *Wired*, July 20, 2011, http://www.wired.com/dangerroom/2011/07/even-dead-osama-has-a-winning-strategy-hint-its-muhammad-alis/.

[37] For additional information, see CRS Report R43612, *The "Islamic State" Crisis and U.S. Policy*, by Christopher M. Blanchard et al.

[38] Remarks by the John Brennan, the Assistant to the President for Homeland Security and Counterterrorism, before the Paul H. Nitze School of Advanced International Studies, June 29, 2011.

[39] For the purposes of this report, *homegrown* describes terrorist activity or plots perpetrated within the United States or abroad by American citizens, lawful permanent residents, or visitors radicalized largely within the United States.

Violent jihadist describes radicalized individuals using Islam as an ideological and/or religious justification for their belief in the establishment of a global caliphate—a jurisdiction governed by a Muslim civil and religious leader known as a caliph—via violent means. *Plots* include schemes by homegrown individuals or groups to either join terrorist organizations abroad or to commit violent attacks. *Attack* describes a plot in which ideologically-driven physical violence was committed by homegrown jihadists. To qualify as an attack, the violence has to harm a person or people in the United States or those targeted as Americans abroad. *Lawful permanent residents* refers to foreign nationals who are legally admitted to reside permanently in the United States. For more information on homegrown violent jihadists, see CRS Report R41416, *American Jihadist Terrorism: Combating a Complex Threat*, by Jerome P. Bjelopera.

[40] For the purposes of this report, "foreign fighters" from the United States are American citizens, lawful permanent residents, or aliens who radicalized in the United States and plotted to or traveled abroad to join a foreign terrorist group.

[41] Nicholas J. Rasmussen, Director of the National Counterterrorism Center, statement for the record for a hearing before the Senate Select Committee on Intelligence, February 12, 2015.

[42] Mark Hosenball, "U.S. Spy Chief Says 40 Americans Who Went to Syria Have Returned," *Reuters*, March 2, 2015.

[43] Christopher M. Piehota. Director, Terrorist Screening Center, Federal Bureau of Investigation, written statement for a House Homeland Security Committee, Subcommittee on Transportation Security hearing, "Safeguarding Privacy and Civil Liberties While Keeping our Skies Safe," September 18, 2014.

[44] See http://www.ise.gov/terrorist-watchlist.

[45] In 2012, Customs and Border Protection (CBP) described commercial air travel as "the primary target of terrorist organizations seeking to attack the homeland or move operatives into the United States.... " See Kevin McAleenan, then-Assistant Commissioner, U.S. Customs and Border Protection, Office of Field Operations, written statement for a House Committee on Homeland Security, Subcommittee on Border and Maritime Security hearing, "Eleven Years Later: Preventing Terrorists from Coming to America," September 11, 2012.

[46] The press release discussed the United Kingdom's decision to raise its threat level from "substantial" to "severe" because of developments in Syria and Iraq. See Department of Homeland Security, press release, "Statement by Secretary Johnson on the United Kingdom's Decision to Raise Their Threat Level," August 29, 2014.

[47] Jeh C. Johnson, Secretary, Department of Homeland Security, written statement for a House Homeland Security Committee hearing, "Worldwide Threats to the Homeland," September 17, 2014.

[48] For details see CBP, "Strengthening Security of the VWP Through Enhancements to ESTA," at http://www.cbp.gov/travel/international-visitors/esta/enhancements-to-esta-faqs. For background see CRS Report RL32221, *Visa Waiver Program*, by Alison Siskin. See also Tom Warrick, Deputy Assistant Secretary for Counterterrorism Policy, Department of Homeland Security, written statement for a House Committee on Foreign Affairs joint subcommittee hearing, "ISIS and the Threat from Foreign Fighters," December 2, 2014.

[49] See http://www.fbi.gov/about-us/investigate/terrorism/terrorism_jttfs.

[50] Tal Kopan, "Holder: DOJ Expanding International Capacity to Stem Foreign Fighters," *Politico,* November 13, 2014. In a capacity that combines interdiction and investigation, in September 2014, DOJ has noted that one of its components, Interpol Washington, announced the creation of a program dedicated to thwarting foreign fighters. It will draw on the investigative work of law enforcement agencies in more than 30 countries. DOJ, "Interpol Washington Spearheads Foreign Terrorist Fighter Program, Serves as Catalyst for Global Information Sharing Network," press release, September 24, 2014.

[51] For more information see CRS Report R42553, *Countering Violent Extremism in the United States*, by Jerome P. Bjelopera.

[52] Brookings Institution, "A National Counterterrorism Center Threat Assessment of ISIL and Al Qaeda in Iraq, Syria, and Beyond," "Proceedings," September 3, 2014.

[53] Nicholas J. Rasmussen, then-Deputy Director National Counterterrorism Center, written statement for a hearing before the Senate Committee on Homeland Security and Governmental Affairs, "Cybersecurity, Terrorism, and Beyond: Addressing Evolving Threats to the Homeland," September 10, 2014.

[54] DOJ, "Attorney General Holder Announces Pilot Program to Counter Violent Extremists," press release, September 15, 2014.

[55] DOJ, "Pilot Programs Are Key to our Countering Violent Extremism Efforts," press release, February 18, 2015.

[56] Defined as an electronic device that accesses or relies on the transfer of bytes of data to perform a mechanical function. The device can access cyberspace (the Internet) through the use of physical connections or wireless signals.

[57] For additional information, see CRS Report RL33123, *Terrorist Capabilities for Cyberattack: Overview and Policy Issues*, by John W. Rollins and Clay Wilson.

[58] See Department of Homeland Security, Office of Inspector General, "Challenges Remain in DHS' Efforts to Security Control Systems," August 2009. For a discussion of how computer code may have caused the halting of operations at an Iranian nuclear facility see CRS Report R41524, *The Stuxnet Computer Worm: Harbinger of an Emerging Warfare Capability*, by Paul K. Kerr, John W. Rollins, and Catherine A. Theohary.

[59] Executive Assistant Director Shawn Henry, *Responding to the Cyber Threat*, Federal Bureau of Investigation, Baltimore, MD, 2011.

[60] Department of Defense Deputy Secretary of Defense William J. Lynn III, "Defending a New Domain," *Foreign Affairs*, October 2010.

[61] Ken Dilanian, "U.S. Spy Agencies to Detail Cyberattacks from Abroad," *Los Angeles Times*, December 6, 2012.

[62] Ibid.

[63] For discussions of federal law and issues relating to cybercrime, see CRS Report 97-1025, *Cybercrime: An Overview of the Federal Computer Fraud and Abuse Statute and Related Federal Criminal Laws*, by Charles Doyle, and CRS Report R41927, *The Interplay of*

Borders, Turf, Cyberspace, and Jurisdiction: Issues Confronting U.S. Law Enforcement, by Kristin Finklea.

[64] Symantec, "Symantec Internet Security Threat Report: Trends for 2010," vol. 16, April 2011. Plain text summary with calculations available at http://www.symantec.com/about/news/release/article.jsp?prid=20110907_02.

[65] For additional information, see CRS Report RL31787, *Information Operations, Cyberwarfare, and Cybersecurity: Capabilities and Related Policy Issues*, by Catherine A. Theohary.

[66] Perlroth, Nicole, "Cyberattack on Saudi Firm Disquiets U.S.," *New York Times*, October 24, 2012, p. A1. Available at http://www.nytimes.com/2012/10/24/business/global/cyberattack-on-saudi-oil-firm-disquiets-us.html?pagewanted=all.

[67] The concept of *attribution* in the cyber world entails an attempt to identify with some degree of specificity and confidence the geographic location, identity, capabilities, and intention of the cyber-aggressor. Mobile technologies and sophisticated data routing processes and techniques often make attribution difficult for U.S. intelligence and law enforcement communities.

[68] Emerging cyber-based technologies that may be vulnerable to the actions of a cyber-aggressor include items that are in use but not yet widely adopted or are currently being developed. For additional information on how the convergence of inexpensive, highly sophisticated, and easily accessible technology is providing opportunities for cyber-aggressors to exploit vulnerabilities found in a technologically laden society, see *Global Trends 2030: Alternative Worlds, National Intelligence Council, Office of the Director of National Intelligence, December 10, 2012.*

[69] Information derived from CRS Report R42114, *Federal Laws Relating to Cybersecurity: Overview of Major Issues, Current Laws, and Proposed Legislation*, by Eric A. Fischer

[70] Information contained in this section was derived from multi-authored reports and memos produced by numerous CRS analysts working on cybersecurity.

[71] The White House, "The Comprehensive National Cybersecurity Initiative," March 5, 2010. For additional information about this Initiative and associated policy considerations, see CRS Report R40427, *Comprehensive National Cybersecurity Initiative: Legal Authorities and Policy Considerations*, by John W. Rollins and Anna C. Henning.

[72] See, for example, Seymour M. Hersh, "Judging the Cyber War Terrorist Threat," *The New Yorker*, November 1, 2010.

[73] Nakashima, Ellen, "Obama Signs Secret Directive to Help Thwart Cyberattacks," *The Washington Post*, Nov. 14, 2012.

[74] The White House, "Cybersecurity," last accessed March 19, 2015, https://www.whitehouse.gov/issues/foreign- policy/cybersecurity.

[75] White House, Office of the Press Secretary, *National Security and Homeland Security Presidential Directive*, May 9, 2007. NSPD-51 is also identified as Homeland Security Presidential Directive (HSPD) 20. A more detailed discussion of national continuity policy is available in CRS Report RS22674, *National Continuity Policy: A Brief Overview*, by R. Eric Petersen. Original document available at https://www.fema.gov/pdf/about/org/ncp/nspd_51.pdf.

[76] NSPD-51 identifies continuity of operations (COOP) as "an effort within individual executive departments and agencies to ensure that Primary Mission-Essential Functions continue to be performed during a wide range of emergencies, including localized acts of nature, accidents, and technological or attack-related emergencies."

[77] NSPD-51 identifies continuity of government (COG) as "a coordinated effort within the federal government's executive branch to ensure that national essential functions continue to be performed during a catastrophic emergency."

[78] The directive notes "that each branch of the federal government is responsible for its own continuity programs," and requires an executive branch official to "ensure that the executive branch's COOP and COG policies ... are appropriately coordinated with those of the legislative and judicial branches in order to ... maintain a functioning federal government."

The legislative branch and the federal judiciary maintain continuity programs consonant with their positions as coequal branches of government. NSPD-51 does not specify the nature of appropriate coordination with continuity planners in the legislative and judicial branch.

[79] 53 *Federal Register* 47491; November 23, 1988.

[80] U.S. Congress, House Committee on Appropriations, Subcommittee on Labor, Health and Human Services, Education, and Related Agencies, Departments of Labor, Health and Human Services, Education, and Related Agencies Appropriations for 2011, Part 6, Statements of Members of Congress and Other Interested Individuals and Organizations, 111th Cong., 2nd sess., May 12, 2010 (Washington: GPO, 2010), pp. 197-204.

[81] See for example, Christopher Nelson, Andrew M. Parker, and Shoshana R. Shelton, et al., *Analysis of the Cities Readiness Initiative* (Santa Monica, CA: RAND Corporation, 2012), pp. 31-34.

[82] For more information, see the BioWatch current services program description in Department of Homeland Security, *Congressional Budget Justification, FY2016,* Office of Health Affairs, pp. OHA-4-5, http://www.dhs.gov/dhs-budget. [83] David Willman, "The Biodefender That Cries Wolf," *Los Angeles Times*, July 8, 2012.

[84] Dr. Alexander Garza, Assistant Secretary for Health Affairs, DHS, "The Truth About BioWatch: The Importance of Early Detection of a Potential Biological Attack," July 12, 2012. Statistics cited in this blog posting were later reported to be inaccurate by a DHS official. See comments of BioWatch Program Manager Dr. Mike Walter before the House Committee on Energy and Commerce, Subcommittee on Oversight and Investigations, *Continuing Concerns over BioWatch and the Surveillance of Bioterrorism*, 113th Cong., 1st sess., June 18, 2013, CQ transcription.

[85] See for example Robert Roos, "Public Health Officials Respond to Critique of BioWatch," *CIDRAP News*, August 17, 2012, http://www.cidrap.umn.edu/cidrap/content/bt/bioprep/news/aug1712biowatch.html.

[86] U.S. Government Accountability Office, *Biosurveillance: DHS Should Reevaluate Mission Need and Alternatives before Proceeding with BioWatch Generation-3 Acquisition*, 12-810, September 10, 2012, http://gao.gov/products/GAO-12-810.

[87] See BioWatch discussions in CRS Reports on annual DHS appropriations, http://www.crs.gov/pages/subissue.aspx? cliid=2345.

[88] DHS, "Cancellation of the BioWatch Autonomous Detection Technology Acquisition," spot report, April 24, 2014. See also David Willman, "Homeland Security Cancels Plans for New BioWatch Technology," *Los Angeles Times*, April 25, 2014.

[89] See BioWatch discussions in CRS Reports on annual DHS appropriations, http://www.crs.gov/pages/subissue.aspx? cliid=2345.

[90] House Committee on Energy and Commerce, Subcommittee on Oversight and Investigations, "Oversight and Investigations Subcommittee Continues Investigation of BioWatch and Surveillance of Bioterrorism," press release, June 18, 2013, with links to committee report and other documents, http://energycommerce.house.gov/news/press- releases.

[91] H.Rept. 113-481, pp. 96-97; S.Rept. 113-198, pp. 109-110.

[92] Food and Drug Administration (FDA), "Food Defense," http://www.fda.gov/Food/FoodDefense.

[93] CRS Report RS22600, *The Federal Food Safety System: A Primer*, by Renée Johnson.

[94] DHS, "Food and Agriculture Sector, Sector Overview," June, 2014, http://www.dhs.gov/food-and-agriculture-sector.

[95] CRS Report R40443, *The FDA Food Safety Modernization Act (P.L. 111-353)*, coordinated by Renée Johnson.

[96] See FDA FSMA implementation information, http://www.fda.gov/Food/GuidanceRegulation/FSMA/default.htm; and CRS Report R43724, *Implementation of the FDA Food Safety Modernization Act (FSMA, P.L. 111-353)*, by Renée Johnson.

[97] FDA, "FSMA Reports and Studies," http://www.fda.gov/Food/GuidanceRegulation/FSMA/ ucm271961.htm.

[98] FDA, "FSMA Proposed Rule for Focused Mitigation Strategies to Protect Food Against Intentional Adulteration," http://www.fda.gov/Food/GuidanceRegulation/FSMA/ ucm378628.htm.

[99] FDA, "President's FY2016 Budget Request: Key Investments for Implementing [FSMA]," fact sheet, February 2, 2015, http://www.fda.gov/food/guidanceregulation/fsma/ucm 432576.htm.

[100] GAO, "Improving Federal Oversight of Food Safety," *High-Risk Series: An Update*, GAO-15-290, February 11, 2015, http://www.gao.gov/highrisk/revamping_food_safety.

[101] GAO, four open recommendations from *Homeland Security: Actions Needed to Improve Response to Potential Terrorist Attacks and Natural Disasters Affecting Food and Agriculture*, GAO-11-652, August 19, 2011, from database of open recommendations, http://www.gao.gov/openrecs.html, searched March 9, 2015.

[102] 1 kV=1,000 volts.

[103] North American Electric Reliability Corporation, "Understanding the Grid," fact sheet, August 2013, http://www.nerc.com/AboutNERC/Documents/Understanding% 20the%20Grid% 20AUG13.pdf. Note that there is no industry consensus as to what voltage rating or other operating characteristic constitutes "high voltage." This report uses 230 kV as the high voltage threshold, but other studies may use a different threshold, such as 115/138 kV, or may include an additional "extra high voltage" category above 345 kV. See, for example, U.S. Department of Energy, *Large Power Transformers and the U.S. Electric Grid*, April 2014, p. 4.

[104] C. Newton, "The Future of Large Power Transformers," *Transmission & Distribution World*, September 1, 1997; William Loomis, "Super-Grid Transformer Defense: Risk of Destruction and Defense Strategies," Presentation to NERC Critical Infrastructure Working Group, Lake Buena Vista, FL, December 10-11, 2001.

[105] North American Electric Reliability Corporation (NERC), *Grid Security Exercise (GridEx II): After-Action Report*, March 2014, p.15; Matthew L. Wald, "Attack Ravages Power Grid. (Just a Test.)," *New York Times*, November 14, 2013.

[106] *RTO Insider*, "Substation Saboteurs 'No Amateurs,'" April 2, 2014, http://www. rtoinsider.com/pjm-grid2020-1113- 03/; Chelsea J. Carter, "Arkansas Man Charged in Connection with Power Grid Sabotage," CNN, October 12, 2013; Max Brantley, "FBI Reports Three Attacks on Power Grid in Lonoke County," *Arkansas Times*, October 7, 2013; Rebecca Smith, "U.S. Risks National Blackout From Small-Scale Attack," *Wall Street Journal*, March 12, 2014.

[107] Federal Energy Regulatory Commission, *Physical Security Reliability Standard*, Docket No. RM14-15-000; Order No. 802, November 20, 2014.

[108] See, for example, Senators Dianne Feinstein, Al Franken, Ron Wyden, and Harry Reid, letter to the Honorable Cheryl LaFleur, Acting Chairman, Federal Energy Regulatory Commission, February 7, 2014, http://www.ferc.gov/industries/electric/indus-act/reliability/chairman-letter-incoming.pdf.

[109] Department of Homeland Security, Transportation Security Administration, *Surface Transportation Security FY2016 Congressional [Budget] Justification*, p. 11.

[110] United States House of Representatives, Committee on Homeland Security, Subcommittee on Transportation Security, Hearing on *TSA's Surface Inspection Program: Strengthening Security or Squandering Resources?*, May 31, 2012, http://homeland.house.gov/hearing/ subcommittee-hearing-tsa%E2%80%99s-surface-inspection-program-strengthening-security-or-squandering.

[111] Department of Homeland Security, Transportation Security Administration, *Surface Transportation Security FY2014 Congressional [Budget] Justification*, p. 18; *FY2015 Congressional [Budget] Justification*, p. 19.

[112] United States Governmental Accountability Office, *Homeland Security: DHS Needs Better Project Information and Coordination Among Four Overlapping Grant Programs*, GAO-12-303, February 2012.

[113] Oriana Zill and Lowell Bergman, "Do the Math: Why the Illegal Drug Business Is Thriving," *PBS Frontline*, http://www.pbs.org/wgbh/pages/frontline/shows/drugs/.

[114] Current means within the past month. U.S. Department of Health and Human Services, Substance Abuse and Mental Health Services Administration, *Results from the 2013 National Survey on Drug Use and Health: Summary of National Findings*, September 2014.

[115] Drug Enforcement Administration, *National Drug Threat Assessment Summary 2014*, November 2014, p. 3.

[116] Drug Enforcement Administration, *Statement of the Honorable Michele Leonhart, Administrator Drug Enforcement Administration, Before the United States House of Representatives Committee on Appropriations, Subcommittee on Commerce, Justice, Science and Related Agencies*, April 2, 2014, p. 2.

[117] Drug Enforcement Administration, *National Drug Threat Assessment Summary 2014*, November 2014, p. 10. [118] See, for example, Nick Miroff, "Tracing the U.S. Heroin Surge Back South of the Border as Mexican Cannabis Output Falls," *The Washington Post*, April 6, 2014.

[119] U.S. Department of Justice, "Attorney General Holder, Calling Rise in Heroin Overdoses 'Urgent Public Health Crisis,' Vows Mix of Enforcement, Treatment," press release, March 10, 2014.

[120] Office of National Drug Control Strategy, *National Southwest Border Counternarcotics Strategy*, 2013, p. 4.

[121] Ibid., pp. 4-9.

[122] U.S. Department of State, *2014 International Narcotics Control Strategy Report: Volume II, Money Laundering and Financial Crimes*, March 2014.

[123] Ibid., p. 161.

[124] The Department of the Treasury defines the BMPE as "a large-scale money laundering system used to launder proceeds of narcotic sales in the United States by Latin American drug cartels by facilitating swaps of dollars in the U.S. for pesos in Colombia through the sale of dollars to Latin America businessmen seeking to buy U.S. goods to export," http://www.fincen.gov/statutes_regs/guidance/html/advis04282006.html.

[125] According to the Department of the Treasury, a money services business is any person or entity engaging in activities including exchanging currency; cashing checks; issuing, selling, or redeeming travelers' checks, money orders, or stored value cards; and transmitting money. For more information, see http://www.fincen.gov/financial_institutions/msb/definitions/msb.html.

[126] According to the U.S. Code of Federal Regulations, stored value are "funds or monetary value represented in digital electronics format (whether or not specially encrypted) and stored or capable of storage on electronic media in such a way as to be retrievable and transferable electronically," 31 C.F.R. §103.11(vv).

[127] Douglas Farah, "Money Laundering and Bulk Cash Smuggling: Challenges for the Mérida Initiative," in *Shared Responsibility: U.S.-Mexico Policy Options for Confronting Organized Crime*, ed. Eric L. Olson, David A. Shirk, and Andrew D. Selee (2010), p. 144.

[128] National Drug Intelligence Center, *National Drug Threat Assessment 2011*. More recent National Drug Threat Assessment Summaries produced by the Drug Enforcement Administration do not contain information on illicit finance.

[129] Ken Stier, "Underground Threat: Tunnels Pose Trouble from Mexico to Middle East," *Time*, May 2, 2009.

[130] Statement of James A. Dinkins, Executive Associate Director, Homeland Security Investigations, U.S. Immigration and Customs Enforcement, before the U.S. Congress, Senate United States Senate Caucus on International Narcotics Control, *Illegal Tunnels on the Southwest Border*, 112th Cong., 1st sess., June 15, 2011.

[131] Department of Homeland Security, Office of Inspector General, "CBP's Strategy to Address Illicit Cross-Border Tunnels," http://www.oig.dhs.gov/assets/Mgmt/2012/OIG_12-132_Sep12.pdf.

[132] U.S. Drug Enforcement Administration, "Second Major Cross-Border Drug Tunnel Discovered South of San Diego This Month: Investigators Seize 32 Tons of Marijuana, Arrest 6 Suspects," press release, November 30, 2011, http://www.justice.gov/dea/divisions/sd/2011/sd113011.shtml.

[133] U.S. Immigration and Customs Enforcement, "ICE-Led Task Force Shutters 2 San Diego-Area Smuggling Tunnels," press release, April 4, 2014.

[134] For more information, see http://www.geophysical.com/militarysecurity.htm.

[135] Statement of Laura E. Duffy, U.S. Attorney, Southern District of California, U.S. Department of Justice, before the U.S. Congress, Senate United States Senate Caucus on International Narcotics Control, *Illegal Tunnels on the Southwest Border*, 112th Cong., 1st sess., June 15, 2011.

[136] Ibid.

[137] See Senate Committee on Appropriations Subcomittee on Homeland Security, *DHS Hearing: Strengthening Trade Enforcement to Protect American Enterprise and Grow American Jobs*. Testimony of CBP Office of International Trade Acting Assistant Commissioner Richard DiNucci.

[138] See U.S. CBP, "C-TPAT: Customs-Trade Partnership Against Terrorism, http://www.cbp.gov/border-security/ports-entry/cargo-security/c-tpat-customs-trade-partnership-against-terrorism. Commercial truck drivers who are Customs- Trade Partnership Against Terrorism (C-TPAT) members also are eligible to join the Free and Secure Trade System (FAST), which permits expedited processing at land ports of entry; and C-TPAT members who are residents of the United States and are known importers that have businesses physically established, located, and managed within the United States may be eligible for the Importer Self-Assessment Program (ISA), which exempts importers from certain post-entry enforcement audits. See ibid., and CBP FAST: Free and Secure Trade for Commercial Vehicles, http://www.cbp.gov/travel/trusted-traveler-programs/fast.

[139] See for example, U.S. Congress, Senate Committee on Homeland Security and Governmental Affairs, *Evaluating Port Security: Progress Made and Challenges Ahead*, 113th Cong., 2nd sess. June 4, 2014.

[140] See for example, U.S. Congress, House Committee on Ways and Means, Subcommittee on Trade, *Supporting Economic Growth and Job Creation through Customs Trade Modernization, Facilitation, and Enforcement*, 112th Cong., 2nd sess. May 17, 2012.

[141] See U.S. Department of Commerce, *Draft Report: Improving Economic Outcomes by Reducing Border Delays*, Facilitating the Vital Flow of Commercial Traffic Across the US-Mexican Border, Washington, DC, 2008, http://grijalva.house.gov/uploads/Draft%20Commerce%20Department%20Report%20on%20Reducing%20Border%20Delays%20Findings%20and%20 Options%20March%202008.pdf.

[142] Secondary inspection may include both non-intrusive imaging (NII) scans and/or physical inspection, in which the container may be opened and unpacked so that materials can be examined.

[143] CRS analysis of data provided by CBP Office of Legislative Affairs, April 28, 2014.

[144] The 100% scanning pilot program is known as the Secure Freight Initiative (SFI). Following DHS's evaluation of the SFI in 2012, the program was scaled back to a single port, Port Qasim, in Pakistan.

[145] The risk-based scanning program is known as the Container Security Initiative (CSI).

[146] Letter from Janet Napolitano, Secretary of Homeland Security, to Hon. Joseph I. Lieberman, Senator, May 2, 2012. The 9/11 Act permits the Secretary to extend the deadline by two years and in additional two-year increments by certifying that two of the following conditions exist: that scanning systems are not available, are insufficiently accurate, cannot be installed, cannot be integrated with existing systems, will significantly impact trade and

the flow of cargo, and/or do not provide adequate notification of questionable or high-risk cargo. In her notification to Congress, Secretary Napolitano certified that the use of systems to scan containers would have a significant and negative impact on trade capacity and cargo flows, and that systems to scan containers cannot be purchased, deployed, or operated at overseas ports due to limited physical infrastructure.

[147] See CBP, *Report to Congress on Integrated Scanning System Pilots (Security and Accountability for Every Port Act of 2006, §231)*. Also see U.S. GAO, *Supply Chain Security: Container Secuirty Programs Have Matured, but Uncertainty Persists over the Future of 100 Percent Scanning*, GAO-12-422T, February 7, 2012, http://www.gao.gov/assets/590/588253.pdf. Also see letter from Janet Napolitano, Secretary of Homeland Security, to Hon. Joseph I. Lieberman, Senator, May 2, 2012.

[148] Spoken response by Kevin McAleenan, Acting Assistant Commissioner, Office of Field Operations, U.S. CBP, U.S. Department of Homeland Security, before the Border and Maritime Security Subcommittee of the Homeland Security Committee, U.S. House, hearing "Balancing Maritime Security and Trade Facilitation: Protecting Our Ports, Increasing Commerce and Securing the Supply Chain—Part I," February 7, 2012. CBP reports that the U.S. government spent a total of about $120 million during the first three years of the Secure Freight Initiative; CBP, *Report to Congress on Integrated Scanning System Pilots*, p. 13.

[149] See Stephen L. Caldwell, Director, Homeland Security and Justice Issues, U.S. Government Accountability Office, testimony before the U.S. Congress, Senate Committee on Homeland Security and Governmental Affairs, *Evaluating Port Security: Progress Made and Challenges Ahead*, 113th Cong., 2nd sess. June 4, 2014.

[150] See for example, U.S. Congress, Senate Committee on Homeland Security and Governmental Affairs, *Evaluating Port Security: Progress Made and Challenges Ahead*, 113th Cong., 2nd sess. June 4, 2014; and U.S. Congress, House Committee on Homeland Security, Subcommittee on Border and Maritime Security, *Balancing Maritime Security and Trade Facilitation: Protecting Our Ports, Increasing Commerce, and Securing the Supply Chain—Part I*, 112th Cong., 2nd sess., February 7, 2012.

[151] H.Rept. 113-481, p. 38.

[152] See, for example, U.S. Congress, House Committee on Homeland Security, Subcommittee on Border and Maritime Security, *Using Technology to Facilitate Trade and Enhance Security at Our Ports of Entry*, 112th Cong., 2nd sess., May 1, 2012. On border wait times, also see GAO, *CBP Action Needed to Improve Wait Time Data and Measure Outcomes of Trade Facilitation Effort*, GAO-13-603, July 24, 2013.

[153] According to a CRS analysis of data provided by CBP Office of Congressional Affairs in January 2013, staffing for enforcement between ports of entry more than doubled between FY2004 and FY2012 (increasing from 10,819 to 21,394), while staffing at ports of entry increased just 20% during this period (from 18,110 to 21,790).

[154] For a fuller discussion, see CRS Report R43147, *Department of Homeland Security: FY2014 Appropriations*, coordinated by William L. Painter.

[155] See Section 560 of the Consolidated and Further Continuing Appropriations Act, FY2013 (P.L. 113-6, Div. D). The FY2013 pilot program permitted five such partnerships in Dallas, TX, Houston, TX, and Miami, FL, and land POEs in El Paso, TX, and Laredo/McAllen, TX.

[156] See Section 559 of the Consolidated Appropriations Act, FY2014 (P.L. 113-76, Div. F).

[157] Ibid.

[158] Legal permanent residents (LPRs) are foreign nationals authorized to live lawfully and permanently within the United States; see CRS Report RL32235, *U.S. Immigration Policy on Permanent Admissions*, by Ruth Ellen Wasem. [159] For a fuller discussion of travel requirements, see CRS Report RL31381, *U.S. Immigration Policy on Temporary Admissions*, by Ruth Ellen Wasem; and CRS Report RL32221, *Visa Waiver Program*, by Alison Siskin.

[160] Individuals are ineligible to participate in a trusted traveler program if they are inadmissible to the United States; provide false or incomplete information on trusted traveler applications; have been convicted of a criminal offense, have outstanding warrants, or are subject to an investigation; or have been found in violation of customs, immigration, or agriculture laws. Trusted travel enrollees are re-checked against certain security databases every 24 hours, every time they enter the United States, and every time they renew their trusted traveler membership.

[161] CBP, "About Global Entry," http://www.cbp.gov/global-entry/about.

[162] CBP, "NEXUS" http://www.cbp.gov/travel/trusted-traveler-programs/nexus.

[163] CBP, "About SENTRI," http://www.cbp.gov/travel/trusted-traveler-programs/sentri.

[164] For information on the Islamic State and foreign fighters, see CRS Report R43612, *The "Islamic State" Crisis and U.S. Policy*, by Christopher M. Blanchard et al.; and CRS Report IN10209, *European Security, Islamist Terrorism, and Returning Fighters*, by Kristin Archick and Paul Belkin.

[165] For example, see U.S. Congress, House Committee on Homeland Security, Subcommittee on Border and Maritime Security, *One Flight Away: An Examination of the Threat Posed by ISIS Terrorists with Western Passports*, 113th Cong., 2nd sess., September 10, 2014; and Jerry Markon, "Visa Waivers Under Scrutiny on Hill," *The Washington Post*, January 28, 2015, p. A2.

[166] The 38 countries are: Andorra, Australia, Austria, Belgium, Brunei, Chile, Czech Republic, Denmark, Estonia, Finland, France, Germany, Greece, Hungary, Iceland, Ireland, Italy, Japan, Latvia, Liechtenstein, Lithuania, Luxembourg, Monaco, Malta, the Netherlands, New Zealand, Norway, Portugal, San Marino, Singapore, Slovakia, Slovenia, South Korea, Spain, Sweden, Switzerland, Taiwan, and the United Kingdom.

[167] ESTA checks the foreign national's information against different immigration, criminal, and security databases.

[168] See U.S. Congress, House Committee on the Judiciary, Subcommittee on Immigration Policy and Enforcement, *Visa Waiver Program Oversight: Risks and Benefits of the Program*, Testimony of Jessica Vaughan, Director of Policy Studies, Center for Immigration Studies, 112th Cong., 1st sess., December 7, 2011.

[169] IAFIS is a national fingerprint and criminal history system. IDENT is a DHS-wide system for the storage and processing of biometric and limited biographic information. IDENT is the primary DHS-wide system for the biometric identification and verification of individuals encountered in DHS mission-related processes. For more information on IAFIS, see Federal Bureau of Investigation, "The Integrated Automated Fingerprint Identification System (IAFIS)," press release, http://www.fbi.gov/hq/cjisd/iafis.htm. For more information on IDENT, see Department of Homeland Security, *Privacy Impact Assessment for the Automated Biometric Identification System (IDENT)*, Washington, DC, July 31, 2006, p. 2.

[170] CRS Report R43356, *Border Security: Immigration Inspections at Ports of Entry*, by Lisa Seghetti.

[171] For an example of this argument, see "Congressman Claims Allowing Poland Visa-Free Travel to the US Would Pose Security Threat," workpermit.com, June 20, 2012, http://www.workpermit.com/news/2012-06-20/us/congressman-claims-allowing-poland-visa-free-travel-to-us-would-pose-security-threat.htm.

[172] For an example of this argument, see David Inserra and Riley Walters, *The Visa Waiver Program: Enhancing Security, Promoting Prosperity*, Heritage Foundation, Issue Brief #4273, Washington, DC, Sept. 16, 2014.

[173] There is not a specific requirement to present an e-passport when entering under the VWP. Any passports issued after October 26, 2006, and used by VWP travelers to enter the United States are required to have integrated chips with information from the data page (e-passports).

[174] The length of validity of a visa is mostly dependent on reciprocity with the United States (i.e., that visas from that country for U.S. citizens are valid for the same period of time). For a

full list of reciprocity schedules, see Department of State, Reciprocity Schedules, at http://travel.state.gov/visa/fees/fees_3272.html.

[175] Testimony of DHS Assistant Secretary David Heyman, U.S. Congress, House Committee on Judiciary, *Implementation of an Entry-Exit System: Still Waiting After All These Years*, 113th Cong., 1st sess., November 13, 2013. Hereinafter: Heyman Testimony, 2013.

[176] CBP, *Secure Borders, Safe Travel, Legal Trade: Fiscal Year 2009-2014 Strategic Plan*, Washington, DC, 2009, p. 15.

[177] See for example Testimony of CBP Deputy Assistant Commissioner John Wagner, U.S. Congress, House Committee on Oversight and Government Affairs, Subcommittee on National Security, *Border Security Oversight, Part III: Border Crossing Cards and B1/B2 Visas*, 113th Cong., 1st sess., November 14, 2013.

[178] By comparison, the enforcement-related budget of the legacy Immigration and Naturalization Service was $380 million in 1986, according to CRS calculations from U.S. Office of Management and Budget, *Budget of the U.S. Government: Appendix*, Washington, DC, 1987. For a fuller discussion of FY2014 appropriations, see CRS Report R43147, *Department of Homeland Security: FY2014 Appropriations*, coordinated by William L. Painter.

[179] See for example, U.S. Congress, House Committee on Homeland Security, Subcommittee on Border and Maritime Security, *A Study in Contrasts: House and Senate Approaches to Border Security*, 113th Cong., 1st sess., July 23, 2013. The Border Patrol published a national strategy for controlling U.S. borders in May 2012, building on three earlier strategies published between 1994 and 2005. The new strategy describes the Border Patrol's approach to risk management and to striking a balance among its traditional emphasis on preventing illegal migration and its post-9/11 priority missions of preventing the entry of terrorists and terrorist weapons, along with the recent U.S. focus on combating transnational criminal organizations. But the strategy does not describe operational plans or address the interaction among the Border Patrol and other federal agencies (including other parts of DHS) with responsibilities at the border.

[180] The border patrol reported 327,577 alien apprehensions along the Southwest border in FY2011, the lowest number since FY1972; see U.S. Border Patrol, *Total Illegal Alien Apprehensions By Fiscal Year*, http://www.cbp.gov/linkhandler/cgov/border_security/border_patrol/usbp_statistics/60_10_app_stats.ctt/60_11_app_stats.pdf.

[181] See, e.g., U.S. Government Accountability Office, *Border Security: Enhanced DHS Oversight and Assessment of Interagency Cooridination is Needed for the Northern Border*, GAO-11-97, December 2010, http://www.gao.gov/new.items/d1197.pdf. Also see CRS Report R42969, *Border Security: Understanding Threats at U.S. Borders*, by Jerome P. Bjelopera and Kristin Finklea.

[182] For a brief overview of challenges with the Advanced Spectroscopic Portal and the Cargo Advanced Automated Radiography System, see Government Accountability Office, *Combating Nuclear Smuggling: DHS Has Developed a Strategic Plan for Its Global Nuclear Detection Architecture, but Gaps Remain*, GAO-11-869T, July 26, 2011.

[183] For background, see CRS Report R41419, *The Helium-3 Shortage: Supply, Demand, and Options for Congress*, by Dana A. Shea and Daniel Morgan.

[184] 72 *Federal Register* 3492-3604, January 25, 2007. Codified at 49 C.F.R. 1572.

[185] 78 *Federal Register* 17782, March 22, 2013.

[186] Comments filed can be viewed at http://www.regulations.gov under docket # USCG-2007-28915.

[187] GAO, *Transportation Worker Identification Credential—Card Reader Pilot Results Are Unreliable; Security Benefits Need to Be Reassessed*, GAO-13-198, May 8, 2013.

[188] U.S. Congress, House Committee on Oversight and Government Reform, Subcommittee on Government Operations, *Federal Government Approaches to Issuing Biometric IDs*, 113th Cong., 1st sess., May 9, 2013.

[189] U.S. Congress, House Committee on Homeland Security, Subcommittee on Border and Maritime Security, *Threat, Risk and Vulnerability: The TWIC Program*, 113th Cong., 1st sess., June 18, 2013.

[190] GAO, *Transportation Security: Action Needed to Strengthen TSA's Security Threat Assessment Process*, GAO-13- 629, July 19, 2013.

[191] GAO, *Transportation Worker Identification Credential—Internal Control Weaknesses Need to Be Corrected to Help Achieve Security Objectives*, May 2011, GAO-11-657.

[192] Keith Laing, "GOP Chairman: TSA Was a 'Big Mistake,'" *The Hill,* March 18, 2015, http://thehill.com/policy/transportation/236130-gop-rep-creating-tsa-was-a-mistake.

[193] Transportation Security Administration, *Screening Partnership Program*, http://www.tsa.gov/ stakeholders/screening-partnership-program.

[194] See P.L. 113-245.

[195] National Commission on Terrorist Attacks upon the United States, *The 9/11 Commission Report*, New York, NY:W.W. Norton & Co., 2004.

[196] See, e.g., American Civil Liberties Union, "ACLU Backgrounder on Body Scanners and 'Virtual Strip Searches,'" January 8, 2010, https://www.aclu.org/technology-and-liberty/aclu-backgrounder-body-scanners-and-virtual-strip- searches.

[197] Department of Homeland Security, Transportation Security Administration, *Fiscal Year 2016 Congressional Justification, Aviation Security*.

[198] U.S. Government Accountability Office, *Aviation Security: Rapid Growth in Expedited Passenger Screening Highlights Need to Plan Effective Security Assessments*, GAO-15-150, December 2014.

[199] See http://www.knowncrewmember.org/Pages/Home.aspx.

[200] Transportation Security Administration, *Press Release: U.S. Airline Flight Attendants to Get Expedited Airport Screening in Second Stage of Known Crewmember Program*, Friday, July 27, 2012, http://www.tsa.gov/press/releases/2012/07/27/us-airline-flight-attendants-get-expedited-airport-screening-second-stage.

[201] U.S. Government Accountability Office, *Aviation Security: TSA Should Limit Future Funding for Behavior Detection Activities*, GAO-14-159, November 2013; Department of Homeland Security, Office of Inspector General, *Transportation Security Administration's Screening of Passengers by Observation Techniques (Redacted)*, OIG-13-91, Washington, DC, May 29, 2013; Department of Homeland Security, Statement of Charles K. Edwards, Deputy Inspector General, Before the United States House of Representatives, Committee on Homeland Security, Subcommittee on Transportation Security, November 13, 2013.

[202] Mary Forgione, "Existing TSA Director Wants to Ease Liquids Ban for Some Passengers," *Los Angeles Times,* November 17, 2014, http://www.latimes.com/travel/deals/la-trb-tsa-airport-screening-20141114-story.html.

[203] Scott Shane, "Lapses Allowed Suspect to Board Plane," *New York Times*, May 4, 2010.

[204] Department of Homeland Security (DHS), "DHS Now Vetting 100 Percent of Passengers On Flights Within Or Bound For U.S. Against Watchlists," Press Release, November 30, 2010.

[205] Department of Homeland Security, Transportation Security Administration, "Privacy Act of 1974; Department of Homeland Security Transportation Security Administration-DHS/TSA-019 Secure Flight Records System of Records," 80 *Federal Register* 233-239, January 5, 2015.

[206] For additional information see CRS Report RL33645, *Terrorist Watchlist Checks and Air Passenger Prescreening*, by William J. Krouse and Bart Elias (out of print—available on request).

[207] Federal Aviation Administration, "Operation and Certification of Small Unmanned Aircraft Systems; Proposed Rule," 80 *Federal Register* 9544-9590, February 23, 2015.

[208] Federal Aviation Administration, *Law Enforcement Guidance for Suspected Unauthorized UAS Operations*, http://www.faa.gov/uas/regulations_policies/media/FAA_UAS-PO_LEA_Guidance.pdf.

[209] Statement of Chief Richard Beary, President of the International Association of Chiefs of Police, Subcommittee on Oversight and Management Efficiency, Committee on Homeland Security, United States House of Representatives, March 18, 2015.

[210] See, e.g., Todd Humphreys, "Statement on the Security Threat Posed by Unmanned Aerial Systems and Possible Countermeasures," submitted to the Subcommittee on Oversight and Management Efficiency, House Committee on Homeland Security, March 16, 2015.

[211] Todd Humphreys, "Statement on the Vulnerability of Civil Unmanned Aerial Vehicles and Other Systems to Civil GPS Spoofing," submitted to the Subcommittee on Oversight, Investigations, and Management of the House Committee on Homeland Security, July 19, 2012; U.S. Government Accountability Office, "Unmanned Aircraft Systems: Use in the National Airspace System and the Role of the Department of Homeland Security," Statement of Gerald L. Dillingham, Ph.D., Director, Physical Infrastructure Issues, Before the Subcommittee on Oversight, Investigations, and Management, Committee on Homeland Security, House of Representatives, July 19, 2012, GAO- 12-889T.

[212] See CRS Report R42701, *Drones in Domestic Surveillance Operations: Fourth Amendment Implications and Legislative Responses*, by Richard M. Thompson II.

[213] See Kyllo v. United States, 533 U.S. 27 (2001).

[214] See California v. Ciraolo, 476 U.S. 207, 213 ("[W]hat a person knowingly exposes to the public ... is not a subject of Fourth Amendment protection") (quoting Katz v. United States, 389 U.S. 347, 351 (1967)).

[215] See, e.g., United States v. Flores-Montano, 541 U.S. 149, 152 (2004) ("The Government's interest in preventing the entry of unwanted persons and effects is at its zenith at the international border").

[216] See, e.g., H.R. 1229, H.R. 1385, S. 635.

[217] Katie Drummond, "Where Have All the MANPADS Gone?," *Wired*, February 22, 2010.

[218] Ibid.; U.S. Department of State, Bureau of Political-Military Affairs, *MANPADS: Combating the Threat to Global Aviation from Man-Portable Air Defense System*, July 27, 2011, http://www.state.gov/t/pm/rls/fs/169139.htm.

[219] For further analysis on emergency and major disaster declarations see CRS Report R43784, *FEMA's Disaster Declaration Process: A Primer*, by Francis X. McCarthy. For more information on the Disaster Relief Fund see CRS Report R43537, *FEMA's Disaster Relief Fund: Overview and Selected Issues*, by Bruce R. Lindsay.

[220] For information on supplemental appropriations for disasters see CRS Report R43665, *Supplemental Appropriations for Disaster Assistance: Summary Data and Analysis*, by Bruce R. Lindsay and Justin Murray.

[221] For further analysis on Stafford Act declarations from 1953 to 2011 see CRS Report R42702, *Stafford Act Declarations 1953-2011: Trends and Analyses, and Implications for Congress*, by Bruce R. Lindsay and Francis X. McCarthy.

[222] For further analysis on disaster assistance under the Budget Control Act see CRS Report R42352, *An Examination of Federal Disaster Relief Under the Budget Control Act*, by Bruce R. Lindsay, William L. Painter, and Francis X. McCarthy.

[223] P.L. 113-2, Making supplemental appropriations for the fiscal year ending September 30, 2013, to improve and streamline disaster assistance for Hurricane Sandy, and for other purposes. For more information on supplemental funding for Hurricane Sandy see CRS Report R42869, *FY2013 Supplemental Funding for Disaster Relief*, coordinated by William L. Painter and Jared T. Brown.

[224] Hurricane Sandy was declared a major disaster on October 30, 2012. Making supplemental appropriations for the fiscal year ending September 30, 2013, to improve and streamline disaster assistance for Hurricane Sandy, and for other purposes (P.L. 113-2) was enacted January 29, 2013.

[225] Information on FirstNet at http://www.firstnet.gov.

[226] Information on IPAWS at https://www.fema.gov/integrated-public-alert-warning-system.

[227] 9-1-1 Implementation Coordination Office (ICO) reauthorized by P.L. 112-96; see 47 U.S. C. §942.

[228] *National Emergency Communications Plan*, 2014, at http://www.dhs.gov/sites/default/files/publications/2014%20National%20Emergency%20Communications%20Plan_October%2029%202014.pdf.

[229] The "whole community" includes individuals and families, including those with access and functional needs; businesses; faith-based and community organizations; nonprofit groups; schools and academia; media outlets; and all levels of government, including state, local, tribal, territorial, and federal partners. See more at FEMA's website at http://www.fema.gov/national-preparedness/whole-community.

[230] White House, *Presidential Policy Directive 8: National Preparedness*, Washington, DC, March 30, 2011, p. 1, http://www.dhs.gov/xabout/laws/gc_1215444247124.shtm.

[231] Ibid.

[232] For more on THIRA, see FEMA's website on the topic at https://www.fema.gov/threat-and-hazard-identification- and-risk-assessment.

[233] Extensive descriptions of the Hurricane Sandy storm and its impacts can be found in Hurricane Sandy Rebuilding Task Force, *Hurricane Sandy Rebuilding Strategy: Stronger Communities, a Resilient Region*, Washington, DC, August 2013, pp. 18-22, at http://portal.hud.gov/hudportal/documents/huddoc?id=HSRebuildingStrategy.pdf; and at Federal Emergency Management Agency, *Hurricane Sandy FEMA After-Action Report*, Washington, DC, July 1, 2013, p. 7, at http://www.fema.gov/media-library/assets/documents/33772.

[234] Executive Order 13632, "Establishing the Hurricane Sandy Rebuilding Task Force," 77 *Federal Register* 74341, December 14, 2012.

[235] Hurricane Sandy Program Management Office, *Hurricane Sandy Rebuilding Strategy: Progress Report, Fall 2014,* Washington, DC, Fall 2014, at http://portal.hud.gov/hudportal/documents/huddoc?id=HurrSandRebStratPRF2014.pdf.

[236] SRIA was enacted as Division B of P.L. 113-2, the Disaster Relief Appropriations Act, 2013.

[237] For example, Section 1109 of SRIA, 127 Stat. 47, required FEMA to review and update its regulations (44 C.F.R.§206.48(b)(2)) concerning the individual assistance factors taken into consideration when evaluating a request for a major disaster declaration by January 29, 2014. For an update on SRIA implementation from FEMA, see their website at https://www.fema.gov/sandy-recovery-improvement-act-2013, as well as Federal Emergency Management Agency, *Sandy Recovery Improvement Act Fact Sheet*, November 2014, at https://www.fema.gov/media-library/assets/documents/85495.

[238] For example, Section 1102 of SRIA, 127 Stat. 42, as codified at 42 U.S.C. §5189f(h), Section 428(h) of the Stafford Act; directs the DHS Inspector General to audit the efficacy of the Public Alterative Procedures.

[239] For further discussion see the *National Health Security Preparedness Index*, http://www.nhspi.org/; and CRS Report RL33579, *The Public Health and Medical Response to Disasters: Federal Authority and Funding*, by Sarah A. Lister. [240] See for example FDA, "Pandemic and All-Hazards Preparedness Reauthorization Act of 2013 (PAHPRA)," http://www.fda.gov/EmergencyPreparedness/Counterterrorism/MedicalCountermeasures/MCMLegalRegulatoryandPolicyFramework/ucm359581.htm.

[241] P.L. 109-417, the Pandemic and All-Hazards Preparedness Act. Actual appropriations for many of these programs have also decreased since 2006.

[242] The Robert T. Stafford Disaster Relief and Emergency Assistance Act, P.L. 93-288, as amended. See CRS Report RL34724, *Would an Influenza Pandemic Qualify as a Major Disaster Under the Stafford Act?*, by Edward C. Liu; and CRS Report RL33053, *Federal Stafford Act Disaster Assistance: Presidential Declarations, Eligible Activities, and Funding*, by Francis X. McCarthy.

[243] See, for example, FEMA Office of Response and Recovery, "Infectious Disease Event," Fact Sheet FP-104-009- 001, October 21, 2014, https://www.fema.gov/media-library/assets/documents/99710.

[244] See for example GAO, *Hurricane Katrina: Allocation and Use of $2 Billion for Medicaid and Other Health Care Needs*, GAO-07-67, February 28, 2007, http://www.gao.gov; CRS Report R41232, *FY2010 Supplemental for Wars, Disaster Assistance, Haiti Relief, and Other Programs*, coordinated by Amy Belasco; and emergency supplemental funding for HHS for the response to the Ebola outbreak in P.L. 113-235, Consolidated and Further Continuing Appropriations Act, 2015, Division G, Title VI.

[245] CRS reports on ACA implementation are available at http://www.crs.gov/pages/subissue.aspx?cliid=3746.

[246] CRS Report RL33579, *The Public Health and Medical Response to Disasters: Federal Authority and Funding*, by Sarah A. Lister.

[247] HHS, "Public Health Emergency Response Initiative," Public Health and Social Services Emergency Fund, Justification of Estimates for Appropriations Committees, FY2016, p. 115, http://www.hhs.gov/budget.

[248] Secretary for Homeland Security Jeh Johnson, interviewed by Steve Watkins, "DHS Head: Cybersecurity, Unity of Effort Top Priority List," *Federal Times*, October 17, 2014. Available at http://www.federaltimes.com/article/20141017/DHS/310170024/.

[249] See H.Rept. 113-481, p.7; and S.Rept. 113-198, p. 16.

[250] For examples of DHS program management and financial management issues, see U.S. Department of Homeland Security, Office of Inspector General, *Major Management Challenges Facing the Department of Homeland Security*, OIG-13-09, November 2012; U.S. Government Accountability Office, *Managing Preparedness Grants and Assessing National Capabilities: Continuing Challenge Impede FEMA's Progress*, GAO-12-526T, March 20, 2012; U.S. Department of Homeland Security, Office of Inspector General, *FEMA's Efforts to Recoup Improper Payments in Accordance with the Disaster Assistance Recoupment Fairness Act of 2011*, OIG-12-127, September 2012.

[251] House Committee on Government Oversight and Reform, Subcommittee on Government Organization, Efficiency and Financial Management, "Department of Homeland Security Financial Management," May 13, 2011. Documents available at http://oversight.house.gov/hearing/financial-management-at-the-department-of-homeland-security/.

[252] Internal control standards seek to ensure that the use of funds comply with applicable laws, that assets are appropriately protected against waste, fraud, and abuse, and that federal agencies have efficient and effective financial and program administration systems that allow for appropriate accountability of funds. Internal control standards are integrated into program management protocols, including quarterly program and financial monitoring, timely submission of single audit reports and grants closeout, and improper payments testing and reporting.

[253] Office of Inspector General, Department of Homeland Security, OIG-15-10, "Independent Auditors' Report on DHS' FY2014 Financial Statements and Internal Control over Financial Reporting," November 2014, p. 1.

[254] Statement of John Roth, Inspector General, Department of Homeland Security, before the House Committee on Homeland Security Subcommittee on Oversight and Management Efficiency, "Assessing DHS' Performance: Watchdog Recommendations to Improve Homeland Security," February 26, 2015, p. 6.

[255] Office of Inspector General, Department of Homeland Security, OIG-15-10, "Independent Auditors' Report on DHS' FY2014 Financial Statements and Internal Control over Financial Reporting," November 2014, p.2

[256] U.S. Congress, House Committee on Appropriations, Subcommittee on Homeland Security, *Homeland Security Headquarters Facilities*, 111th Cong., 2nd sess., March 25, 2010 (Washington: GPO, 2010), pp. 335-366.

[257] "St. Elizabeths Development Revised Baseline," document provided by DHS, June 12, 2013.

[258] "Prospectus—Construction: Department of Homeland Security Consolidation at St. Elizabeths, Washington DC," PDC-0002-WA14, p. 14 as downloaded from GSA.gov.

[259] U.S. Department of Homeland Security, *Strategic Plan Fiscal Years 2012-2016* (Washington, DC: February 2012), pp. 25-26, available at http://www.dhs.gov/xlibrary/assets/dhs-strategic-plan-fy-2012-2016.pdf.

[260] A September 2014, article in the *Washington Post* reported that: "During the Obama years, the outflow of personnel has accelerated, according to the FedScope database of federal employees maintained by the Office of Personnel Management. Between 2010 and 2013, the number of annual departures of permanent employees from DHS increased 31 percent, compared with a 17 percent increase for the government overall. Members of the Senior Executive Service—the government's top career managers—also are leaving DHS at a much higher rate. In 2013, SES departures were up 56 percent from the year before. By contrast, the rate for the government as a whole was virtually unchanged." (Jerry Markon, Ellen Nakashima and Alice Crites, "Top-level Turnover Makes It Harder for DHS to Stay on Top of Evolving Threats," *Washington Post*, September 21, 2014, available at http://www.washingtonpost.com/politics/top- level-turnover-makes-it-harder-for-dhs-to-stay-on-top-of-evolving-threats/2014/09/21/ca7919a6-39d7-11e4-9c9f-ebb47272e40e_story.html.) In response, Secretary Jeh Johnson issued a statement that noted, in part: "In fact, over the last nine months there have been 12 presidential appointments to senior-level positions in this Department. Each of these appointees [has] pledged to serve until at least the end of this Administration. In fact, 90 percent of all positions at the SES level and above across this 240,000-person Department are now filled." (U.S. Department of Homeland Security, DHS Press Office, "Statement by Secretary Johnson About Today's *Washington Post* Story on DHS," September 22, 2014, available at http://www.dhs.gov/news/2014/09/22/statement-secretary-johnson-about-todays-washington-post-story-dhs). The current incumbents of executive positions in the department, including those officials who are serving in an "Acting" capacity, are listed on a "Leadership" page on the DHS website, available at http://www.dhs.gov/leadership.

[261] Vacancies in executive positions at DHS have been discussed during hearings conducted by the House of Representatives and the Senate. For example, see U.S. Congress, House Committee on Homeland Security, *Help Wanted at DHS: Implications of Leadership Vacancies on the Mission and Morale*, Hearing, 113th Cong., 1st sess., (Washington: GPO, December 12, 2013), available at http://www.gpo.gov/fdsys/pkg/CHRG-113hhrg87376/pdf/CHRG-113hhrg87376.pdf. U.S. Senate, Committee on Homeland Security and Governmental Affairs, *Nomination of Hon. Jeh C. Johnson*, Hearing, 113th Cong., 1st sess., (Washington: GPO, November 13, 2013), available at http://www.gpo.gov/fdsys/pkg/CHRG-113shrg86634/pdf/CHRG-113shrg86634.pdf.

[262] U.S. Office of Personnel Management, "A Guide to the Strategic Leadership Succession Management Model," (Washington, DC: OPM, March 2009), p. 1, available at http://archive.opm.gov/hcaaf_resource_center/assets/Lead_Guide.pdf.

[263] Ibid., p. 5.

[264] U.S. Congress, Senate Committee on Homeland Security and Governmental Affairs, Subcommittee on Oversight of Government Management, the Federal Workforce, and the District of Columbia, Hearing, *Keeping the Nation Safe Through the Presidential Transition*, 110th Cong., 2nd sess. (Washington: GPO, September 18, 2008), p. 30, available at http://www.gpo.gov/fdsys/pkg/CHRG-110shrg45577/pdf/CHRG-110shrg45577.pdf.

[265] U.S. Congress, House Committee on Oversight and Government Reform, Subcommittee on Government Management, Organization, and Procurement, Hearing, *Passing the Baton: Preparing for the Presidential Transition*, 110th Cong., 2nd sess. (Washington: GPO, September 24, 2008), available at http://www.gpo.gov/fdsys/pkg/CHRG- 110hhrg49494/pdf/CHRG-110hhrg49494.pdf.

[266] Ibid., pp. 210-211.

[267] National Academy of Public Administration, A Report by a Panel of the National Academy of Public Administration, "Addressing the 2009 Presidential Transition at the Department of Homeland Security" (Washington: NAPA, June 2008), pp. 82-86, available at http://www.politicalappointeeproject.org/sites/default/files/napadhhs.pdf.

[268] On January 28, 2015, the Congressional Research Service requested information from DHS on its succession plan and current succession management activities underway, but the department has not yet provided a response.

[269] The Department of Homeland Security Office of the Chief Human Capital Officer webpage is available at http://www.dhs.gov/organization/ochco-office-chief-human-capital-officer.

[270] This section of the Federal Employee Viewpoint Survey includes nine questions: (63) How satisfied are you with your involvement in decisions that affect your work?; (64) How satisfied are you with the information you receive from management on what's going on in your organization?; (65) How satisfied are you with the recognition you receive for doing a good job?; (66) How satisfied are you with the policies and practices of your senior leaders?; (67) How satisfied are you with your opportunity to get a better job in your organization?; (68) How satisfied are you with the training you receive for your present job?; (69) Considering everything, how satisfied are you with your job?; (70) Considering everything, how satisfied are you with your pay?; and (71) Considering everything, how satisfied are you with your organization?

[271] U.S. Office of Personnel Management, "2014 Federal Employee Viewpoint Survey Employees Influencing Change," Published Reports, select "Federal Employee Viewpoint Survey 2014: FedView Report by Agency," then select the second PDF file, Question 69. The published reports page is available at http://www.fedview.opm.gov/2014/Published/ and includes information on the survey methodology. The specific percentages for each response category were: "Very satisfied" (14.3%), "Satisfied" (38.8%), "Neither Satisfied nor Dissatisfied" (20.9%), "Dissatisfied" (15.9%), and "Very Dissatisfied" (10.1%).

[272] Ibid. Question 71. The specific percentages for each response category were: "Very satisfied" (9.6%), "Satisfied" (32.1%), "Neither Satisfied nor Dissatisfied" (23.1%), "Dissatisfied" (20.0%), and "Very Dissatisfied" (15.1%).

[273] The results for the earlier years are included with the 2014 results.

[274] The Unlocking Federal Talent Dashboard is available to agencies with an assigned user name and password at https://unlocktalent.gov/.

[275] The "Employee Engagement and Satisfaction" page will allow managers to "view employee scores (i.e., rating satisfaction with supervisors and peers, with their jobs and pay levels)" by office or department and easily compare office "scores to government-wide averages, or, compare them to earlier years' scores as a way of gauging progress-or lack of progress-over time." U.S. Office of Personnel Management, "OPM Releases UnlockTalent.gov Dashboard," News Release, July 15, 2014, available at http://www.opm.gov/news/releases/2014/07/opm-releases-unlocktalentgov- dashboard/.

[276] See Jerry Markon, "DHS Tackles Endless Morale Problems With Seemingly Endless Studies," *Washington Post*, February 20, 2015, available at http://www.washingtonpost.com/politics/homeland-security-has-done-little-for-low- morale-but-study-it—repeatedly/2015/02/20/f626eba8-b15c-11e4-886b-c22184f27c35_story.html.

[277] U.S. Department of Homeland Security, "Homeland Security Advisory Council—New Tasking," 79 *Federal Register* 64399, October 29, 2014, available at http://www.gpo.gov/fdsys/pkg/FR-2014-10-29/pdf/2014-25660.pdf.

[278] According to the report, "employee engagement has three primary elements: (1) emotional and rational commitment to the job and the organization; (2) discretionary effort that produces sustained goal-directed performance; and (3) satisfaction from the job and its context." U.S. Merit Systems Protection Board, "Federal Employee Engagement: The Motivating Potential of Job Characteristics and Rewards" (Washington: MSPB, December 2012), p. 2, available at http://www.mspb.gov/netsearch/viewdocs.aspx?docnumber =780015&version=782964.

[279] Ibid., pp. 33-34.

[280] U.S. Congress, House Committee on Homeland Security, *Help Wanted at DHS: Implications of Leadership Vacancies on the Mission and Morale*, Hearing, 113th Cong., 1st sess. (Washington: GPO, December 12, 2013), pp. 58- 59, available at http://www.gpo.gov/fdsys/pkg/CHRG-113hhrg87376/pdf/CHRG-113hhrg87376.pdf.

[281] U.S. Senate, Committee on Homeland Security and Governmental Affairs, *Nomination of Hon. Jeh C. Johnson*, Hearing, 113th Cong., 1st sess. (Washington: GPO, November 13, 2013), p. 20, available at http://www.gpo.gov/fdsys/pkg/CHRG-113shrg86634/pdf/CHRG-113shrg86634.pdf.

[282] A Management Directive and an Instruction Guide for the program were issued by DHS in August 2008. U.S. Department of Homeland Security, DHS Directives System, Directive 084-01, "Department of Homeland Security Loaned Executive Program," August 4, 2008, available at http://www.dhs.gov/xlibrary/assets/mgmt/mgmt-directive- 084-01-loaned-executive-program.pdf. U.S. Department of Homeland Security, DHS Directives System, Instruction 084-01-001, "Instruction Guide on the Department of Homeland Security Loaned Executive Program," August 7, 2008, available at http://www.dhs.gov/xlibrary/assets/mgmt/mgmt-loaned-executive-program-instruction-guide.pdf.

[283] U.S. Department of Homeland Security, "Loaned Executive Program," February 6, 2015, available at http://www.dhs.gov/loaned-executive-program.

[284] U.S. Department of Homeland Security, DHS Press Office, "DHS Loaned Executive Program Begins to Improve the Travel Experience for Commercial Aviation Travelers," November 14, 2014, available at http://www.dhs.gov/news/2014/11/14/dhs-loaned-executive-program-begins-improve-travel-experience-commercial-aviation.

[285] The executive will serve a six-month assignment with the option for a renewal of six months. See "Senior Advisor, Lifeline Functions Restoration, FEMA Region VIII," available at http://www.dhs.gov/sites/default/files/publications/Policy-PSO/SeniorAdvisorLifeline FunctionsRestoration_FEMARegionVIIIE.pdf.

[286] The civil servants were selected from the Leadership Directory database and were generally in General Schedule (GS) grades GS-13 and above. Respondents were not identified.

[287] National Academy of Public Administration and ICF International, "Federal Leaders Digital Insight Study," January 13, 2015, p. 1, available at http://napawash.org/images/reports/2015/Federal_Leaders_Digital_Insights_Study.pdf. The definition did not include the underlying information technology systems "that provide infrastructure or computing platforms." (Hereinafter referred to as Digital Insight Study.)

[288] Digital Insight Study, p. 3. ICF administered the survey between August 28, 2014, and September 26, 2014, and sent it to 8,967 Federal Leaders by electronic mail.

[289] Examples of such offices or positions that were listed in the report were: Offices/Directors of Digital Strategy/Digital Programs/Digital Trends/Digital Communications; Innovation Offices; Digital Diplomacy/e- Diplomacy Office; Departments/Centers for New Media; Social Media Engagement Specialists/Managers; Customer Relations Officers/Managers; E-Commerce/Shoppers Insight Division; and Cyber Czar.

[290] Digital Insight Study, pp. 9-10.

[291] Digital Insight Study, p. 10.

[292] U.S. Office of Personnel Management, "2014 Federal Employee Viewpoint Survey Employees Influencing Change," Published Reports, select "Federal Employee Viewpoint Survey 2014: FedView Report by Agency," then select the second PDF file, Question 68. The published reports page is available at http://www.fedview.opm.gov/2014/Published/ and includes information on the survey methodology. The specific percentages for each response category were: "Very satisfied" (9.0%), "Satisfied" (34.6%), "Neither Satisfied nor Dissatisfied" (23.6%), "Dissatisfied" (19.5%), and "Very Dissatisfied" (13.4%).

[293] For specific details on the Interagency Council on Veterans Employment and the Veterans Employment Initiative, see U.S. President (Obama), "Employment of Veterans in the Federal Government," Executive Order 13518, 74 *Federal Register* 58533-58536,

November 13, 2009, available at http://www.gpo.gov/fdsys/pkg/FR-2009-11-13/pdf/E9-27441.pdf.

[294] Ibid, p. 58535.

[295] U.S. Department of Homeland Security, "Veterans and Homeland Security," August 26, 2014, available at http://www.dhs.gov/veterans-and-homeland-security.

[296] U.S. Department of Homeland Security, "Departmental Management and Operations, Strategic Context, Fiscal Year 2016 Congressional Justification" (Washington: DHS, February 2015), p. DMO-6, embedded within the "Congressional Budget Justification FY2016," available at http://www.dhs.gov/sites/default/files/publications/DHS_FY2016_Congressional_Budget_Justification.pdf.

In: Homeland Security
Editor: Malcolm Leonard Moreno

ISBN: 978-1-63484-754-4

Chapter 2

DEPARTMENT OF HOMELAND SECURITY APPROPRIATIONS: FY2016*

William L. Painter and Barbara L. Schwemle

SUMMARY

This report discusses the FY2016 appropriations for the Department of Homeland Security (DHS) and provides an overview of the Administration's FY2016 request. The report makes note of many budgetary resources provided to DHS, but its primary focus is on funding approved by Congress through the appropriations process. It also includes an appendix with definitions of key budget terms used throughout the suite of Congressional Research Service reports on homeland security appropriations. It also directs the reader to other reports providing context for and additional details regarding specific component appropriations and issues engaged through the FY2016 appropriations process.

The Administration requested $41.4 billion in adjusted net discretionary budget authority for DHS for FY2016, as part of an overall budget that the Office of Management and Budget estimates to be $64.8 billion (including fees, trust funds, and other funding that is not annually appropriated or does not score against discretionary budget limits). The request amounted to a $1.7 billion, or 4.4%, increase from the $39.7

* This is an edited, reformatted and augmented version of a Congressional Research Service publication R44053, prepared for Members and Committees of Congress, dated August 7, 2015.

billion enacted for FY2015 through the Department of Homeland Security Appropriations Act, 2015 (P.L. 114-4).

The Administration also requested an additional $6.7 billion not reflected above for the Federal Emergency Management Agency (FEMA) in disaster relief funding, as defined by the Budget Control Act (BCA, P.L. 112-25), and a $160 million transfer from the Navy to the Coast Guard for overseas contingency operations (OCO) funding. Neither the disaster relief funding nor the OCO funding is considered when calculating the total amount of adjusted net discretionary budget authority, as neither count against the discretionary spending limit.

On June 18, 2015, the Senate Committee on Appropriations reported out S. 1619, accompanied by S.Rept. 114-68. S. 1619 would include $40.2 billion in adjusted net discretionary budget authority for FY2016. This was $1.2 billion (2.9%) below the level requested by the Administration, but over $0.5 billion (1.4%) above the enacted level for FY2015. The Senate committee-reported bill included the administration-requested levels for disaster relief funding and OCO funding covered by BCA adjustments—the latter as an appropriation in the DHS appropriations bill rather than the requested transfer.

On July 14, 2015, the House Committee on Appropriations reported out H.R. 3128, accompanied by H.Rept. 114-215. H.R. 3128 would include $39.3 billion in adjusted net discretionary budget authority for FY2016. This was almost $2.1 billion (5.0%) below the level requested by the Administration, and $337 million (0.8%) below the FY2015 enacted level. While the House-reported bill included the administration-requested level for disaster relief funding, overseas contingency operations funding for the Coast Guard covered by BCA adjustments was provided in the House-passed Department of Defense appropriations act as a transfer from the Navy— therefore it is not included in the total funding in this bill for DHS.

INTRODUCTION

This report describes and analyzes annual appropriations for the Department of Homeland Security (DHS) for FY2016. It compares the enacted FY2015 appropriations for DHS, the Administration's FY2016 budget request, and the appropriations proposed by Congress thus far. This report identifies additional informational resources, reports, and products on DHS appropriations that provide additional context for the discussion. The suite of CRS reports on homeland security appropriations tracks legislative action and congressional issues related to DHS appropriations, with particular attention paid to discretionary funding amounts.

The reports do not provide in-depth analysis of specific issues related to mandatory funding—such as retirement pay—nor do they systematically follow other legislation related to the authorization or amending of DHS programs, activities, or fee revenues.

Discussion of appropriations legislation involves a variety of specialized budgetary concepts. The *Appendix* to this report explains several of these concepts, including budget authority, obligations, outlays, discretionary and mandatory spending, offsetting collections, allocations, and adjustments to the discretionary spending caps under the Budget Control Act (P.L. 112-25). A more complete discussion of those terms and the appropriations process in general can be found in CRS Report R42388, *The Congressional Appropriations Process: An Introduction*, by Jessica Tollestrup, and the Government Accountability Office's *A Glossary of Terms Used in the Federal Budget Process*.[1]

Note on Data and Citations

Except in summary discussions and when discussing total amounts for the bill as a whole, all amounts contained in the suite of CRS reports on homeland security appropriations represent budget authority and are rounded to the nearest million. However, for precision in percentages and totals, all calculations were performed using unrounded data.

Data used in this report for FY2015 amounts are derived from the Department of Homeland Security Appropriations Act, 2015 (P.L. 114-4) and the explanatory statement that accompanied H.R. 240 as printed in the *Congressional Record* of January 13, 2015, pages H275-H322. Contextual information on the FY2016 request is generally from the *Budget of the United States Government, Fiscal Year 2016*, the FY2016 DHS congressional budget justifications, and the FY2016 DHS *Budget in Brief*.[2] However, most data used in CRS analyses in reports on DHS appropriations is drawn from congressional documentation to ensure consistent scoring whenever possible. Data on the FY2016 budget request and Senate-reported recommended funding levels are from S. 1619 and S.Rept. 114-68. Information on the House-reported recommended funding levels is from H.R. 3128 and H.Rept. 114-215.

Summary of DHS Appropriations

Generally, the homeland security appropriations bill includes all annual appropriations provided for DHS, allocating resources to every departmental component. Discretionary appropriations[3] provide roughly two-thirds to three-fourths of the annual funding for DHS operations, depending how one accounts for disaster relief spending and funding for overseas contingency operations. The remainder of the budget is a mix of fee revenues, trust funds, and mandatory spending.

Appropriations measures for DHS typically have been organized into five titles.[4] The first four are thematic groupings of components:

- Title I, *Departmental Management and Operations,* the smallest of the first four titles, contains appropriations for the Office of the Secretary and Executive Management (OSEM), the Office of the Under Secretary for Management (USM), the Office of the Chief Financial Officer, the Office of the Chief Information Officer (CIO), Analysis and Operations (A&O), and the Office of the Inspector General (OIG).
  - The Administration requested $1,396 million in FY2016 net discretionary budget authority for components included in this title.[5] The appropriations request was $255 million (22.3%) more than was provided for FY2015.
  - Senate-reported S. 1619 envisions the components included in this title receiving $1,346 million in net discretionary budget authority. This would be $50 million (3.6%) less than requested, but $205 million (18.0%) more than was provided in FY2015.
  - House-reported H.R. 3128 envisions the components included in this title receiving $1,217 million in net discretionary budget authority, a $179 million (12.8%) decrease from the request and $76 million (6.7%) above FY2015.
- Title II, *Security, Enforcement, and Investigations,* comprising roughly three-quarters of the funding appropriated for the department, contains appropriations for Customs and Border Protection (CBP), Immigration and Customs Enforcement (ICE), the Transportation Security Administration (TSA), the Coast Guard (USCG), and the Secret Service.

- The Administration requested $32,481 million in FY2016 net discretionary budget authority for components included in this title, as part of a total budget for these components of $39,431 million for FY2016.[6] The appropriations request was $807 million (2.5%) more than was provided for FY2015.
- Senate-reported S. 1619 envisions the components included in this title receiving $32,484 million in net discretionary budget authority. This would be $3 million (0.01%) more than requested, and $810 million (2.6%) more than was provided in FY2015.
- House-reported H.R. 3128 envisions the components included in this title receiving $32,182 million in net discretionary budget authority. This would be $299 million (0.9%) less than requested, and $508 million (1.6%) more than was provided in FY2015.

- Title III, *Protection, Preparedness, Response, and Recovery,* the second-largest of the first four titles, contains appropriations for the National Protection and Programs Directorate (NPPD), the Office of Health Affairs (OHA), and the Federal Emergency Management Agency (FEMA).
  - The Administration requested $6,222 million in FY2016 net discretionary budget authority for components included in this title, as part of a total budget for these components of $19,020 million for FY2016.[7] The appropriations request was $267 million (4.5%) more than was provided for FY2015.
  - Senate-reported S. 1619 envisions the components included in this title receiving $6,291 million in net discretionary budget authority. This would be $69 million (1.1%) more than requested, and $336 million (5.6%) more than was provided in FY2015.
  - House-reported H.R. 3128 envisions the components included in this title receiving $6,146 million in net discretionary budget authority. This would be $100 million (1.6%) less than requested, and $167 million (2.8%) more than was provided in FY2015.
- Title IV, *Research and Development, Training, and Services,* the second-smallest of the first four titles, contains appropriations for the U.S. Citizenship and Immigration Services (USCIS), the Federal Law Enforcement Training Center (FLETC), the Science and Technology Directorate (S&T), and the Domestic Nuclear Detection Office (DNDO).

- The Administration requested $1,554 million in FY2016 net discretionary budget authority for components included in this title, as part of a total budget for these components of $5,427 million for FY2016. The appropriations request was $251 million (13.9%) less than was provided for FY2015.
- Senate-reported S. 1619 envisions the components included in this title receiving $1,461 million in net discretionary budget authority. This would be $93 million (6.0%) less than requested, and $344 million (19.1%) less than was provided in FY2015.
- House-reported H.R. 3128 envisions the components included in this title receiving $1,503 million in net discretionary budget authority. This would be $30 million (2.0%) less than requested, and $292 million (16.3%) less than was provided in FY2015.

A fifth title contains general provisions, the impact of which may reach across the entire department, impact multiple components, or focus on a single activity. Rescissions of prior-year appropriations—cancellations of budget authority that reduce the net funding level in the bill— are found here. The Administration proposed rescinding $255 million in prior-year appropriations as part of its FY2016 budget request. Senate-reported S. 1619 included $1,359 million in rescissions, while House-reported H.R. 3128 included $1,692 million.

HOMELAND SECURITY APPROPRIATIONS

The following tables present comparisons of FY2015 enacted and FY2016 requested appropriations for the department by thematic grouping. References to titles refer to the organization of the funding in the FY2015 appropriations cycle, not the Administration's budget request.

The tables summarize the appropriations provided for each component, subtotaling the resources provided through the appropriations legislation. Indented text and bracketed numbers indicate resources either provided through provisions separate from the base appropriations for the component, or that do not count as net discretionary budget authority (see below). A subtotal for each component of total estimated resources that would be available under the legislation and from other sources (such as fees, mandatory spending, and trust funds) for the given fiscal year is also provided. At the bottom of each table, three totals indicate the total for the title on its own, the total for title's components in the entire bill, and the projected total FY2016 funding for the title's components from all sources (such as fees not governed by the bill, trust funds, etc.).

DHS and "Adjusted" Net Discretionary Budget Authority

The annual DHS budget proposal includes a variety of funding mechanisms. For example, the FY2016 request envisions an appropriations bill that includes

- appropriations that are offset by agency collections, such as user fees;
- funding that is effectively not subject to the discretionary spending limits due to special designation;
- appropriations that are considered to be mandatory spending; and
- appropriations that are contingent on certain things happening.[8]

The appropriations bill also may include rescissions—cancellation of budget authority that otherwise would be available for obligation and thus is treated as negative spending. Also credited to the discretionary spending in the bill are two elements of "permanent indefinite discretionary spending" that are not included in the actual appropriations bill but are included in the discretionary spending total of the bill because of scorekeeping practices.

These numbers can be totaled in several different ways to summarize what is in the bill. For DHS, net discretionary budget authority includes all discretionary budget authority credited to the bill (thus excluding specially designated funding and mandatory spending), net of offsets (including any offsetting collections and fees).

In DHS budget documents, net discretionary budget authority does not take into account the impact of rescissions. However, adjusted net discretionary budget authority does take rescissions into account. This is the total that counts against discretionary spending limits, and it is the total used most commonly in debate on appropriations. To avoid confusion when readers interpret DHS documents, CRS reporting on DHS appropriations uses the DHS terminology to describe that total.

Departmental Management and Operations

Table 1. Budgetary Resources for Departmental Management and Operations Components, FY2015 and FY2016 (budget authority in millions of dollars)

	FY2015		FY2016	
Component/Appropriation	Enacted	Request	Senate-Reported S. 1619	House-Reported H.R. 3128
Office of the Secretary and Executive Management	133	134	133	132
Office of the Under Secretary for Management	188	193	185	194
DHS Headquarters Consolidation	—	216[b]	—	—
DHS Headquarters Consolidation (Title V)	[49]	—	[212]	[44]
Office of the Chief Financial Officer	52	54	53	56
Financial Systems Modernization (Title V)	[34]	[43[c]]	[36]	[53]
Office of the Chief Information Officer	288	321	304	308
Analysis and Operations	256	269	263	265
Office of the Inspector General	119	142	134	141
Transfer to OIG from FEMA's DRF (Title III)[a]	[24]	[24]	[24]	[24]
Net Discretionary Budget Authority: Title I	1,035	1,329	1,074	1,096
Component/Appropriation	FY2015		FY2016	
Net Discretionary Budget Authority: Total for Departmental Management and Operations Components	1,141	1,396	1,346	1,217
Total Gross Budgetary Resources for Departmental Management and Operations Components	1,141	1,396	1,346	1,217

Source: CRS analysis of P.L. 114-4 and its explanatory statement as printed in the Congressional Record of January 13, 2015, pp. H275-H322, the FY2016 DHS Budget-in-Brief, S. 1619, S.Rept. 114-68, H.R. 3128 and H.Rept. 114-215.

Notes: Table displays rounded numbers, but all operations were performed with unrounded data. Therefore, amounts may not sum to totals. FEMA = Federal Emergency Management Agency; DRF = Disaster Relief Fund.

[a] The DHS Office of the Inspector General (OIG) also receives transfers from FEMA to pay for oversight of disaster-related activities that are reflected in the last two lines in these tables, including $24 million in FY2015 and $24 million requested for FY2016.

[b] This amount includes more than $11 million in support costs for the facility, which generally has been appropriated in the Coast Guard's Operating Expenses account.

[c] The Administration requested funding for this activity under the Office of the Chief Financial Officer.

Security, Enforcement, and Investigations

Table 2. Budgetary Resources for Security, Enforcement, and Investigations, FY2015 and FY2016 (budget authority in millions of dollars)

	FY2015		FY2016	
Component/Appropriation	Enacted	Request	Senate-reported S. 1619	House-reported H.R. 3128
Customs and Border Protection				
Salaries and Expenses	8,460	9,124	8,779	8,695
Small Airport User Fee[a]	9	9	9	9
Automation Modernization	808	867	854	846
Border Security Fencing, Infrastructure, and Technology	382	373	373	439
Air and Marine Operations	750	747	755	785
Facilities Management	289	342	314	341
COBRA FTA funding (Title V)[b]	[138]	[180]	[220]	[180]
Title II Appropriation	10,699	11,463	11,084	11,116
Total Appropriation	10,837	11,643	11,304	11,296
Fees, Mandatory Spending, and Trust Funds	1,884	1,977	1,977	1,977
Total Budgetary Resources (including Title V)	12,721	13,620	13,281	13,273
Immigration and Customs Enforcement				
Salaries and Expenses	5,933	5,887	5,762	5,736
Automation and Infrastructure Modernization	26	74	53	74
Construction	0	5	0	5
Appropriation	5,959	5,965	5,815	5,815
Fees, Mandatory Spending, and Trust Funds	345	322	322	322
Total Budgetary Resources	6,304	6,287	6,137	6,137
Transportation Security				
Administration				
Aviation Security (net funding)	3,574	3,500	3,453	3,429
Surface Transportation Security	124	124	123	107
Intelligence and Vettingc (net funding)	219	228	225	216
Transportation Security Support	917	931	919	901
Appropriation	4,834	4,783	4,719	4,653
Fees, Mandatory Spending, and Trust Funds	2,395	2,564	2,579	2,579

Table 2. (Continued)

Component/Appropriation	FY2015 Enacted	FY2016 Request	Senate-reported S. 1619	House-reported H.R. 3128
Total Budgetary Resources	7,229	7,347	7,299	7,233
U.S. Coast Guard				
Operating Expenses[d]	7,043	6,823	6,996	6,899
Overseas Contingency Operations	[213]	0	[160]	0
Adjustment (included in Operating Expenses)[d]				
Environmental Compliance and Restoration	13	13	13	13
Reserve Training	115	111	111	111
Acquisition, Construction, and Improvements	1,225	1,017	1,573	1,301
Research, Development, Testing, and Evaluation	18	18	18	18
Health Care Fund Contributiona	177	169	169	169
Discretionary Appropriation	8,378	8,151	8,721	8,512
Fees, Mandatory Spending, and Trust Funds	1,664	1,822	1,822	1,822
Total Budgetary Resources U.S. Secret Service	10,255	9,973	10,703	10,334
Salaries and Expenses	1,616	1,867	1,837	1,833
Acquisition, Construction, and Improvements	50	72	87	73
Appropriation	1,666	1,939	1,924	1,906
Fees, Mandatory Spending, and Trust Funds	260	265	265	265
Total Budgetary Resources	1,926	2,204	2,189	2,171
Net Discretionary Budget Authority: Title II	31,536	32,301	32,264	32,002
Net Discretionary Budget Authority:	31,674	32,481	32,484	32,182
Total for Security, Enforcement, and Investigations Components				
Total Gross Budgetary Resources for Security, Enforcement, and Investigations Components	38,434	39,431	39,609	39,147

Source: CRS analysis of P.L. 114-4 and its explanatory statement as printed in the Congressional Record of January 13, 2015, pp. H275-H322, the FY2016 DHS Budget-in-Brief, S. 1619, S.Rept. 114-68, H.R. 3128 and H.Rept. 114-215.

Notes: Table displays rounded numbers, but all operations were performed with unrounded data. Amounts, therefore, may not sum to totals. Fee revenues included in the "Fees, Mandatory Spending, and Trust Funds" lines are projections, and do not include budget authority provided through general provisions.

[a] This item is considered permanent indefinite discretionary spending and, therefore, scores as being in the bill, despite not being explicitly appropriated in the bills' legislative language.

[b] Sec. 556 of the Senate-reported bill and Sec. 551 of the House reported bill authorize CBP to expend certain fee revenues collected pursuant to the Colombia Free Trade Act. These provisions score as discretionary budget authority, and so are reflected separately from other fees.

[c] Formerly entitled "Transportation Threat Assessment and Credentialing."

[d] Overseas contingency operations funding is included in the Operating Expenses appropriation, but is not added to the appropriations total in accordance with the appropriations committees' practices for subtotaling this account. This funding is reflected in the total gross budgetary resources for the Coast Guard, not the total net discretionary budget authority.

Protection, Preparedness, Response, and Recovery

Table 3. Budgetary Resources for Protection, Preparedness, Response, and Recovery, FY2015 and FY2016 (budget authority in millions of dollars)

	FY2015	FY2016		
Component/Appropriation	Enacted	Request	Senate-reported S. 1619	House-reported H.R. 3128
National Protection and Programs				
Directorate				
Management and Administration	62	64	58	56
Infrastructure Protection and Information	1,189	1,312	1,297	1,245
Security				
Federal Protective Service[a]	[1,343]	[1,443]	[1,443]	[1,443]
Office of Biometric Identity Management	252	284	283	283
Appropriation	1,502	1,659	1,638	1,585
Fees, Mandatory Spending, and Trust Funds	1,343	1,443	1,443	1,443
Total Budgetary Resources	2,845	3,103	3,082	3,028
Office of Health Affairs				

Table 3. (Continued)

Component/Appropriation	FY2015 Enacted	FY2016 Request	Senate-reported S. 1619	House-reported H.R. 3128
Appropriation	129	124	123	125
Fees, Mandatory Spending, and Trust Funds	0	0	0	0
Total Budgetary Resources	129	124	123	125
Federal Emergency Management				
Agency				
Salaries and Expenses	934	949	929	956
Grants and Training	2,530	2,231	2,530	2,530
Radiological Emergency Preparedness	-2	*	*	*
U.S. Fire Administration	44	42	44	44
Disaster Relief Fund	596	662	662	662
Major Disasters Adjustment	[6,438]	[6,713]	[6,713]	[6,713]
Transfer to Office of Inspector General	[-24]	[-24]	[-24]	[-24]
Subtotal: Net Total Disaster Relief	[7,009]	[7,351]	[7,351]	[7,351]
Funding[b]				
Flood Hazard Mapping and Risk Analysis	100	279	190	100
National Flood Insurance Funda	[179]	[181]	[181]	[181]
Pre-disaster Mitigation Fund	25	200	100	25
Emergency Food and Shelter	120	100	100	120
Appropriation[c]	4,347	4,462	4,554	4,437
Fees, Mandatory Spending, and Trust Funds	4,538	4,666	4,666	4,666
Total Budgetary Resources	15,299	15,817	15,909	15,791
Net Discretionary Budget Authority: Title III[c]	5,979	6,246	6,315	6,147
Net Discretionary Budget Authority: Total for Protection, Preparedness, Response and Recovery Components	5,955	6,222	6,291	6,123
Total Gross Budgetary Resources for Protection, Preparedness, Response and Recovery Components	18,250	19,020	19,114	18,920

Source: CRS analysis of P.L. 114-4 and its explanatory statement as printed in the Congressional Record of January 13, 2015, pp. H275-H322, the FY2016 DHS Budget-in-Brief, S. 1619, S.Rept. 114-68, H.R. 3128 and H.Rept. 114-215.

Notes: * = rounds to zero. Table displays rounded numbers, but all operations were performed with unrounded data. Amounts, therefore, may not sum to totals.

Fee revenues included in the "Fees, Mandatory Spending, and Trust Funds" lines are projections, and do not include budget authority provided through general provisions.

[a] This line is wholly offset by fees and, therefore, does not add to the total appropriation.

[b] This line is a subtotal of the "Disaster Relief Fund" line and the "Disaster Relief Adjustment"—it represents the total resources provided to the DRF. The "Disaster Relief Fund" line is included in the "Appropriation" line, but the "Disaster Relief Adjustment" line is not.

[c] For consistency across tables, this line does not include the $24 million transfer from the DRF—its impact is reflected in the budgetary resource totals below.

Research and Development, Training, and Services

Table 4. Budgetary Resources for Research and Development, Training, and Services FY2015 andFY2016 (budget authority in millions of dollars)

	FY2015	FY2016		
Component/Appropriation	Enacted	Request	Senate-reported S. 1619	House-reported H.R. 3128
U.S. Citizenship and Immigration Services				
E-Verify	124	120	120	120
Immigrant Immigration Programs	—	10	—	—
Immigrant Integration Grants (Title V; authority to use fees)	[10]	—	[10]	[10]
U Visa fee proposal (Title V)	—	21	—	—
Appropriation	124	151	120	120
Fees, Mandatory Spending, and Trust Funds	3,097	3,874	3,491	3,491
Total Budgetary Resources	3,231	4,025	3,620	3,620
Federal Law Enforcement Training Center				
Salaries and Expenses	230	239	219	212
Acquisition, Construction, Improvements, and	28	28	26	28
Related Expenses				
Appropriation	258	267	246	239
Fees, Mandatory Spending, and Trust Funds	0	0	0	0
Total Budgetary Resources	258	267	246	239
Science and Technology Directorate				

Table 4. (Continued)

Component/Appropriation	FY2015 Enacted	FY2016 Request	Senate-reported S. 1619	House-reported H.R. 3128
Management and Administration	130	132	130	132
Research, Development, Acquisition, and Operations	974	647	634	655
Appropriation	1,104	779	765	787
Fees, Mandatory Spending, and Trust Funds	0	0	0	0
Total Budgetary Resources	1,104	779	765	787
Domestic Nuclear Detection Office				
Management and Administration	37	38	38	38
Research, Development, and Operations	198	196	196	196
Systems Acquisition	73	123	87	123
Appropriation	308	357	320	357
Fees, Mandatory Spending, and Trust Funds	0	0	0	0
Total Budgetary Resources	308	357	320	357
Net Discretionary Budget Authority: Title IV	1,795	1,533	1,451	1,503
Net Discretionary Budget Authority: Total for Research and Development, Training, and Services Components	1,805	1,554	1,461	1,513
Total Gross Budgetary Resources for Research and Development, Training, and Services Components	4,902	5,427	4,951	5,003

Source: CRS analysis of P.L. 114-4 and its explanatory statement as printed in the Congressional Record of January 13, 2015, pp. H275-H322, the FY2016 DHS Budget-in-Brief, S. 1619, S.Rept. 114-68, H.R. 3128 and H.Rept. 114-215.

Notes: Table displays rounded numbers, but all operations were performed with unrounded data. Amounts, therefore, may not sum to totals. Fee revenues included in the "Fees, Mandatory Spending, and Trust Funds" lines are projections, and do not include budget authority provided through general provisions.

Crosscutting Issues for the Department of Homeland Security[9]

Discretionary Spending Limits

Most of the DHS budget is outside of the defense budget function (050). As a result, the department competes with the rest of the federal nondefense budget for discretionary spending allocations under the budget controls imposed by the Budget Control Act.[10] The funding to be allocated among the appropriations subcommittees is not anticipated to rise at the same rate as envisioned in the Administration's budget request. House Homeland Security Subcommittee Chairman John Carter described the tension this creates at a subcommittee hearing on the request:

> To begin, the $1.5 billion increase [proposed for DHS] absorbs almost 75% of non-defense, discretionary spending available under the limits of the Budget Control Act of 2013. Mr. Secretary ... the Congress intends to live within the confines of the law even if the Administration does not. As a result, I doubt DHS's budget will rise as steeply as the request proposes.[11]

Federal Pay Issues

The Administration proposed a 1.3% pay increase for all civilian federal employees and members of the military in its FY2016 budget request. Almost all DHS employees are considered civilians, with the significant exception of Coast Guard military personnel.

The Senate Appropriations Committee report stated that "the committee assumes the COLA for civilian employees across the Department will be absorbed within amounts appropriated in this act."[12] Likewise, the House Appropriations committee report indicated that funding was not provided for the civilian pay increase, but that if the administration provides a civilian pay increase that it would "be absorbed within other amounts appropriated for FY2016."[13] The House Appropriations Committee report indicated that the military pay raise was fully funded.[14]

The House report also stated that the FY2017 budget request was to also include estimated amounts, by component, and the standards and criteria for bonuses and performance awards.

S. 1619 and H.R. 3128, as reported, included general provisions[15] that would prohibit the obligation of appropriated funds for any structural pay reform that affects more than 100 full-time positions or costs more than $5 million in a single year until the end of the 30-day period that begins when the Secretary notifies Congress about (1) the number of FTE positions affected by the change, (2) funding required for the change for the current year and through the Future Years Homeland Security Program, (3) the justification for the change, and (4) an analysis of the compensation alternatives to the change that the department considered.

Execution of Personnel Funding

Hiring Process Delays

The Senate Appropriations Committee report stated that although Congress has provided for the increased personnel that the department has consistently requested,[16] "DHS has failed to bring those funded positions on board for a myriad of reasons including delays in obtaining suitability determinations and a backlog in polygraphs."[17] According to the committee, hiring difficulties are exacerbated by qualified applicants who have withdrawn from the process or accepted other positions by the time an offer of employment is made. Hiring times have increased department-wide (from 146 days in 2013 to 163 days in 2014) and at CBP (from 278 days in 2013 to 308 days in 2014). While noting that the U.S. Secret Service improved its hiring times (from 327 days in 2013 to 295 days in 2014), the committee report stated that the hiring process "still takes an inordinately long time."

The Senate report directed the department to report on its strategy to reduce hiring times and time to hire statistics within 60 days after the act's enactment. In addition, DHS and its major components were directed to develop metrics to track the status of hiring actions, including measuring the time spent on actions within each step of the process.[18] The USM was directed to provide a briefing on the development of the metrics within 90 days after the act's enactment.

According to the House Appropriations Committee report, "Chronic and systemic personnel shortfalls and lengthy hiring times jeopardize DHS's homeland security mission" and attrition rates are outpacing hiring in several components of the department. The report stated that DHS expects to end FY2015 "more than 6,000 FTEs below the number for which funds were provided" and would have to hire more than 7,000 FTEs between July 2015 and September 30, 2015, to reach the FTE level requested for FY2016. Given these circumstances, the report states that, for FY2016, "the Committee is unconvinced DHS will be able to spend the funds requested in the budget" and therefore, "reduce[d] funding in various agencies to reflect a more realistic and achievable number of FTEs."[19]

Going forward, the House report mandated two actions. First, the USM was directed to prepare "a root cause analysis" of the attrition and hiring shortfalls, "develop a corrective action plan" that will include metrics to measure the outcomes of initiatives, and provide monthly updates, beginning on January 15, 2016, to the committee on the results of the initiatives. Second, the department was again directed to provide a report,[20] on a strategy for reducing hiring times and provide data on those hiring times by component, by quarter, within 30 days after the act's enactment and thereafter, each quarter. The committee required that the report include additional content on hiring times[21] and metrics.[22]

Determining Personnel Requirements

The Senate Appropriations Committee report stated that the committee seeks "to understand how the Department proposes to balance real technology needs against manpower costs" and has requested "reports and briefings on the right balance of people, technology, and infrastructure" to support DHS operations.[23]

The House Appropriations Committee report believes that "the lack of a rigorous and consistent methodology to determine" the department's personnel requirements and costs is a "strategic problem." To address this matter, the committee directed USM to require the OCFO "to conduct an analysis of force structure that identifies the operations in which DHS personnel are expected to perform, the effects they must achieve, the attributes the forces must possess, and what kind and size of force is needed to execute the operations successfully."[24] The committee also directed that the OCFO provide quarterly briefings on the progress of the study and apply recommendations from its analysis to the FY2018 budget request, with personnel funding shortfalls noted.

Reception and Representation Expenses

Several DHS components have specific limitations placed on their funding for "reception and representation expenses." These limits range from $2,000 for the Office of the Under Secretary for Management in House-reported H.R. 3128 to 34,425 for Customs and Border protection in both Senate and House-reported bills. Thirteen such limitations, totaling $177,505, appear in Senate-reported S. 1619, and 14 such limitations, totaling $166,955, appear in House-reported H.R. 3128. Aside from the specific direction provided in the Senate- and House-reported legislation, both committee reports provided additional direction. The Senate Appropriations Committee report continued to require quarterly reports on obligations for all reception and representation expenses and stated that the funds should not be used "to purchase unnecessary collectibles or memorabilia."[25] The House committee report directed the department to review representation allowances for all DHS agencies to ensure the equitable alignment of funds with responsibilities, and submit any proposed changes with the FY2017 budget request.[26]

APPENDIX. APPROPRIATIONS TERMS AND CONCEPTS

Budget Authority, Obligations and Outlays

Federal government spending involves a multistep process that begins with the enactment of budget authority by Congress. Federal agencies then obligate funds from enacted budget authority to pay for their activities. Finally, payments are made to liquidate those obligations; the actual payment amounts are reflected in the budget as outlays.

Budget authority is established through appropriations acts or direct spending legislation and determines the amounts that are available for federal agencies to spend. The Antideficiency Act[27] prohibits federal agencies from obligating more funds than the budget authority enacted by Congress. Budget authority also may be indefinite, as when Congress enacts language providing "such sums as may be necessary" to complete a project or purpose. Budget authority may be available on a one-year, multiyear, or no-year basis. One-year budget authority is only available for obligation during a specific fiscal year; any unobligated funds at the end of that year are no longer available for spending. Multiyear budget authority specifies a range of time during which funds may be obligated for spending, and no-year budget authority is available for obligation for an indefinite period of time.

Obligations are incurred when federal agencies employ personnel, enter into contracts, receive services, and engage in similar transactions in a given fiscal year. *Outlays* are the funds that are actually spent during the fiscal year.[28] Because multiyear and no-year budget authorities may be obligated over a number of years, outlays do not always match the budget authority enacted in a given year. Additionally, budget authority may be obligated in one fiscal year but spent in a future fiscal year, especially with certain contracts.

In sum, budget authority allows federal agencies to incur obligations and authorizes payments, or outlays, to be made from the Treasury. Discretionary agencies and programs, and appropriated entitlement programs, are funded each year in appropriations acts.

Discretionary and Mandatory Spending

Gross budget authority, or the total funds available for spending by a federal agency, may be composed of discretionary and mandatory spending.

Discretionary spending is not mandated by existing law and is thus appropriated yearly by Congress through appropriations acts. The Budget Enforcement Act of 1990[29] defines discretionary appropriations as budget authority provided in annual appropriations acts and the outlays derived from that authority, but it excludes appropriations for entitlements. Mandatory spending, also known as direct spending, consists of budget authority and resulting outlays provided in laws other than appropriations acts and is typically not appropriated each year. Some mandatory entitlement programs, however, must be appropriated each year and are included in appropriations acts. Within DHS, Coast Guard retirement pay is an example of appropriated mandatory spending.

Offsetting Collections[30]

Offsetting funds are collected by the federal government, either from government accounts or the public, as part of a business-type transaction such as collection of a fee. These funds are not considered federal revenue. Instead, they are counted as negative outlays. DHS *net discretionary budget authority*, or the total funds that are appropriated by Congress each year, is composed of discretionary spending minus any fee or fund collections that offset discretionary spending.

Some collections offset a portion of an agency's discretionary budget authority. Other collections offset an agency's mandatory spending. These mandatory spending elements are typically entitlement programs under which individuals, businesses, or units of government that meet the requirements or qualifications established by law are entitled to receive certain payments if they establish eligibility. The DHS budget features two mandatory entitlement programs: the Secret Service and the Coast Guard retired pay accounts (pensions). Some entitlements are funded by permanent appropriations, and others are funded by annual appropriations. Secret Service retirement pay is a permanent appropriation and, as such, is not annually appropriated. In contrast, Coast Guard retirement pay is annually appropriated. In addition to these entitlements, the DHS budget contains offsetting Trust and Public Enterprise Funds. These funds are not appropriated by Congress. They are available for obligation and included in the President's budget to calculate the gross budget authority.

302(a) and 302(b) Allocations

In general practice, the maximum budget authority for annual appropriations (including DHS) is determined through a two-stage congressional budget process. In the first stage, Congress sets overall spending totals in the annual concurrent resolution on the budget. Subsequently, these totals are allocated among the appropriations committees, usually through the statement of managers for the conference report on the budget resolution. These amounts are known as the *302(a) allocations*. They include discretionary totals available to the House and Senate Committees on Appropriations for enactment in annual appropriations bills through the subcommittees responsible for the development of the bills.

In the second stage of the process, the appropriations committees allocate the 302(a) discretionary funds among their subcommittees for each of the appropriations bills. These amounts are known as the *302(b) allocations*. These allocations must add up to no more than the 302(a) discretionary allocation and form the basis for enforcing budget discipline, since any bill reported with a total above the ceiling is subject to a point of order. The 302(b) allocations may be adjusted during the year by the respective Appropriations Committee issuing a report delineating the revised suballocations as the various appropriations bills progress toward final enactment.

Table A-1 shows comparable figures for the 302(b) allocation for FY2015, based on P.L. 114-4, and the President's request for FY2016. House and Senate allocations for the Homeland Security appropriations bill will be added as they become available.

Table A-1. FY2015 and FY2016 302(b) Discretionary Allocations for DHS

FY2015	FY2016 Request	FY2016 House	FY2016 Senate	FY2016 Enacted
Comparable	Comparable	Allocation	Allocation	Comparable
39.670[a]	41,194b	39,330[b]	40,213	

Source: CRS analysis of the explanatory statement accompanying H.R. 240 as printed in the Congressional Record of January 13, 2015, pp. H275-H322, and the FY2015 DHS Budget-in-Brief.

[a] This authority does not include the $213 million for overseas contingency operations or the $6,438 million for disaster relief covered by adjustments to the discretionary spending caps set by the Budget Control Act.

[b] This authority does not include the $6,713 million requested for disaster relief covered by adjustments to the discretionary spending caps set by the Budget Control Act. This allocation was originally $39,230 million—it was adjusted upward by a committee amendment on July 8, 2015.

The Budget Control Act, Discretionary Spending Caps, and Adjustments

The FY2012 appropriations bills were the first appropriations bills governed by the Budget Control Act, which established discretionary security and nonsecurity spending caps for FY2012 and FY2013. The bill also established overall caps that govern the actions of appropriations committees in both chambers. Subsequent legislation, including the Bipartisan Budget Act of 2013,[31] amended those caps. For FY2015, the overall cap on discretionary spending is $1,014 billion. Separate limitations are made for defense and nondefense spending—roughly $521 billion and $492 billion, respectively. Most of the budget for DHS is considered nondefense spending.

In addition, the Budget Control Act allows for adjustments that would raise the statutory caps to cover funding for overseas contingency operations/Global War on Terror, emergency spending, and, to a limited extent, disaster relief and appropriations for continuing disability reviews and control of health care fraud and abuse.

Three of the four justifications outlined in the Budget Control Act for adjusting the caps on discretionary budget authority have played a role in DHS's appropriations process. Two of these—emergency spending and overseas contingency operations/Global War on Terror—are not limited.

The third justification—disaster relief—is limited. Under the Budget Control Act, the allowable adjustment for disaster relief is determined by the Office of Management and Budget (OMB), using the following formula:

> Limit on disaster relief cap adjustment for the fiscal year = Rolling average of the disaster relief spending over the last ten fiscal years (throwing out the high and low years) + the unused amount of the potential adjustment for disaster relief from the previous fiscal year.

For FY2014, OMB determined the allowable adjustment for disaster relief was $12,143 million,[32] of which only $5,717 million was exercised. In February 2015, OMB noted the FY2015 allowable adjustment for disaster assistance was $18,430 million: $11,913 million from the rolling average and $6,517 million in carryover from FY2014.[33] FY2015 was the first year in which more than $1 billion of allowable adjustment for disaster relief carried over from the previous fiscal year.

End Notes

[1] U.S. Government Accountability Office, A Glossary of Terms Used in the Federal Budget Process, GAO-05-734SP, September 1, 2005, http://www.gao.gov/products/GAO-05-734SP.

[2] On April 14, 2016, the Administration submitted technical amendments to its budget request, but it presented no adjustments to its totals for the department. Therefore, modifications to authorization for Customs and Border Protection to use certain fee revenues are not reflected in this report.

[3] Generally speaking, those provided through annual legislation. For more detail, see the Appendix.

[4] Although the House and Senate generally produce symmetrically structured bills, this is not always the case. Additional titles are sometimes added by one of the chambers to address special issues. For example, the FY2012 House full committee markup added a sixth title to carry a $1 billion emergency appropriation for the Disaster Relief Fund (DRF). The Senate version carried no additional titles beyond the five described above. For FY2016, the House- and Senate-reported versions of the DHS appropriations bill were generally symmetrical.

[5] In addition to the appropriations provided in Title I, under the request, the DHS Office of Inspector General (OIG) would receive $24 million in a transfer from the Disaster Relief Fund appropriation, and $43 million for financial systems modernization in general provisions. Funding for DHS headquarters consolidation is included in these totals, although funding is often provided in general provisions.

[6] In addition to the appropriations provided in Title II, under the request, U.S. Customs and Border Protection would receive $180 million in budget authority from a general provision that grants them the authority to expend fees raised under the Colombia Free Trade Act. Other resources that contribute to the budget for these components include mandatory spending, fee revenues, and trust funds.

[7] In addition to the appropriations provided in Title III, under the request, the Disaster Relief Fund would receive would receive $6,713 million in budget authority that is accounted for by an adjustment to the discretionary spending limits set by the Budget Control Act (P.L. 112-25). Another $1,443 million is provided through offsetting collections to the Federal Protective Service—neither of these are included in the net discretionary budget total. Other resources that contribute to the budget for these components include mandatory spending, fee revenues, and trust funds, including the National Flood Insurance Fund.

[8] Projections of the budget authority provided by these provisions may vary between the Office of Management and Budget and the Congressional Budget Office, but both include such appropriations in calculations of discretionary budget authority.

[9] These sections coauthored with Barbara L. Schwemle, Analyst in American National Government, Government and Finance Division.

[10] For more detail on the Budget Control Act and its implications on the appropriations process, see CRS Report R41965, The Budget Control Act of 2011, by Bill Heniff Jr., Elizabeth Rybicki, and Shannon M. Mahan.

[11] Rep. John Carter, opening statement for Budget Hearing—Department of Homeland Security, House Appropriations Committee Subcommittee on Homeland Security, March 26, 2015, at http://docs.house.gov/meetings/AP/AP15/20150326/103205/HHRG-114-AP15-20150326-SD001.pdf.

[12] S.Rept. 114-68, p. 21.

[13] H.Rept. 114-215, p. 3.

[14] H.Rept. 114-215, p. 57.

[15] Sec. 506 and Sec. 552, respectively.

[16] The Senate committee report noted particularly requests for border security and cybersecurity personnel. (S.Rept. 114-68, p. 19.)

[17] S.Rept. 114-68, p. 19.

[18] The Senate committee report noted that the Federal Emergency Management Agency already tracks the status of hiring actions. (S.Rept. 114-68, p. 20.)

[19] The report stated that the committee recommended the requested number of mission-critical positions in Customs and Border Protection and the U.S. Secret Service. (H.Rept. 114-215, p. 13 and p. 4.)

[20] The explanatory statement that accompanied P.L. 114-4 directed DHS to provide such a report. The committee received the report on June 22, 2015, but determined that it "failed to fully comply with the requirement" because of incomplete data on hiring times and a lack of information on metrics. (H.Rept. 114-215, p. 13.)

[21] With regard to hiring, the number of days associated with each step in the hiring process, including announcements in progress, announcements posted, interviews pending, offers pending, individuals selected, security approvals, and personnel entering on duty should be included.

[22] With regard to metrics, data on the number of days reduced by implementing an initiative, the numbers of onboard personnel at the beginning and end of the reporting period, and the number of separations for the reporting period should be included.

[23] S.Rept. 114-68, p. 5.

[24] H.Rept. 114-215, p. 13.

[25] S.Rept. 114-68, p. 9.

[26] H.Rept. 114-21527 31 U.S.C. §§1341, 1342, 1344, 1511-1517.

[27] 31 U.S.C. §§1341, 1342, 1344, 1511-1517.

[28] Appropriations, outlays, and account balances for various appropriations accounts can be viewed in the end-of-year reports published by the U.S. Treasury titled Combined Statement of Receipts, Outlays, and Balances of the United States Government. The DHS portion of the report can be accessed at http://fms.treas.gov/annualreport/cs2005/c18.pdf.

[29] P.L. 101-508, Title XIII.

[30] Prepared with assistance from Bill Heniff Jr., Analyst in American National Government.

[31] P.L. 113-67.

[32] Office of Management and Budget, OMB Sequestration Preview Report to the President and Congress for Fiscal Year 2015, Washington, DC, March 10, 2014, p. 9.

[33] Office of Management and Budget, OMB Sequestration Update Report to the President and Congress for Fiscal Year 2016, Washington, DC, February 2, 2015, p. 12.

In: Homeland Security
Editor: Malcolm Leonard Moreno

ISBN: 978-1-63484-754-4

Chapter 3

DHS APPROPRIATIONS FY2016: SECURITY, ENFORCEMENT AND INVESTIGATIONS*

William L. Painter, Lisa Seghetti, Alison Siskin, Bart Elias and John Frittelli

SUMMARY

This report is part of a suite of reports that discuss appropriations for the Department of Homeland Security (DHS) for FY2016. It specifically discusses appropriations for the components of DHS included in the second title of the homeland security appropriations bill— Customs and Border Protection (CBP), Immigration and Customs Enforcement (ICE), the Transportation Security Administration (TSA), U.S. Coast Guard (USCG), and the U.S. Secret Service (USSS). Collectively, Congress has labeled these components in recent years as "Security, Enforcement, and Investigations."

The report provides an overview of the Administration's FY2016 request for Security, Enforcement, and Investigations, and the appropriations proposed by the House and Senate appropriations committees thus far. Rather than limiting the scope of its review to the second title, the report includes information on provisions throughout the proposed bill and report that directly affect these functions.

---

* This is an edited, reformatted and augmented version of a Congressional Research Service publication, No. R44215, dated October 2, 2015.

> Security, Enforcement, and Investigations is the largest of the four titles that carry the bulk of the funding in the bill. The Administration requested $32,481 million for these components in FY2016, $807 million more than was provided for FY2015. Although 78.5% of the administration's $41.4 billion request for the department in net discretionary budget authority, the proposed additional funding is 46.7% of the total net increase requested. The largest budget increase proposed in the request for these five agencies was $806 million (7.4%) for CBP, while the largest budget decrease proposed was $227 million (2.8%) for the USCG..
>
> Senate-reported S. 1619 envisions the components included in this title receiving $32,484 million in net discretionary budget authority. This would be $3 million (0.01%) more than requested, and $810 million (2.6%) more than was provided in FY2015.
>
> House-reported H.R. 3128 envisions the components included in this title receiving $32,182 million in net discretionary budget authority. This would be $299 million (0.9%) less than requested, and $508 million (1.6%) more than was provided in FY2015.
>
> Additional information on the broader subject of FY2016 funding for the department can be found in CRS Report R44053, *Department of Homeland Security Appropriations: FY2016,* as well as links to analytical overviews and details regarding appropriations for other components.

This report is part of a suite of reports that discuss appropriations for the Department of Homeland Security (DHS) for FY2016. It specifically discusses appropriations for the components of DHS included in the second title of the homeland security appropriations bill—Customs and Border Protection (CBP), Immigration and Customs Enforcement (ICE), the Transportation Security Administration (TSA), U.S. Coast Guard (USCG), and the U.S. Secret Service (USSS). Collectively, Congress has labeled these components in recent years as "Security, Enforcement, and Investigations."

The report provides an overview of the Administration's FY2016 request for Security, Enforcement, and Investigations, and the appropriations proposed by Congress thus far. Rather than limiting the scope of its review to the second title, the report includes information on provisions throughout the proposed bill and report that directly affect these functions.

The suite of CRS reports on homeland security appropriations tracks legislative action and congressional issues related to DHS appropriations, with particular attention paid to discretionary funding amounts. The reports do not provide in-depth analysis of specific issues related to mandatory funding—such as retirement pay—nor do they systematically follow other legislation related to the authorization or amending of DHS programs, activities, or fee revenues.

Discussion of appropriations legislation involves a variety of specialized budgetary concepts. The Appendix to CRS Report R44053, Department of Homeland Security Appropriations: FY2016 explains several of these concepts, including budget authority, obligations, outlays, discretionary and mandatory spending, offsetting collections, allocations, and adjustments to the discretionary spending caps under the Budget Control Act (P.L. 112-25). A more complete discussion of those terms and the appropriations process in general can be found in CRS Report R42388, *The Congressional Appropriations Process: An Introduction*, by Jessica Tollestrup, and the Government Accountability Office's *A Glossary of Terms Used in the Federal Budget Process.*[1]

Note on Data and Citations

Except in summary discussions and when discussing total amounts for the bill as a whole, all amounts contained in the suite of CRS reports on homeland security appropriations represent budget authority and are rounded to the nearest million. However, for precision in percentages and totals, all calculations were performed using unrounded data.

Data used in this report for FY2015 amounts are derived from the Department of Homeland Security Appropriations Act, 2015 (P.L. 114-4) and the explanatory statement that accompanied H.R. 240 as printed in the Congressional Record of January 13, 2015, pp. H275-H322.

Contextual information on the FY2016 request is generally from the Budget of the United States Government, Fiscal Year 2016, the FY2016 DHS congressional budget justifications, and the FY2016 DHS Budget in Brief.[2] However, most data used in CRS analyses in reports on DHS appropriations is drawn from congressional documentation to ensure consistent scoring whenever possible. Information on the FY2016 budget request and Senate-reported recommended funding levels is from S. 1619 and S.Rept. 114-68. Information on the House-reported recommended funding levels is from H.R. 3128 and H.Rept. 114-215.

SUMMARY OF DHS APPROPRIATIONS

Generally, the homeland security appropriations bill includes all annual appropriations provided for DHS, allocating resources to every departmental component. Discretionary appropriations[3] provide roughly two-thirds to three-fourths of the annual funding for DHS operations, depending how one accounts for disaster relief spending and funding for overseas contingency operations. The remainder of the budget is a mix of fee revenues, trust funds, and mandatory spending.[4]

Appropriations measures for DHS typically have been organized into five titles.[5] The first four are thematic groupings of components: Departmental Management and Operations; Security, Enforcement, and Investigations; Protection, Preparedness, Response, and Recovery; and Research and Development, Training, and Services. A fifth title contains general provisions, the impact of which may reach across the entire department, impact multiple components, or focus on a single activity.

The following pie chart presents a visual comparison of the share of annual appropriations in each title, highlighting the components discussed in this report.

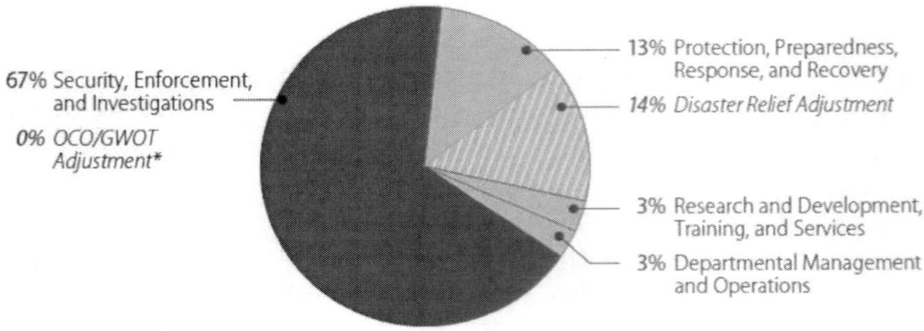

Source: CRS analysis of data from U.S. Department of Homeland Security, *FY2016 Budget in Brief.*

Notes: *—The Administration requested $160 million to be transferred to DHS under the Overseas Contingency Operations / Global War on Terror (OCO/GWOT) allowable adjustment under the Budget Control Act. This amount rounds to zero for this calculation, and thus does not appear in the chart. Titles in italics and patterned wedges represent funding covered under adjustments to discretionary spending limits under the Budget Control Act.

Figure 1. Proportion of Requested DHS Discretionary Budget Authority by Title; (funding in general provisions distributed to recipient components).

Security, Enforcement, and Investigations

As noted above, the Security, Enforcement, and Investigations title (Title II) of the DHS appropriations bill includes over three-quarters of the net discretionary budget authority provided in the legislation, and provides funding for many of DHS's largest operational components: CBP, ICE, TSA, USCG, and USSS. Some provisions in Title V, General Provisions, may affect the total funding provided for some of these components.

The Administration requested $32,481 million in FY2016 net discretionary budget authority for components included in this title, as part of a total budget for these components of $39,431 million for FY2016.[6] The appropriations request was $807 million (2.5%) more than was provided for FY2015.

Senate-reported S. 1619 envisions the components included in this title receiving $32,484 million in net discretionary budget authority. This would be $3 million (0.01%) more than requested, and $810 million (2.6%) more than was provided in FY2015.

Senate-reported S. 1619 also included $160 million in overseas contingency operations funding for the Coast Guard. This amount, originally requested by the administration through the Department of Defense, is covered by an adjustment under the Budget Control Act (BCA), and does not add to the total adjusted net discretionary budget authority in the bill.

House-reported H.R. 3128 envisions the components included in this title receiving $32,182 million in net discretionary budget authority. This would be $299 million (0.9%) less than requested, and $508 million (1.6%) more than was provided in FY2015.

House-reported H.R. 3128 does not include $160 million in overseas contingency funding for the Coast Guard. House-passed H.R. 2685, the Department of Defense Appropriations Act, 2016, already included that funding, as well as language to authorize transfer of that funding to the Coast Guard.

Not in the Bill, but Still on the Tab

Both CBP and the USCG receive a small fraction of their budget authority through a mechanism known as permanent indefinite discretionary spending, through which the components receive funding through permanent budget authority in other laws. However, this spending is considered discretionary rather than mandatory, and counts against any procedural and statutory limits on discretionary spending—including the 302(b) suballocation to the Homeland Security Subcommittee. Because of this budgetary treatment, this permanent indefinite discretionary spending is reflected in the Appropriations Committee reports and scored with the rest of the department's discretionary budget, even though it does not actually appear in the appropriations measures themselves. Most discussion in the public forum of the funding provided through annual DHS appropriations measures does not make a distinction between permanent indefinite discretionary spending and the spending that is actually included in the bill. For the sake of clarity of discussion in this report, all discretionary budget authority scored against the bill is considered as being included in the bill.

Table 1 lists the enacted funding level for the individual components funded under Security, Enforcement, and Investigations for FY2015, as well as the amounts requested for these accounts by the Administration and recommended by the Senate-reported bill for FY2016. The table includes information on funding under Title II as well as other provisions in the bill.

Table 1. Budgetary Resources for Security, Enforcement, and Investigations, FY2015 and FY2016 (budget authority in millions of dollars)

	FY2015	FY2016		
Component/Appropriation	Enacted	Request	Senate-reported S. 1619	House-reported H.R. 3128
Customs and Border Protection				
Salaries and Expenses	8,460	9,124	8,779	8,695
Small Airport User Fee[a]	9	9	9	9
Automation Modernization	808	867	854	846
Border Security Fencing, Infrastructure, and Technology	382	373	373	439
Air and Marine Operations	750	747	755	785
Facilities Management	289	342	314	341
COBRA FTA funding (Title V)[b]	[138]	[180]	[220]	[180]
Title II Appropriation	10,699	11,463	11,084	11,116

	FY2015	FY2016		
Component/Appropriation	Enacted	Request	Senate-reported S. 1619	House-reported H.R. 3128
Total Appropriation	10,837	11,643	11,304	11,296
Fees, Mandatory Spending, and Trust Funds	1,884	1,977	1,977	1,977
Total Budgetary Resources (including Title V)	12,721	13,620	13,281	13,273
Immigration and Customs Enforcement				
Salaries and Expenses	5,933	5,887	5,762	5,736
Automation and Infrastructure Modernization	26	74	53	74
Construction	0	5	0	5
Appropriation	5,959	5,965	5,815	5,815
Fees, Mandatory Spending, and Trust Funds	345	322	322	322
Total Budgetary Resources	6,304	6,287	6,137	6,137
Transportation Security Administration				
Aviation Security (net funding)	3,574	3,500	3,453	3,429
Surface Transportation Security	124	124	123	107
Intelligence and Vetting[c] (net funding)	219	228	225	216
Transportation Security Support	917	931	919	901
Appropriation	4,834	4,783	4,719	4,653
Fees, Mandatory Spending, and Trust Funds	2,395	2,564	2,579	2,579
Total Budgetary Resources	7,229	7,347	7,299	7,233
U.S. Coast Guard				
Operating Expenses[d]	7,043	6,823	6,996	6,899
Overseas Contingency Operations Adjustment (included in Operating Expenses)[d]	[213]	0	[160]	0

Table 1. (Continued)

	FY2015	FY2016		
Component/Appropriation	Enacted	Request	Senate-reported S. 1619	House-reported H.R. 3128
Environmental Compliance and Restoration	13	13	13	13
Reserve Training	115	111	111	111
Acquisition, Construction, and Improvements	1,225	1,017	1,573	1,301
Research, Development, Testing, and Evaluation	18	18	18	18
Health Care Fund Contribution[a]	177	169	169	169
Discretionary Appropriation	8,378	8,151	8,721	8,512
Fees, Mandatory Spending, and Trust Funds	1,664	1,822	1,822	1,822
Total Budgetary Resources	10,255	9,973	10,703	10,334
U.S. Secret Service				
Salaries and Expenses	1,616	1,867	1,837	1,833
Acquisition, Construction, and Improvements	50	72	87	73
Appropriation	1,666	1,939	1,924	1,906
Fees, Mandatory Spending, and Trust Funds	260	265	265	265
Total Budgetary Resources	1,926	2,204	2,189	2,171
Net Discretionary Budget Authority: Title II	31,536	32,301	32,264	32,002
Net Discretionary Budget Authority: Total for Security, Enforcement, and Investigations Components	31,674	32,481	32,484	32,182
Total Gross Budgetary Resources for Security, Enforcement, and Investigations Components	38,434	39,431	39,609	39,147

Source: CRS analysis of P.L. 114-4 and its explanatory statement as printed in the *Congressional Record* of January 13, 2015, pp. H275-H322, the FY2016 DHS *Budget-in-Brief,* S. 1619, S.Rept. 114-68, H.R. 3128, and H.Rept. 114-215.

Notes: Table displays rounded numbers, but all operations were performed with unrounded data. Amounts, therefore, may not sum to totals. Fee revenues included in the "Fees, Mandatory Spending, and Trust Funds" lines are projections, and do not include budget authority provided through general provisions. Bracketed amounts do not add to discretionary appropriations totals for Title II due to their location in the bill or their structure.

[a] This item is considered permanent indefinite discretionary spending and, therefore, scores as being in the bill, despite not being explicitly appropriated in the bills' legislative language.

[b] Sec. 556 of the Senate-reported bill and Sec. 551 of the House reported bill authorize CBP to expend certain fee revenues collected pursuant to the Colombia Free Trade Act. These provisions score as discretionary budget authority, and so are reflected separately from other fees.

[c] Formerly entitled "Transportation Threat Assessment and Credentialing."

[d] Overseas contingency operations funding is included in the Operating Expenses appropriation, but is not added to the appropriations total in accordance with the appropriations committees' practices for subtotaling this account. This funding is reflected in the total gross budgetary resources for the Coast Guard, not the total net discretionary budget authority.

CUSTOMS AND BORDER PROTECTION (CBP)[7]

CBP is responsible for security at and between ports of entry (POE) along the border, with a dual mission of preventing the entry of terrorists and instruments of terrorism, while also facilitating the flow of legitimate travel and trade into and out of the United States. CBP officers inspect people (immigration enforcement) and goods (customs enforcement) at POEs to determine if they are authorized to enter the United States. CBP officers and U.S. Border Patrol (USBP) agents enforce more than 400 laws and regulations at the border to prevent illegal entries.

CBP's major programs include Border Security Inspections and Trade Facilitation, which encompasses risk-based targeting and the inspection of travelers and goods at POEs; Border Security and Control between Ports of Entry, which includes the Border Patrol; Air and Marine Interdiction; Automation Modernization, which includes customs and immigration information technology systems; Border Security Fencing, Infrastructure, and Technology (BSFIT); Facilities Management; and a number of immigration and customs user Fee Accounts. See **Table 1** for account-level detail for all of the agencies in Title II, and **Table 2** for subaccount-level detail for CBP appropriations and funding for FY2015-FY2016.

FY2016 Request

For FY2016, the Administration requested an appropriation of $13,620 million in gross budget authority for CBP, including $11,643 million in net discretionary budget authority through appropriations legislation.[8]

The bullets below highlight select program changes from the FY2015 enacted level.

- An increase of $267 million for ports of entry (POE) operations.
- An increase of almost $15 million to fund training for new and incumbent CBP officers, Agriculture Specialists, Import Specialists, and Entry Specialists assigned to the ports of entry.
- An increase of more than $86 million to fund the refreshment and refurbishment of Non-Intrusive Inspection (NII) technology equipment.[9]
- An increase of more than $153 million for border security and control between ports of entry.
- A decrease of $9.0 million in infrastructure and technology along the borders. The decrease is in the Development and Deployment account, which funds activities associated with procuring new technology, among other things.
- An increase of almost $53 million for the construction and sustainment of CBP facilities. The increased funding was requested for a backlog of unmet maintenance and repair requirements of CBP facilities.
- A decrease of $3 million for Air and Marine Operations.

The Administration also requested additional appropriations for an unaccompanied alien children (UAC) Contingency Fund, to be provided in the event that the number of UAC crossing the border in FY2016 exceeds the number that crossed in FY2015 (See "Unaccompanied Alien Children" below for further discussion).

Senate-Reported S. 1619

The Senate Appropriations Committee recommended $13,281 million in gross budget authority for CBP, $339 million (2.5%) below the Administration's request and $560 million (4.4%) above the FY2015 enacted level. Senate-reported S. 1619 included $11,304 million in net discretionary budget authority for CBP.[10]

The Senate-reported bill recommended a decrease of $137 million (3.4%) below the Administration's request for POE operations (i.e., Inspections, Trade, and Travel Facilitation at Ports of Entry). The committee, however, did not recommend funding the Administration's request for additional CBP officers. The committee noted that the number of CBP officers is below the committee recommended funding level of 23,775 and is unlikely to reach such level until late FY2016.

The Senate-reported bill recommended funding to support 21,370 Border Patrol agents, which is the same number that was funded in the FY2015 bill. Like CBP officers, the committee noted that the number of Border Patrol agents is below the committee recommended funding level and is unlikely to reach such level until late FY2016. The committee noted the issues CBP has been having in hiring and retaining Border Patrol agents. The Senate report recommended increased funding for one of the issues the Administration cited for the delay in hiring new Border Patrol agents, a lack of polygraph examiners. Polygraph examiners are necessary to complete the background investigation of applicants. The committee recommended an increase of more than $1 million for additional examiners.[11]

House-Reported H.R. 3128

The House Appropriations Committee recommended $13,273 million in gross budget authority for CBP, $347 million (2.5%) below the Administration's request, $553 million (4.3%) over the FY2015 enacted level, and $8 million less than what the Senate Appropriations Committee approved. House-reported H.R. 3128 included $11,296 million in net discretionary budget authority for CBP.[12]

The House-reported bill included a 50% decrease below the Administration's request for the CBP Commissioner's office.[13] The committee noted that CBP failed to provide a timely response to requests for information about hiring, attrition, and funding for full time equivalent (FTE) positions.

For POE operations (i.e., Border Security Inspections and Trade Facilitation), the House-reported bill included a decrease of $183 million below the Administration's request, an increase of $191 million over the FY2015 enacted level, and $34 million below the recommended amount in the Senate-reported bill. The relatively lower amount recommended by the House committee includes a "projected underexecution of funds for personnel."[14]

For operations along the border (i.e., Border Security and Control Between Ports of Entry), the House-reported bill included a decrease of $199 million (4.9%) below the Administration's request, a decrease of $45 million (1.2%) below the FY2015 enacted level, and $61 million (1.2%) below the Senate Appropriations Committee proposal. The majority of the committee's recommended reduction from the Administration's request is due to the denial of the requested unaccompanied alien children (UAC) contingency fund (see "Unaccompanied Alien Children" below). Another portion of the reduction was due to the pay raise that was assumed in the President's budget.[15] The committee also recommended reducing the level of funding for the recommended 21,370 Border Patrol agents because, according to the committee, it is probable that CBP will not reach that number until the end of the fiscal year.[16]

The House-reported bill recommended $439 million for the Border Security Fencing, Infrastructure, and Technology account. This amount was an increase of $66 million (17.7%) more than the Administration's request, an increase of $57 million (14.9%) over the FY2015 enacted level, and an increase of $66 million (15.3%) over the Senate-reported bill. The committee noted the Administration's practice of carrying over unobligated amounts from prior years while requesting "significant amounts of new funding." Thus, the committee's recommendation included a decrease of the amount that was carried over in the Administration's request for FY2016 but recommended a portion of the committee's amount be carried over into FY2017 and FY2018.[17]

While the total appropriation included for BSFIT was higher than requested, the House-reported bill reduced the amount of multi-year funding provided for BSFIT by $150 million from the budget request. In a change from FY2015, the House Appropriations Committee provided only a portion of the BSFIT appropriation as three-year funding, thus reducing the amount that could be carried over into future fiscal years. In prior years, the entire BSFIT appropriation was provided as a three-year appropriation. Title V of the bill also included rescissions totaling almost $99 million from appropriations provided in prior years for BSFIT, which would reduce the existing level of carryover.

The House-reported bill included $785 million for CBP's Office of Air and Marine operations (OAM), an increase of $38 million (5%) over the Administration's request, an increase of $34 million (4.6%) over the FY2015 enacted level, and $30 million (4.6%) more than what was recommended by the Senate Appropriations Committee.

Table 2. U.S. Customs and Border Protection Account Detail, FY2015-FY2016 (budget authority in rounded millions of dollars)

	FY2015	FY2016		
Appropriation / Sub-Appropriation	**Enacted**	**Request**	**Senate-Reported S. 1619**	**House-Reported H.R. 3128**
Salaries and Expenses	8,460	9,124	8,779	8,695
Headquarters Management and Administration	*1,368*	*1,506*	*1,447*	*1,458*
Border Security Inspections and Trade Facilitation	*3,187*	*3,560*	*3,412*	*3,378*
Border Security and Control Between POE	*3,904*	*4,058*	*3,921*	*3,859*
Small Airport User Fee[a]	9	9	9	9
Automation Modernization	808	867	854	846
Border Security Fencing, Infrastructure, and Technology	382	373	373	439
Air and Marine Operations	750	747	755	785
Facilities Management	289	342	314	341
Total Net Appropriation, CBP, Title II	**10,699**	**11,463**	**11,084**	**11,116**
Estimated Fees, Mandatory Spending and Trust Funds (including CFTA collections)	2,022	2,157	2,197	2,157
Total CBP Budget Authority	**12,721**	**13,620**	**13,281**	**13,273**

Source: CRS analysis of P.L. 114-4 and its explanatory statement as printed in the *Congressional Record* of January 13, 2015, pp. H275-H322, the FY2016 DHS *Budget-in-Brief,* S. 1619, S.Rept. 114-68, H.R. 3128, and H.Rept. 114-215.

Notes: Table displays rounded numbers, but all operations were performed with unrounded data: therefore, amounts may not sum to totals.

[a] This is permanent indefinite discretionary spending, and therefore scores as being in the bill, despite not being explicitly appropriated in the bills' legislative language.

Issues for Congress

This section does not discuss policy-related issues; rather it focuses on issues that potentially may impact CBP's appropriations.

Unaccompanied Alien Children

Over the past several years, the number of unaccompanied alien children (UAC, unaccompanied minors) that were apprehended by the Border Patrol for illegally crossing the Southwest border substantially increased. In FY2014, that number reached a peak, with the Border Patrol apprehending over 68,000 unaccompanied minors along the Southwest border. In the FY2015 budget cycle, appropriators grappled with the increased number of unaccompanied children who came across the border illegally and its impact on CBP's operations and resources. While the current number of unaccompanied children coming across the border has dropped compared to this time last year, the Administration also requested contingent appropriations in the event the number rose unexpectedly in FY2016. The amount provided would ultimately depend on the number of apprehended UAC transferred to the Department of Health and Human Services, ranging from no additional funding for CBP if the number of UAC transferred did not exceed the number transferred in FY2015, to $117 million if it did, to $134 million if the number of UAC transferred exceeds 160% of FY2015's total.[18]

While the budget appendix indicates the trigger for the contingent appropriation is a determination that the number of UAC transferred to HHS is higher than the previous fiscal year, not all UACs detained and cared for by DHS are transferred to HHS. For example, of the 15,600 UACs from Mexico that were apprehended in FY2014, only 1,150 were transferred to HHS.

Neither the Senate-reported nor the House-reported bill recommends funding the UAC Contingency Fund.

Border Enforcement Personnel

CBP's front-line enforcement personnel include CBP officers at ports of entry, agriculture specialists, U.S. Border Patrol agents, air interdiction agents, and marine interdiction agents. Taken together, these personnel numbers grew from 31,695 in FY2005 to 46,666 in FY2013, an increase of 14,971 (47%). Border Patrol agents accounted for the greatest share of this growth, with an increase of 10,106 agents during this period.[19]

Proportionally among all CBP personnel, the number of CBP officers grew the least during this period, increasing from 17,881 in FY2005 to 21,775 in FY2013, a 22% increase. However, in the Homeland Security Appropriations Act, 2014 (P.L. 113-76), Congress appropriated $256 million to increase CBP officers at ports of entry by no fewer than 2,000 by the end of FY2015.

For FY2016, the Administration proposed, through legislation,[20] to hire 2,700 additional CBP officers, including 1,400 officers through revenues generated by user fee increases. The user fee increases proposed by the Administration include a $2.00 increase in the Immigration User Fees (IUF).[21] Additionally, the Administration proposed to begin charging the IUF fee to every sea passenger, including individuals whose trip originated from an exempt region.[22]

With respect to commercial traffic, the Administration, through legislation,[23] has proposed increasing the fees associated with the Consolidated Omnibus Budget Reconciliation Act of 1985 (COBRA fees)[24] and the Express Consignment Clearance Facility (ECCF) fees.[25]

As previously mentioned, Senate-reported S. 1619 and House-reported H.R. 3128 did not recommend funding to support the Administration's request for additional CBP officers.

Public-Private Partnerships at POEs

The FY2013 DHS appropriations act (Division D of P.L. 113-6) established a pilot program to permit CBP to enter into up to five public-private partnerships (PPPs) to support customs and immigration services at certain ports of entry (e.g., air ports of entry). In general, PPPs may provide low-cost alternatives to increase POE personnel and/or to add or improve port of entry infrastructure. The provision authorizing CBP to enter into these PPPs was extended in FY2014 and FY2015, although modified to permit CBP to accept donations of real and personal property (including monetary donations) from private parties and state and local government entities for the purpose of constructing or expanding POE facilities.

Both Senate-reported S. 1619 and House-reported H.R. 3128 recommended increasing the number of air ports of entry pilots from five to ten.[26]

Preclearance Facilities

In April 2013, DHS reached an agreement with the government of the United Arab Emirates (UAE) to set up a preclearance facility in the Abu Dhabi International Airport. Some Members of Congress raised objections to the proposed Abu Dhabi program because no U.S. air carriers fly directly from

Abu Dhabi to the United States, arguably giving the UAE-owned Etihad Airlines a competitive advantage over U.S.-owned carriers, and because UAE is not a signatory to the United Nations Refugee Convention.[27] Since FY2014, appropriators have prohibited funding for preclearance operations in new locations unless an economic impact analysis of the new location on U.S. air carriers has been conducted and provided to the committee, among other conditions.[28] Both the Senate- and House-reported bills for the FY2016 DHS appropriations recommended a similar prohibition.[29]

Immigration and Customs Enforcement (ICE)[30]

ICE focuses on enforcement of immigration and customs laws within the United States. ICE has two main components: Homeland Security Investigations (HSI) and Enforcement and Removal Operations (ERO). HSI is responsible for disrupting and dismantling criminal organizations (many of which are transnational) engaged in activities including terrorist financing and money laundering, intellectual property theft, human trafficking, cybercrime, child exploitation, and drug trafficking. HSI enforces export laws and enforces trade agreement noncompliance, and is responsible for investigating and enforcing violations of the immigration laws (e.g., alien smuggling, hiring unauthorized alien workers). ERO is the government agency responsible for locating, detaining if appropriate, and removing foreign nationals who have overstayed their visas, entered illegally, or have become deportable.

FY2016 Request

For FY2016, the Administration requested $5,965 million in net budget authority, a 0.1% increase from the FY2015 enacted amount. The Administration requested $6,287 million in gross budget authority for ICE which represented a decrease of 0.3% from the FY2015 enacted amount.

Senate-Reported S. 1619

For FY2016, Senate-reported S. 1619 provided $5,815 million in net budget authority for ICE, which would have resulted in $6,137 million in gross budget authority for the component. The Senate-reported bill included 2.5%

less than the President's request in net budget authority, which would have resulted in the component receiving 2.4% less in gross budget authority.

House-Reported H.R. 3128

House-reported H.R. 3128 also included $5,815 million in net budget authority, which likewise would have resulted in $6,137 million in gross budget authority for the component—although the House appropriations committee did recommend a different distribution of resources.

Table 3. Immigration and Customs Enforcement (ICE) Sub-Account Detail, FY2015-FY2016 (budget authority in rounded millions of dollars)

	FY2015	FY2016		
Appropriation / Sub-Appropriation	**Enacted**	**Request**	**Senate-reported S. 1619**	**House-reported H.R. 3128**
Salariesand Expenses	**5,933**	**5,887**	**5,762**	**5,736**
HQ Management andAdministration	347	342	340	295
Office of Principal Legal Advisor	217	248	243	231
Investigations	1,860	1,905	1,898	1,864
Investigations—Domestic	*1,700*	*1,767*	*1,760*	*1,728*
Investigations—International	*160*	*139*	*138*	*136*
International Operations	*111*	*108*	*107*	*104*
Visa Security Program	*50*	*31*	*31*	*33*
Intelligence	76	80	79	80
Enforcement and Removal Operations	3,431	3,311	3,202	3,267
Custody Operations	*2,533*	*2,407*	*2,296*	*2,389*
Fugitive Operations	*143*	*129*	*143*	*128*
Criminal Alien Program	*327*	*320*	*317*	*317*
Alternatives to Detention	*110*	*122*	*122*	*110*
Transportation and Removal Program	*319*	*324*	*324*	*323*

Table 3. (Continued)

	FY2015	FY2016		
Appropriation / Sub-Appropriation	**Enacted**	**Request**	**Senate-reported S. 1619**	**House-reported H.R. 3128**
Unaccompanied Alien Children Contingency Funding	—	*8*[a]	—	—
Automation and Infrastructure Modernization	**26**	**74**	**53**	**74**
Construction	**0**	**5**	**0**	**5**
ICE Appropriations	**5,959**	**5,965**	**5,815**	**5,815**
Fee Accounts	345	322	322	322
ICE Gross Budget Authority	6,304	6,287	6,137	6,137

Source: CRS analysis of P.L. 114-4 and its explanatory statement as printed in the *Congressional Record* of January 13, 2015, pp. H275-H322, the FY2016 DHS *Budget-in-Brief,* S. 1619, S.Rept. 114-68, H.R. 3128, and H.Rept. 114-215.

Notes: Table displays rounded numbers, but all operations were performed with unrounded data: therefore, amounts may not sum to totals.

[a] This is the CBO score of a requested appropriation, the final value of which is contingent on factors beyond the control of Congress. See "Unaccompanied Alien Children (UAC)" below for more details.

Issues for Congress

ICE is responsible for many different activities due to the breadth of the civil and criminal violations of law that fall under its jurisdiction. As a result, how ICE resources can be allocated so as best to achieve its mission is continuously debated. Nonetheless, most of the discussion regarding ICE appropriations focuses on Enforcement and Removal Operations (ERO) and issues regarding identifying and removing foreign nationals who have violated U.S. immigration law rather than on HSI and its activities.

Custody Management

ICE's Office of Enforcement and Removal Operations provides custody management of the aliens who are in removal proceedings or who have been ordered removed from the United States. ERO also is responsible for ensuring that aliens ordered removed actually depart from the United States.

The number of foreign nationals detained by ICE has been an area of Congressional attention. Since FY2007, the appropriations committees have included direction either in report language or legislative language describing or directing the average number of detention beds to be maintained by ICE in a given fiscal year. The amount of detention beds set by Congress is seen by some as a "detention mandate," i.e., that ICE must, on average, detain daily the same number of aliens as the bed space specified by Congress.

The Administration requested funding for 34,040 beds, 31,280 adult beds and 2,760 family beds.[31] Both S. 1619 and H.R. 3128 provided funding to maintain 34,000 beds.

Due to the cost of detaining aliens, and the fact that many non-detained aliens with final orders of removal do not leave the country, there has been interest in developing alternatives to detention for certain types of aliens who do not require a secure detention setting. ICE's Alternatives to Detention (ATD) program provides less restrictive alternatives to detention, using such tools as electronic monitoring devices (e.g., ankle bracelets), home visits, work visits, and reporting by telephone, to monitor aliens who are out on bond while awaiting hearings during removal proceedings or the appeals process. The Administration requested $122 million for the ATD program, an increase of $12 million from the FY2015 enacted amount. While the House-reported bill funded the ATD program at the FY2015 level, the Senate-reported bill fully funded the President's request.

Office of the Principal Legal Advisor (OPLA)

Among other duties, lawyers in ICE's Office of the Principal Legal Advisor (OPLA) represent the government's position in removal proceedings before the Department of Justice, Executive Office for Immigration Review (EOIR). In FY2015, Congress appropriated additional funds to EOIR to hire 35 immigration judges and support staff to reduce the backlog of pending removal cases.[32] The President's budget requested $248 million for OPLA, an increase of $31 million over the FY2015 appropriated amount to increase the number of attorneys. Both the House and Senate bills increased funding for OPLA over the FY2015 appropriated amount; the Senate Appropriations Committee recommended $243 million for OPLA while the House Appropriations Committee recommended $231 million.[33]

Unaccompanied Alien Children (UAC)

ICE is responsible for the transportation of undocumented and unaccompanied alien children (UAC) arriving in the United States and representing the government's position in removal proceedings before the Department of Justice, Executive Office for Immigration Review (EOIR). ICE is also responsible for the physical removal of all foreign nationals, including UAC, who have final orders of removal or who have elected voluntary departure while in removal proceedings. In FY2014, there was a large increase in the number of UAC apprehensions, which caused a strain on agency resources. However, UAC apprehensions have decreased significantly in FY2015.[34]

While the current number of unaccompanied children coming across the border has dropped compared to this time last year, the Administration also requested contingent appropriations for costs associated with transporting UAC in the event the number rose unexpectedly in FY2016. The amount provided would ultimately depend on the number of apprehended UAC transferred to the Department of Health and Human Services, ranging from no additional funding for ICE if the number of UAC transferred did not exceed the number transferred in FY2015, to almost $7 million if it did, to over $27 million if the number of UAC transferred exceeds 160% of FY2015's total.[35]

Neither the House-reported nor Senate-reported bill contained contingency funding for this purpose.

ICE Public Advocate

In 2012, ICE created the Public Advocate Office "to assist individuals and representatives who have concerns about ICE operations and policies in the field."[36] The office was created in response to critiques that the agency was unresponsive to the complaints of those who were detained or investigated. However, some contend that the program is not productive and is not a proper use of ICE resources.[37] The FY2015 DHS Appropriations Act (P.L. 114-4) specified that no funds under the act could be used to fund the position of Public Advocate within ICE. Both H.R. 3128 and S. 1619 contained the same limitation. Nonetheless, some argue that the position of Public Advocate was simply renamed Deputy Assistant Director of Custody Programs and Community Outreach, and that the functions of the disbanded Public Advocate Office are currently being performed under the umbrella of "community outreach."[38]

TRANSPORTATION SECURITY ADMINISTRATION[39]

TSA, created in 2001 by the Aviation and Transportation Security Act (ATSA, P.L. 107-71), is charged with protecting air, land, marine, and rail transportation systems within the United States to ensure the freedom of movement for people and goods. In 2002, TSA was transferred from the Department of Transportation to DHS with the passage of the Homeland Security Act (P.L. 107 296). TSA's responsibilities include protecting the aviation system against terrorist threats, sabotage, and certain other criminal acts through the deployment of passenger and baggage screeners; detection systems for explosives, weapons, and other threats; and other security technologies. TSA also has certain responsibilities for marine and land modes of transportation including assessing the risk of terrorist attacks to all non-aviation transportation assets, including seaports; issuing regulations to improve security; and enforcing these regulations to ensure the protection of these transportation systems. TSA is further charged with serving as the primary liaison for transportation security to the law enforcement and intelligence communities.

Table 4. TSA Requested Budgetary Resources, FY2016 (budget authority in millions of dollars)

Funding Source	FY2016 Request
Total Offsetting Fees	2,581
Aviation Passenger Security Fee	*2,132*
Aviation Security Capital Fund (Mandatory)	*250*
Credentialing Fees (including Mandatory Alien Flight Student Program)	*199*
Discretionary appropriations	4,766
Total Budgetary Resources	7,347

Sources: CRS analysis of the FY2016 DHS congressional justifications.

Note: These are OMB-developed numbers; due to differences between OMB and CBO methodologies and issues related to authorization of fee increases, these numbers are not congruent with other CBO-based numbers presented in this report.

The TSA budget is one of the most complex components of the DHS Appropriations bill. Net direct discretionary appropriations represent only a portion of the budgetary resources it has available. An airline security fee collection offsets a portion of aviation security costs, including $250 million dedicated to capital investments in screening technology. Other fees offset the costs of transportation threat assessment and credentialing. Table 4 presents a breakdown of TSA's total additional budgetary resources requested from all non-appropriated sources and those provided through direct appropriations, as accounted for in the DHS budget justifications. Due to differences between OMB and CBO methodologies and issues related to authorization of fee increases, these amounts are not completely congruent with other amounts presented in committee documents or this report.

FY2016 Request

The FY2016 President's request specified a gross total of $7,347 million for TSA, $118 million above the FY2015 enacted amount (see Table 5). The administration anticipates that roughly $2,581 million will be offset through fee collections, including the aviation passenger security fee charged on airline ticket purchases and various credentialing fees. The aviation passenger security fee is set at $5.60 per one way trip. TSA anticipates total aviation passenger security fee collections of $3,382 million in FY2016, but language in the Bipartisan Budget Act of 2013 (P.L. 113-67) requires that $1,250 million of that be deposited in the Treasury general fund for deficit reduction, while additional amounts are to be treated as offsetting collections for TSA expenditures.

The request included $5,615 million for Aviation Security, including the Federal Air Marshals Service, $24 million less than the FY2015 enacted amount. The request identified more than $110 million in savings, and a decrease of 1,666 screener positions as a result of efficiencies from risk-based screening practices, as well as a decrease of $14 million for equipment maintenance savings. These savings more than offset pay inflation and increases to retirement contribution costs for TSA screeners and air marshals as well as increases in funding for checkpoint technologies and for airport management, information technology, and support activities. TSA indicated that a focus of FY2016 activities will be on extending the life of existing screening technologies through various software patches and upgrades.

The request for Intelligence and Vetting activities ($427 million) includes an increase of $128 million reflecting anticipated increases in the utilization of credentialing programs including the Transportation Worker Identification Credential (TWIC), the Hazardous Materials (HAZMAT) driver threat assessment program, and the TSA Pre-Check program. These costs are recovered through fees set to recoup the cost of administering background checks, conducting threat assessments, and issuing appropriate credentials. In the case of the TWIC and HAZMAT threat assessments, the anticipated revenue increases reflect projected increases in enrollment numbers as well as the additional recovery of fees previously retained by vendors. For Pre-Check, TSA anticipates more than 900,000 applications in FY2016 resulting in fee collections of $80 million.

The amount requested for Surface Transportation Security activities ($124 million) is in line with the FY2015 enacted amount, while the request for Transportation Security Support ($931 million) included a $14 million increase, including $3 million for internal cybersecurity remediation.

Senate-Reported S. 1619

The Senate-reported bill specified a gross total of $7,299 million for TSA, $70 million more than the FY2015 enacted level but $48 million less than requested. The Senate Appropriations Committee recommended $5,583 million for aviation security, $32 million less than requested. The committee report specified $2,843 million for screener compensation and benefits, $29 million less than requested, and $593 million for airport management, information technology, and support, $3 million less than requested. The report also specified $112 million for checkpoint support, $15 million more than requested, to provide for procurement and field testing of carry-on screening technologies, checkpoint reconfiguration, and checkpoint surveillance technologies. The bill included a cap of 43,000 full-time equivalent screeners.

The committee report specified $23 million for the Federal Flight Deck Officer (FFDO) program and crew training, $3 million more than requested. However, it included $790 million for the Federal Air Marshals Service (FAMS), $27 million less than requested.

The Senate-reported bill specified $123 million for surface transportation security, $1 million less than requested, and $225 million for intelligence and vetting, $2 million less than requested. The bill included $919 million for transportation security support, $12 million less than requested.

House-Reported H.R. 3128

The House-reported bill specified a gross total of $7,232 million for TSA, $115 million less than requested. In addition to targeted reductions from the requested amount, the House bill reduced personnel compensation amounts TSA-wide undoing the pay raise adjustment assumed in the request. The House-reported bill retains the existing cap of 45,000 full-time equivalent screeners.

The House-reported bill recommended $5,559 million for aviation security, $55 million less than requested. The House Appropriations Committee report specified $29 million less than requested for screening personnel, $7 million less than requested for airport management and support, and $12 million less than requested for FAMS. It also recommended $21 million for the FFDO program and crew training, $1 million more than requested.

The bill specified $107 million for surface transportation security, $17 million less than requested, based on projected under-execution of funds for surface inspectors and visible intermodal prevention and response (VIPR) teams, despite a paring down of the VIPR program in FY2015. Additionally, the bill recommended $415 million for intelligence and vetting, $11 million less than requested, and $901 million for transportation security support, $30 million less than requested.

Table 5. TSA Gross Budget Authority by Budget Activity, FY2015-FY2016
(gross budget authority in rounded millions of dollars)

	FY2015	FY2016		
Appropriation / Sub-Appropriation	**Enacted**	**Request**	**Senate-reported S. 1619**	**House-reported H.R. 3128**
Aviation Security	5,639	5,615	5,583	5,559
Screening Partnership Program (SPP)	*167*	*167*	*167*	*167*
Screener Personnel Compensation andBenefits	*2,924*	*2,872*	*2,843*	*2,843*
Screener Training andOther	*225*	*227*	*239*	*223*
Checkpoint Support	*88*	*97*	*112*	*96*
EDS/ETD Purchase/Installation	*84*	*83*	*83*	*83*

	FY2015	FY2016		
Appropriation / Sub-Appropriation	**Enacted**	**Request**	**Senate-reported S. 1619**	**House-reported H.R. 3128**
Screening Technology Maintenance andUtilities	*295*	*281*	*281*	*281*
Aviation Regulation and Other Enforcement	*350*	*349*	*347*	*345*
Airport Management, IT, and Support	*588*	*596*	*593*	*589*
FFDO and Flight Crew Training	*22*	*20*	*23*	*21*
Air Cargo	*106*	*106*	*105*	*105*
Federal Air Marshals	*790*	*817*	*790*	*805*
Intelligence and Vetting (formerly Threat Assessment and Credentialing (TTAC))	299	427	424	415
Intelligence	*52*	*52*	*52*	*48*
Secure Flight	*100*	*106*	*105*	*101*
Other Vetting / Screening Administration and Operations	*68*	*70*	*68*	*67*
Credentialing Fees	*80*	*199*	*199*	*199*
Surface Transportation Security	124	124	123	107
Operations and Staffing	*29*	*29*	*28*	*27*
Security Inspectors	*95*	*95*	*94*	*79*
Transportation Security Support	917	931	919	901
HQ Administration	*269*	*277*	*273*	*257*
Information Technology	*449*	*452*	*447*	*447*
Human Capital Services	*199*	*202*	*199*	*198*
Aviation Security Capital Fund (ASCF) (mandatory)	250	250	250	250
TSA Gross Total	**7,229**	**7,347**	**7,299**	**7,232**

Sources: CRS analysis of P.L. 114-4 and its explanatory statement as printed in the *Congressional Record* of January 13, 2015, pp. H275-H322, the FY2016 DHS *Budget-in-Brief,* S. 1619 and S.Rept. 114-68, and H.R. 3128 and H.Rept. 114-215.

Notes: Table displays rounded numbers, but all operations were performed with unrounded data: therefore, amounts may not sum to totals.

Issues for Congress

Balancing Risk-Based Screening Efficiencies with Screening Effectiveness

TSA had previously been directed by Congress to develop a strategy to increase the number of airline passengers eligible for expedited screening to 50% by the end of CY2014.[40] As noted above, these risk-based initiatives to expand expedited screening have resulted in annual savings of more than $110 million largely from the reduced labor costs of conducting expedited screening as opposed to standard screening.

However, various reports have raised concerns whether this push for increased efficiency at airport passenger checkpoints has impacted screening effectiveness. Although the primary means for being granted expedited screening is by voluntarily submitting detailed biographical information to TSA to be vetted for acceptance into its Pre-Check program, other passengers may receive expedited screening based on threat assessments performed by the Secure Flight system, or based on an initiative known as managed inclusion, which integrates random selection with behavioral observation and sometimes the use of explosives detection canine teams. Potential vulnerabilities have been identified in each of these approaches, although generally, policymakers have pushed for restricting expedited screening to only those passengers vetted under the voluntary Pre-Check program and refining that program as needed.

A January 2015 DHS Office of the Inspector General (OIG) report had recommended various undisclosed steps for TSA to improve its process for vetting TSA Pre-Check program applicants and members, as well as program effectiveness, communications, and coordination.[41] Additionally, a March 2015 DHS OIG report[42] identified potential vulnerabilities in Secure Flight vetting used as the basis for granting passengers access to Pre-Check expedited screening lanes and concluded that Secure Flight vetting should not be used as a basis for expedited screening. The report detailed a case in which a convicted felon linked to a domestic terrorist group was granted expedited screening, even though a TSA document checker recognized the notorious individual from media coverage and notified a supervisor that the traveler's past crimes were disqualifying for Pre-Check expedited screening.

As a result of its investigation, the DHS OIG recommended TSA limit expedited screening to passengers that it determines are members of trusted populations. TSA did not concur, and continues to use Secure Flight risk assessments to select passengers. In addition TSA continues to use managed inclusion, in which passengers without a Pre-Check indicator on their boarding pass may be randomly selected for expedited screening if assessed to be low risk by a behavior detection officer, and/or an explosives detection canine team.

While TSA continues to use these alternative techniques to increase the proportion of passengers processed through expedited screening, the Senate Appropriations Committee report cautioned that "[a]s the process expands and TSA seeks to cast a wider net, it's not clear that additional populations granted expedited screening meet comparable levels of security."[43] Similarly the House Appropriations Committee report noted that "TSA's reliance on Managed Inclusion and other methods to attain its expedited screening goals introduces a partially-vetted population into a process intended for travelers who have voluntarily submitted to prior in-depth vetting."[44] It, however, remained supportive of the Pre-Check program, and urged TSA to seek out partnerships with airports and private entities to expand Pre-Check enrollment, evaluate the impact of membership costs on enrollments, and examine other opportunities to strengthen and expand Pre-Check. Similarly, the Senate committee expressed its support of TSA efforts to partner with third party providers to draw upon private industry expertise to increase program awareness and ease of enrollment.

Appropriations committees have also expressed concern about the effectiveness of TSA's behavioral detection techniques. The House committee noted that it remained skeptical of their value, indicating that $25 million in FY2015 appropriations has been withheld until TSA completes and reports on ongoing operational tests to provide evidence that behavioral indicators can be successful utilized in operational settings to identify passengers that may pose a threat to aviation security.

Moreover, the House committee asserted that recently leaked results of covert testing of screening effectiveness have renewed serious concerns regarding screening technologies and techniques, noting that these results raise fundamental questions about TSA's overall risk mitigation strategy and layered approach to security. House report language directed TSA to brief the committee on its aviation security risk mitigation strategy and provide semiannual updates on covert testing activities, results, and corrective actions to address identified deficiencies. Similarly, the Senate committee requested quarterly briefings on covert testing activities, detailing metrics and mitigation actions taken in response.

In addition, H.Rept. 114-215 highlighted TSA's ongoing difficulties in acquiring and deploying checkpoint screening technologies. It noted that, in

FY2015, Congress withheld $25 million in response to GAO findings regarding TSA's acquisition and deployment of advanced imaging technology (AIT) whole-body scanners. The committee reported that it continues to await a statutorily mandated report from TSA addressing GAO's findings.

Airport Worker Vetting and Screening

In addition to concerns over the effectiveness of passenger screening, oversight bodies have focused some attention on lapses in airport worker vetting and screening. In June 2015, DHS OIG reported that, while TSA vetting processes were generally effective, TSA records for vetting airport workers with unescorted access to secured areas of airports and aircraft were often inaccurate or incomplete, and TSA lacked assurance that all credentialed airport workers had been properly vetted.[45] The report noted that TSA failed to identify 73 airport workers with links to terrorism because policies restricted TSA access to certain categories of watchlist data. It also concluded that TSA relies on airports to perform criminal history and work authorization checks. The report noted that TSA has limited oversight of airports and thus lacks the ability to assure that submitted data is complete and accurate and that all credentialed workers are properly vetted. It recommended that TSA take corrective actions and work with other federal agencies and airports to improve initial and recurrent vetting of airport workers.

Additionally, the Aviation Security Advisory Committee (ASAC), an industry body that advises TSA on policies and regulatory matters, recommended that TSA and airports improve security audits and internal controls regarding airport-issued identification; consider biometric standards for identification; expand the use of closed circuit television and other surveillance technologies; and tighten access controls and reduce access points at airports.[46] The group also recommended that TSA and airports do more to promote employee engagement in security, report concerns through anonymous tip lines, and adopt other airport security best practices. The group recommended examination of risk-based screening techniques for certain employee groups serve as a means to enhance security along with other risk-based measures. The Senate Appropriations Committee report included language directing TSA to brief the committee on its progress in implementing these recommendations.

Deployment and Installation of Checked Baggage Explosives Detection Systems

The Aviation and Transportation Security Act (ATSA, P.L. 107-71) mandated 100% screening of checked baggage. To meet this mandate, TSA has deployed about 1,800 explosives detection systems and 2,600 explosives trace detections units to about 450 commercial passenger airports. Most airports are now equipped and designed to utilize the most efficient technologies and resources to screen baggage. However, as many of the units deployed to meet the 100% screening mandate are reaching the end of their useful service life, TSA has shifted its priorities to replacing aging equipment with new, more capable next generation units and has requested additional flexibility in appropriations language allowing it to use Aviation Security Capital Fund (ASCF) monies for this purpose. Prior to FY2012, the ASCF was restricted to funding airport security improvement projects such as modifications to accommodate screening equipment installations. The Senate- and House-reported bills both included language that would permit TSA to use ASCF funds to procure and install explosives detection screening equipment as well. The Senate-reported bill also included language requiring TSA to include anticipated labor savings from deploying next generation high speed explosives detection systems in its report on savings from various efficiencies. The House committee report encouraged TSA to expeditiously pursue the development, testing, and deployment of more effective and efficient baggage screening systems.

With regard to ASCF funds, the Senate committee report noted that TSA has not established a process or program to reimburse certain airports that incurred eligible costs for modifying baggage handling systems to accommodate in-line baggage screening without having entered into formal reimbursable agreements with TSA. Senate report language directs TSA to develop a process to validate the eligibility of submitted claims and establish a plan for reimbursing valid claims. [47] Similarly, the House committee report noted that at least 16 reimbursement claims from airports for systems installed prior to 2008 are currently unresolved and directed TSA to develop a plan to resolve these claims and provide Congress with a reimbursement plan within 60 days of enactment. The House committee report also noted that several growing airports have requested ASCF funding for new in-line baggage screening projects and instructed TSA to find an appropriate funding balance for these new projects and for replacement in-line projects at established airports in a manner that will not deter airport growth.[48]

Budgetary Diversions and Oversight

The House committee expressed concern over what it described as historic under-execution of funds appropriated for staffing across the agency. It noted that TSA's past inability to maintain staffing at appropriated levels has resulted in diverting these funds for other purposes, including unplanned and unbudgeted activities, without congressional oversight. For this reason, the House report recommended various reductions below the requested amount. In addition, based on projected under-execution of funds for personnel, the House bill included the following rescissions of FY2015 appropriated funds: $30 million from aviation security; $22 million from surface transportation security; $8 million from intelligence and vetting; and $26 million from transportation security support. The Senate bill would rescind $28 million from FY2015 aviation security funding and $5 million from unobligated prior year balances for surface transportation.

The House and Senate bills both contain DHS-wide language that would place restrictions and conditions on the reprogramming of funds.[49]

Consolidation of Vetting Functions and Databases

The budget request specified almost $43 million for funding of Technology Infrastructure Modernization (TIM), an ongoing multiyear major acquisition project to consolidate the various vetting systems. TSA reported that TIM achieved initial operating capability in FY2014, initially integrating almost 2 million TWIC records. Additional integration is planned through FY2018, resulting in all vetting activities being integrated into TIM, creating a repository of more than 14 million records. The system proposes to incorporate a new standardized vetting, adjudication, and redress rule that is currently being reviewed by the administration and will interact with other DHS and Department of Justice databases to improve access to identification information, criminal records, and terrorist threat data. While TIM endeavors to improve vetting across a broad array of transportation credentialing and threat assessment programs, its size and complexity makes it a challenging and costly undertaking. While TIM development has progressed over the past four years, it is roughly three years behind schedule based on stated objectives in the FY2012 request to have the system fully functional by FY2015, a milestone that TSA now projects will be met in FY2018.

The House committee report expressed concern that unanticipated schedule delays and cost escalation have resulted in TSA scaling back the functionality and capabilities originally envisioned for TIM. The report asked for a briefing from TSA detailing its revised plans, an updated schedule, lifecycle cost estimates, and a description of the functionality of the end-state system envisioned under the TIM program.

U.S. COAST GUARD[50]

The Coast Guard is the lead federal agency for the maritime component of homeland security. As such, it is the lead agency responsible for the security of U.S. ports, coastal and inland waterways, and territorial waters. The Coast Guard also performs missions that are not related to homeland security, such as maritime search and rescue, marine environmental protection, fisheries enforcement, and aids to navigation.

FY2016 Request

The President requested $8,151 million in discretionary appropriations for the Coast Guard, $227 million (2.7%) less than enacted for FY2015. The request includes $6,823 million for operating expenses ($221 million, or 3.1%, below FY2015)[51] and $1,017 million for acquisition, construction, and improvements ($208 million, or 17.0%, below FY2015).

Senate-Reported S. 1619

The Senate Appropriations Committee recommended $8,721 million for the Coast Guard, $570 million (7%) more than the President requested. The Senate reported bill includes $6,996 million for operating expenses ($174 million, or 2.5% above the request)—including $160 million in overseas contingency operations funding. It also included $1,573 million for acquisition, construction and improvements ($556 million, or 54.7%, above the request). This additional funding is driven by a $640 million recommendation to fund acquiring a ninth national security cutter.

House-Reported H.R. 3128

The House Appropriations Committee recommended $8,512 million for the Coast Guard, $361 million (4.4%) more than the President requested. The

House-reported bill includes $6,899 million for operating expenses, $77 million (1.1%) more than the President requested.[52] It also included $1,301 million for acquisition, construction, and improvements ($284 million, or 27.9%, more than the request)—including $95 million above the request to acquire an additional long-range surveillance aircraft, $71 million above the request to accelerate acquisition of an offshore patrol cutter, and $83 million above the request—nearly triple the President's proposal—to improve certain Coast Guard facilities, including housing and aids to navigation.

Table 6. Coast Guard Operating (OE) and Acquisition (ACI) Sub-Account Detail, FY2015-FY2016
(budget authority in rounded millions of dollars)

	FY2015	FY2016		
Appropriation / Sub-Appropriation	**Enacted**	**Request**	**Senate-reported S. 1619**	**House-reported H.R. 3128**
Operating Expenses	**7,043**	**6,823**	**6,996**	**6,899**
Military pay and allowances	3,450	3,466	3,480	3,487
Civilian pay and benefits	782	800	793	793
Training and recruiting	198	206	206	206
Operating funds and unit level maintenance	1,009	1,010	1,013	1,019
Centrally managed accounts	336	330	330	330
Intermediate and depot level maintenance	1,057	1,010	1,015	1,065
OCO / GWOT	213	—a	160	—
Tricare (Legislative Proposal)	—	1	—	—
Acquisition, Construction, and Improvements	**1,225**	**1,017**	**1,573**	**1,301**
Vessels	**824**	**534**	**1,070**	**616**
Aircraft	**180**	**200**	**200**	**295**
Other Acquisition Programs	**59**	**65**	**65**	**68**
Shore Facilities and Aids to Navigation	**41**	**101**	**121**	**184**
Military Housing	**6**	**—**	**—**	**21**
Personnel and Related Support	**115**	**117**	**117**	**117**

Source: CRS analysis of P.L. 114-4 and its explanatory statement as printed in the *Congressional Record* of January 13, 2015, pp. H275-H322, the FY2016 DHS *Budget-in-Brief*, S. 1619, S.Rept. 114-68, H.R. 3128, and H.Rept. 114-215.

Notes: Table displays rounded numbers, but all operations were performed with unrounded data: therefore, amounts may not sum to totals.

[a] The Administration requested a transfer of $160 million from Navy Operations and Maintenance for USCG support of Operation Enduring Freedom.

Issues for Congress

Vessels and Aircraft

As has been the case in recent years, there are significant differences among proposed budgets in the number of new vessels and aircraft that the Coast Guard would procure during the 2016 fiscal year. The Senate recommends that the Coast Guard procure a ninth national security cutter (NSC) and thus recommends several hundred million dollars more than the President requested for the NSC acquisition program. The original plan was to acquire eight national security cutters and the House report states that "funding for additional NSCs beyond the program of record would be neither operationally necessary nor warranted, would create potentially unsustainable operational funding requirements in the future, and could potentially threaten funding for other Coast Guard acquisition priorities."[53] There are also significant differences in recommended funds for the Offshore Patrol Cutter and Fast Response Cutters.

The House recommends $95 million more than requested to procure a thirteenth HC-130J long range surveillance aircraft. The Senate agrees with the President's requested amount.

Also under the acquisition, construction, and improvements account, the House recommends $83 million more than requested for certain Coast Guard shore facilities, including construction of a new ship-lift facility, Coast Guard housing, training centers, and boat piers.

Oil Spill Prevention

As the Commandant noted in his testimony on the FY2016 budget request,[54] the production of shale oil in North Dakota and Texas has significantly changed where and how crude oil is transported on U.S. waterways. This change could have implications for the risk of oil spills. Generally, much less crude oil is now being imported by tanker ships while much more is being transported domestically by barge. For instance, from 2011 to 2014, tons of petroleum transported on the nation's inland waterways increased 26%, and for the first five months of 2015, it increased another 3% compared to the first five months of 2014.[55] Petroleum has now surpassed coal as the leading commodity (measured in tons) transported on U.S. inland waterways. According to oil spill data compiled by the Coast Guard,[56] from 1995 to 2011 (latest year available), barges spilled about 2.7 times more oil in U.S. waters than did tanker ships. (Over this time frame, the number of oil spill incidents and the amount spilled annually have declined significantly for both barges and tankers.)[57]

In view of the significant increase in the movement of crude oil by barge, the Coast Guard is in the process of finalizing a new safety inspection regime for barges that Congress called for in 2004 (the Coast Guard and Maritime Transportation Act of 2004, P.L. 108-293, Section 415). This includes establishing structural standards for vessels as well as standards for the number and qualifications of crew members. Section 409 of the 2004 Act also authorized the Coast Guard to evaluate an hours-of-service limit for crews on tugs that push barge tows. Congress has been concerned with the pace at which the Coast Guard is carrying out the directive on towing vessels. In the Coast Guard authorization Act of 2010 (P.L. 111-281, Section 701), Congress requested that all rulemakings related to oil pollution prevention, including towing vessel inspection, be finalized within 18 months of enactment (April 2012), but this deadline was not met and some final rules have yet to be issued as of July 2015. According to a barge industry newsletter, the Coast Guard submitted its proposed final rule to DHS for review in April 2015.[58]

In previous appropriations, the Administration has requested and Congress has appropriated additional funds for personnel in the Coast Guard's Marine Safety Office for the purpose of reducing a backlog of rulemakings and strengthening the Coast Guard's safety inspection function.

Emission Control Areas (ECAs)

The United States has established a 200-mile perimeter from its coastlines in which vessels must reduce their emissions while sailing in these waters. To meet a stricter requirement that was triggered on January 1, 2015, ships are switching to cleaner-burning (lower-sulfur) fuel when they reach this zone. The Coast Guard is responsible for enforcing correct fuel use in this zone.

The House Committee Report requested that the Coast Guard provide information on ECA enforcement actions taken since January 1, 2015, as well as the number of reports by vessels that cleaner burning fuel was not available and hence the number of waivers or exemptions granted to vessels.

In addition to this information, Congress may also seek information on the number of vessels that have experienced engine stall-outs when switching to cleaner fuels. Reportedly, ships have experienced loss of propulsion during the switchover as well as subsequently while operating with the cleaner fuel. This is said to be due to "thermal shock"—the cleaner fuel is more viscous than bunker fuel and does not need to be heated before entering the engine.[59] The temperature difference is believed to cause fuel pump seizures and leaks. In

September 2014, the Coast Guard issued a safety alert to vessels off California waters to the potential for loss of propulsion (California regulations for ship emissions predate national requirements).[60] The safety alert states that from June 2013 to June 2014, there were 15 loss of propulsion incidents in California waters related to fuel switching, potentially creating serious safety and environmental protection concerns.

The need to reduce emissions in ECAs has also generated interest in using liquefied natural gas (LNG) as a ship fuel. Some cargo ships serving U.S. non-contiguous trades have converted to LNG. Ferries, cruise ships, and other vessels that sail entirely or mostly in ECA waters also are interested in LNG as fuel. For safety and security reasons, LNG-fueled ships present budget issues for the Coast Guard. The Coast Guard is developing regulations as to the placement of LNG fuel tanks on vessels, the protocol for LNG refueling operations in ports, and spill response requirements.[61]

Electronic Navigation

A primary and resource intensive function of the Coast Guard is installing and maintaining aids to navigation (ATON). This includes buoys, beacons, and other visual aids that mark and guide vessels through waterway channels. There are about 50,000 federally owned visual aids, according to the Coast Guard, and an equal number of non-federal visual aids. Because storms or ice can move buoys out of place and channels can move due to shoaling, the Coast Guard services about 134 buoys and fixed aids to navigation on an average day.[62] Part of the Coast Guard's fleet includes 68 "buoy tenders," which are vessels designed for the proper positioning of channel markers. Mariners continue to rely on these physical visual aids even though their vessels are typically equipped with virtual or electronic aids, such as GPS, AIS (automatic identification system), and electronic charts. These technologies, in essence, allow channel markings to be made known to a vessel operator by electronic transmission (e-navigation), either enhancing or potentially replacing a physical aid to navigation. The increase in size of the largest ships transiting U.S. harbors, as well as a general increase in the number of vessels on many waterways, places a premium on the accuracy of aids to navigation. The Coast Guard has begun testing electronic aids to navigation on the West Coast and Mississippi River.[63]

ATON activities consume about 20% of the Coast Guard's discretionary budget. While e-navigation offers the potential of significant savings in maintaining physical aids to navigation, key questions have yet to be answered. What is the reliability and resiliency of e-navigation? Should e-navigation replace physical aids or merely supplement them? Are they as accessible to recreational craft? Are there cyber-security concerns associated with e-navigation? The Coast Guard's ATON budgetary needs in coming years will depend on the answers to these questions.[64]

The Senate Committee report requests a Coast Guard report on the feasibility and advisability of using e-navigation in U.S. areas of the Arctic Ocean.[65]

Use of Unmanned Aircraft Systems (UAS)

The Coast Guard's FY2016 budget justification indicates that the agency is testing the use of small unmanned aircraft for search and rescue, patrols and general maritime surveillance. The Coast Guard has tested both smaller, hand-held UAS and larger UAS to extend the surveillance range of its patrol vessels. In April 2015, the Coast Guard announced that it would be testing UAS in the Arctic for missions such as surveying ice conditions, marine environmental monitoring, marine safety, and search and rescue.[66] The test unmanned aircraft could be launched from land or a Coast Guard cutter.

The House Committee report recommends an additional $12 million above the President's request for the use of UAS aboard national security cutters.[67] Like e-navigation, greater use of UAS potentially offers significant efficiencies in the vessels, aircraft, and crews needed to perform various Coast Guard missions.

U.S. SECRET SERVICE

The U.S. Secret Service (USSS) has two concurrent missions—criminal investigations and protection of certain people, places, and events. Criminal investigation activities encompass financial crimes, identity theft, counterfeiting, computer fraud, and computer-based attacks on the nation's financial, banking, and telecommunications infrastructure, among other areas. The protection mission entails protecting current and former Presidents, Vice Presidents, their spouses and minor children, as well as distinguished foreign visitors to the United States, and certain other individuals.[68] The USSS also secures the White House, Vice President's residence and foreign missions in the District of Columbia, and coordinates security for National Special Security Events.[69]

FY2016 Request

The FY2016 appropriations request for the Secret Service was $1,939 million, a net increase of $273 million (16.4%) above the FY2015 enacted level. This increase was largely driven by a $300 million increase in funding designated for the USSS protection mission, including $117 million more for protection of persons and facilities, and $178 million more to ramp up operations in preparation for protection of Presidential candidates and nominees.

Part of the basis for this increase was the report of the USSS Protective Mission Panel, which was established in October 2014 to review the security of the White House complex after several high-profile incidents. The response to that report's findings through appropriations legislation is discussed below.

Senate-Reported S. 1619

Senate-reported S. 1619 included $1,924 million for the USSS, $15 million (0.8%) below the requested level, but $258 million (15.5%) above the amount appropriated in FY2015. The Senate Appropriations Committee recommended $37 million (3.6%) less than requested for protection of persons and facilities, but still proposed funding that was $80 million (8.9%) higher than FY2015. The Senate Appropriations Committee recommended fully funding the request for protection of Presidential candidates and nominees.

House-Reported H.R. 3128

House-reported H.R. 3128 included $1,906 million for the USSS, $33 million (1.7%) below the requested level, but $240 million (14.4%) above the amount appropriated in FY2015. The House Appropriations Committee recommended $33 million (3.2%) less than requested for protection of persons and facilities, slightly more than the Senate Appropriations Committee, and $84 million (9.4%) higher than FY2015. Like the Senate Appropriations Committee, the House Appropriations Committee recommended fully funding the request for protection of Presidential candidates and nominees.

Table 7. Budget Authority for the U.S. Secret Service, FY2015-FY2016 (budget authority in rounded millions of dollars)

	FY2015	**FY2016**		
Appropriation / Sub-Appropriation	**Enacted**	**Request**	**Senate-reported S. 1619**	**House-reported H.R. 3128**
Salaries and Expenses	**1,616**	**1,867**	**1,837**	**1,833**
Protection	990	1,290	1,252	1,248
Protection of persons and facilities	*893*	*1,009*	*972*	*977*
Protective intelligence activities	*68*	*73*	*72*	*64*
National Special Security Events	*5*	*5*	*5*	*5*
Presidential candidate nominee protection	*26*	*204*	*204*	*204*
Investigations	381	325	337	336
Domestic field operations	*338*	*291*	*295*	*295*
International Field Office Administration, Operations and Training	*34*	*34*	*34*	*33*
Forensic Support to the National Center for Missing and Exploited Children	*8*	—	*8*	*8*
Headquarters, Management and Administration	188	195	192	193
Information Integration and Technology Transformation	1	1	1	1
James J. Rowley Training Center	55	56	55	54
Acquisition, Construction, and Improvements	**50**	**72**	**86**	**73**
Facilities	5	26	26	29
Next Generation Limo	—	—	—	9
Information Integration and Technology Transformation	45	45	61	35
Total	**1,666**	**1,939**	**1,924**	**1,906**

Sources: CRS analysis of P.L. 114-4 and its explanatory statement as printed in the *Congressional Record* of January 13, 2015, pp. H275-H322, the FY2016 DHS *Budget-in-Brief,* S. 1619, S.Rept. 114-68, H.R. 3128, and H.Rept. 114-215.

Note: Table displays rounded numbers, but all operations were performed with unrounded data: therefore, amounts may not sum to totals.

Issues for Congress

Protective Mission Panel Recommendations

The USSS Protective Mission Panel was established in October, 2014 to make recommendations on upgrading security White House complex. The executive summary to the report, released in December 2014, included a series of recommendations that fell within three general areas: training and personnel; perimeter security, technology and operations; and leadership. However, not all of the panel's recommendations were released publicly—several in the "perimeter security, technology and operations" category were classified.[70] An additional $25 million, representing initial funding for some of the panel's recommendations, was included in the FY2015 DHS Appropriations Act (P.L. 114-4), including funding to upgrade security infrastructure at the White House complex and Vice President's Residence.[71]

$87 million in additional investments were proposed by the Administration, including $66 million in salaries and expenses and $21 million in acquisition funding to support the training facility of the USSS—the James J. Rowley Training Center. The request for acquisition funds included $8 million for a scale mock-up of the White House grounds, $8 million to renovate or replace the existing canine training facility, and $5 million to renovate shooting ranges and tactical training areas.

While the Senate Appropriations Committee also recommended providing the funding level requested for Rowley Training Center improvements, in its report it described the cost estimates for the canine training facility and White House mock-up as "inaccurate," and recommended $13 million for construction of a new canine training facility, and less than $1 million for a feasibility study and design plan for the White House mock-up. Full funding was recommended for the range and tactical area renovations, and the remainder of the funding provided—slightly more than $2 million—was to be applied to deferred maintenance needs at the training center.[72]

The House Appropriations Committee recommended $29 million in facilities funding, $3 million more than requested. Like the Senate Appropriations Committee, it proposed a different allocation of the budget authority between projects than had been requested. Like the Senate Appropriations Committee, the House Appropriations Committee recommended $13 million for the new canine facility construction, full funding for ranges and tactical training area upgrades, and funding to address backlogged maintenance. Almost $3 million was recommended for the White House mock-up, but the House-reported bill withholds over $2 million of those funds from obligation until a feasibility study and design plan are completed and approved by the National Capital Planning Commission. The House committee also required a detailed obligation plan for the facilities funding before it could be used.[73]

End Notes

[1] U.S. Government Accountability Office, *A Glossary of Terms Used in the Federal Budget Process*, GAO-05-734SP, September 1, 2005, http://www.gao.gov/products/GAO-05-734SP.

[2] On April 14, 2016, the Administration submitted technical amendments to its budget request, but it presented no adjustments to its totals for the department. Therefore, modifications to authorization for Customs and Border Protection to use certain fee revenues are not reflected in this report.

[3] Generally speaking, those provided through annual legislation.

[4] A detailed analysis of this breakdown between discretionary appropriations and other funding is available in CRS Report R44052, *DHS Budget v. DHS Appropriations: Fact Sheet.*

[5] Although the House and Senate generally produce symmetrically structured bills, this is not always the case. Additional titles are sometimes added by one of the chambers to address special issues. For example, the FY2012 House full committee markup added a sixth title to carry a $1 billion emergency appropriation for the Disaster Relief Fund (DRF). The Senate version carried no additional titles beyond the five described above. For FY2015, the House- and Senate-reported versions of the DHS appropriations bill were generally symmetrical.

[6] In addition to the appropriations provided in Title II, under the request, U.S. Customs and Border Protection would receive $180 million in budget authority from a general provision that grants them the authority to expend fees raised under the Colombia Free Trade Act. Other resources that contribute to the budget for these components include mandatory spending, fee revenues, and trust funds.

[7] Prepared by Lisa Seghetti, Section Research Manager, Domestic Social Policy Division.

[8] In addition to the appropriations traditionally carried in Title II for CBP, authorization to use fees collected under section 601(b) of the United States-Colombia Trade Promotion Agreement Implementation Act (P.L. 112-42) was also requested, which CBO estimated would provide $180 million in additional budget authority.

[9] N II equipment includes x-ray and gamma ray imaging systems and related technologies. NII scanning produces a high-resolution image of container contents that is reviewed by law enforcement officers to detect hidden cargo and other anomalies that suggest container contents do not match reported manifest data. If an officer detects an abnormality, containers may be "cracked open" for a physical examination. For a fuller discussion, see CRS Report R43014, *U.S. Customs and Border Protection: Trade Facilitation, Enforcement, and Security*, by V ivian C. Jones and Lisa Seghetti.

[10] In addition to the appropriations traditionally carried in Title II for CBP, this total includes authorization provided in Title V to use fees collected under section 601(b) of the United States-Colombia Trade Promotion Agreement Implementation Act (P.L . 112-42), which CBO estimated would provide $180 million in additional budget authority.

[11] Rept. 114-68, p. 33.

[12] In addition to the appropriations traditionally carried in Title II for CBP, this total includes authorization provided in Title V to use fees collected under section 601(b) of the United States-Colombia Trade Promotion Agreement Implementation Act (P.L. 112-42), which CBO estimated would provide $180 million in additional budget authority.

[13] This subaccount is located in the Headquarters, Management and Administration account and is not reflected in Table 2.

[14] H.Rept. 114-215, p. 28.

[15] Further discussion of pay issues is included in CRS Report R44053, *Department of Homeland Security Appropriations: FY2016*, coordinated by William L. Painter.

[16] H.Rept. 114-215, p. 29.

[17] H.Rept. 114-215, p. 31.

[18] For budgetary purposes, OMB scored this provision as costing $24 million, while CBO scored it using a different methodology at $79 million.

[19] The number of Border Patrol agents grew from 11,264 in FY2005 to 21,408 in FY2011, before falling back to 21,388 in FY2012 and 21,370 in FY2013.

[20] The Administration will seek the appropriate authorizing Congressional committees to advance its legislative proposals.

[21] IUF collects fees from arriving individuals for the costs of inspections activities at airports and sea ports. 8 U.S.C. 1356(h).

[22] Exempt regions include the United States and its territories.

[23] The Administration will seek the appropriate authorizing Congressional committees to advance its legislative proposals.

[24] CBP collects several different types of customs-related user fees, including fees paid by passengers and by cargo carriers and importers for the provision of customs services. These fees are often referred to as COBRA fees because they were passed as part of the Consolidated Omnibus Budget Reconciliation Act of 1986 (COBRA, P.L. 99-272). Under 19 U.S.C. 58c(f)(1)-(3), a portion of these fees directly reimburses CBP for certain customs functions, including overtime compensation and certain benefits and premium pay for CBP officers, certain preclearance services, foreign language proficiency awards, and—to the extent funds remain available—certain officer salaries. Another portion of COBRA fees—merchandise processing fees—is deposited in CBP's Customs User Fee Account to pay for additional customs revenue functions but is only available to the extent provided for in appropriations acts.

[25] ECCF fees reimburses CBP for the costs associated with express clearance of goods.

[26] See S.Rept. 114-68, section 547 and H.R. 3128, section 559.

[27] See for example, Letter from Hon. Michael McCaul, Hon. Bennie Thompson, Hon. Bill Shuster, et al. to Janet Napolitano, Secretary of Homeland Security, April 18, 2013; and U.S. Congress, House Committee on Foreign Affairs, Subcommittee on Terrorism, Nonproliferation, and Trade, *The Abu Dhabi Pre-Clearance Facility: Implications for U.S. Business and National Security*, 113th Cong., 1st sess., July 10, 2013.

[28] See section 555 of P.L. 114-4 and section 564 of P.L. 113-76.

[29] See section 551 of S. 1619 and section 548 of H.R. 3128.

[30] Prepared by Alison Siskin, Specialist in Immigration Policy, Domestic Social Policy Division.

[31] On average the average daily rate an adult bed is $123.54, while the average daily rate for a family bed is $342.73. FY2016 *DHS Congressional Budget Justifications*.

[32] See Explanatory Statement Submitted By Mr. Rogers of Kentucky, Chairman of the House Committee on Appropriations Regarding the House Amendment to the Senate Amendment

on H.R. 83, *Congressional Record*, daily edition, vol. 160, part 151 (December 11, 2014), p. H9345.

[33] S.Rept. 114-68 reported that the funding increases the number of attorneys by 150, while H.Rept. 114-68 stated that the amount "funds the agency's request to hire 311 additional attorneys.... "

[34] For a discussion of the issue of unaccompanied alien children, see CRS Report R43599, *Unaccompanied Alien Children: An Overview*, by William A. Kandel and Lisa Seghetti.

[35] For budgetary purposes, OMB scored this provision as costing $3 million, while CBO scored it using a different methodology at $8 million.

[36] Department of Homeland Security, *Teleconference Recap: A Conversation with U.S. Immigration and Customs Enforcement (ICE) Public Advocate*, Washington, DC, March 28, 2012, http://www.dhs.gov/teleconference-recapconversation-us-immigration-and-customs-enforcement-ice-public-advocate.

[37] See, for example, Stephen Dinan, "Senate Democrats Join Push to Cut Obama's Illegal Immigrant Advocate," *The Washington Times*, March 12, 2013, http://www.washingtontimes.com/news/2013/mar/12/senate-spending-billincludes-elimination-of-new-i/?page=all.

[38] See U.S. Congress, House Committee on the Judiciary, *Enforcing the President's Constitutional Duty to Faithfully Execute the Laws*, Testimony Of Representative Diane Black, 113th Cong., 2nd sess., February 26, 2014.

[39] Prepared by Bart Elias, Specialist in Aviation Policy, Resources, Science, and Industry Division.

[40] See P.L. 113-76.

[41] Department of Homeland Security, Office of Inspector General, *Security Enhancements Needed to the Pre-Check Initative (Unclassified Summary)*, January 28, 2015.

[42] Department of Homeland Security, Office of Inspector General, *Allegation of Granting Expedited ScreeningThrough TSA Pre-Check Improperly (OSC File No. DI-14-3679) (Redacted)*, March 16, 2015.

[43] S.Rept. 114-68, p. 65.

[44] H.Rept. 114-215, p. 49.

[45] Department of Homeland Security, Office of Inspector General, *TSA Can Improve Aviation Worker Vetting (Redacted)*, June 4, 2015.

[46] Aviation Security Advisory Committee, *Final Report of the Aviation Security Advisory Committee's Working Group on Airport Access Control*, April 8, 2015, https://www.tsa.gov/sites/default/files/assets/pdf/Intermodal/asac_employee_screening_wg_final_report_8apr15.pdf.

[47] S.Rept. 114-66-67.

[48] H.Rept. 114-215.

[49] See H.R. 3128, Sec. 503 and S. 1619 Sec. 503.

[50] Prepared by John Frittelli, Specialist in Transportation Policy, Resources, Science, and Industry Division.

[51] The Administration did not include overseas contingency operations funding for the Coast Guard in the DHS appropriations request, instead seeking $160 million by transfer from the Navy, which is not included in this total.

[52] Like the request, the House-passed FY2016 appropriations bill for the Department of Defense includes a $160 million transfer of overseas contingency operations funding from the Navy to the Coast Guard.

[53] H.Rept. 114-215, p. 59.

[54] Testimony of Paul F. Zukunft, Commandant U.S. Coast Guard, House Coast Guard and Maritime Transportation Subcommittee, Coast Guard FY2016 Budget Request, February 25, 2015, p. 2.

[55] Army Corps of Engineers, Navigation Data Center, Internal U.S. Waterway Monthly Indicators; http://www.navigationdatacenter.us/wcsc/wcsc.htm.

[56] U.S. Coast Guard, Polluting Incidents In and Around U.S. Waters, A Spill/Release Compendium: 1969-2011 (Washington, DC: January 2013); http://homeport.uscg.mil/.

[57] For further information, see CRS Report R43653, *Shipping U.S. Crude Oil by Water: Vessel Flag Requirements and Safety Issues*, by John Frittelli.

[58] See *AWO Letter*, June 12, 2015, http://awo.informz.net/informzdataservice/onlineversion/ind/bWFpbGluZ2luc3RhbmNlaWQ9NDQxOTgxMyZzdWJzY3JpYmVyaWQ9ODQ2NzA0NzEw.

[59] Ship and Bunker, "Fuel Switching-Related Power Losses Persist in ECAs," March 30, 2015; Bunkerworld, "Surge In Engine Blackouts Feared at ECA Borders in 2015," September 22, 2014.

[60] U.S. Coast Guard, *Marine Safety Information Bulletin 14-01*, September 9, 2014; http://www.mxsocal.org/pdffiles/D11-MSIB-14-01_LossOfPropulsion-FuelSwitching Safety_ 9SEP14%20 (3).pdf.

[61] In February 2015, the Coast Guard issued interim guidelines for LNG bunkering operations; http://www.regulations.gov/#!documentDetail;D=USCG-2013-1084-0031.

[62] Coast Guard 2016 Budget in Brief; http://www.uscg.mil/budget/docs/2016_Budget_in_Brief.pdf.

[63] *Professional Mariner*, "U.S. Coast Guard Begins Testing Synthetic Aids, Virtual Buoys," August 2014.

[64] For further information on developments in navigation technology, see *Coast Guard Proceedings*, Summer 2015 issue; http://www.uscg.mil/proceedings/archive/2015/Vol72_No2_Sum2015.pdf.

[65] S.Rept. 114-68, p. 76.

[66] 80 *Federal Register* 18431, April 6, 2015.

[67] H.Rept. 114-215, p. 59.

[68] The scope of Secret Service protectees is defined in 18 U.S.C. 3056.

[69] For more information, see CRS Report RL34603, *The U.S. Secret Service: History and Missions*, by Shawn Reese.

[70] Joseph Hagin, Thomas Perrelli, and Danielle Gray, et al., Executive Summary to Report from the from the United States Secret Service Protective Mission Panel to the Secretary of Homeland Security, Unites States Secret Service Protective Mission Panel, Washington, DC, December 15, 2014, p. 7, http://www.dhs.gov/publication/executivesummary-report-usss-protective-mission-panel.

[71] "Explanatory Statement Submitted by Mr. Rogers of Kentucky, Chairman of the House Committee on Appropriations, Regarding H.R. 240," *Congressional Record*, January 13, 2015, p. H284.

[72] S.Rept. 114-68, pp. 89-90.

[73] H.Rept. 114-215, pp. 66-67.

In: Homeland Security
Editor: Malcolm Leonard Moreno
ISBN: 978-1-63484-754-4

Chapter 4

COMPARING DHS APPROPRIATIONS BY COMPONENT, FY2016: FACT SHEET*

William L. Painter

Generally, the homeland security appropriations bill includes all annual appropriations for the Department of Homeland Security (DHS), providing resources to every departmental component. *Table 1* and *Figure 1* show DHS's new discretionary budget authority enacted for FY2015 and requested by the Administration for FY2016, as well as the funding levels provided in the Senate-reported and House-reported homeland security appropriations bills broken down by component—from largest to smallest appropriations request.

Total discretionary appropriations (as opposed to mandatory appropriations or other revenue available without annual congressional action) in *Table 1* do not include resources provided through adjustments under the Budget Control Act (BCA)[1] in the individual component lines. These are accounted for separately from the total discretionary appropriations and are displayed at the bottom of the table. As the table and figure reflect new discretionary budget authority, neither appropriated mandatory spending nor rescissions of prior-year budget authority are reflected in the component totals.

---

* This is an edited, reformatted and augmented version of a Congressional Research Service publication R44051, prepared for Members and Committees of Congress, dated August 6, 2015.

Table 1. DHS Appropriations by Component, FY2015 and FY2016 (in millions of dollars of discretionary budget authority, rounded)

Component	FY2015 Enacted	FY2016 Request	Senate-Reported S. 1619	House-Reported H.R. 3128
Customs and Border Protection (CBP)	$10,837	$11,643	$11,304	$11,296
U.S. Coast Guard (USCG)	8,378[a]	8,151[b]	8,721[c]	8,512
Immigration and Customs Enforcement (ICE)	5,959	5,965	5,815	5,815
Transportation Security Administration (TSA)	4,834	4,783	4,719	4,653
Federal Emergency Management Agency (FEMA)	4,347[d]	4,462[e]	4,554[e]	4,436[e]
U.S. Secret Service (USSS)	1,666	1,939	1,924	1,906
National Protection and Programs Directorate (NPPD)	1,502	1,659	1,638	1,585
Departmental Management	743	961	924	787
Science & Technology Directorate (S&T)	1,104	779	765	787
Domestic Nuclear Detection Office (DNDO)	308	357	320	357
Analysis & Operations (A&O)	256	269	263	265
Federal Law Enforcement Training Center (FLETC)	258	267	246	239
Office of the Inspector General (OIG)	119	142	134	141
U.S. Citizenship and Immigration Services (USCIS)	124	151	120	120
Office of Health Affairs (OHA)	129	124	123	125
Total Discretionary Appropriations without Rescissions	*$40,565*	*$41,653*	*$41,572*	*$41,024*
Adjustments under the Budget Control Act	6,651	6,713	6,873	6,713
Total New Discretionary Budget Authority	$47,215	$48,366	$48,445	$47,737
General Provisions: Rescissions (not reflected above or visually in figure)	*-894*	*-255*	*-1,359*	*-1,692*
Total Net Discretionary Appropriations	$39,670	$41,398	$40,213	$39,332

Source: Congressional Research Service (CRS) analysis of P.L. 114-4 and its explanatory statement as printed in the Congressional Record of January 13, 2015, pp. H275-H322, the FY2016 DHS Budget-in-Brief, S. 1619, S.Rept. 114-68, H.R. 3128 and H.Rept. 114-215.

Notes: Table does not reflect non-appropriated resources available to DHS components.

[a] $213 million in FY2015 funding for overseas contingency operations for the Coast Guard under an adjustment to the discretionary spending limits is not shown in this table entry, but is reflected in Figure 1.

[b] $160 million in proposed FY2016 funding for overseas contingency operations for the Coast Guard under an adjustment to the discretionary spending limits to be provided as a transfer from the Navy is not shown in this table entry.

[c] $160 million in proposed FY2016 funding for overseas contingency operations in the Senate-reported DHS appropriations bill for the Coast Guard under an adjustment to the discretionary spending limits is not shown in this table entry, but is reflected in Figure 1.

[d] $6,438 million in FY2015 funding for disaster relief costs provided through FEMA's Disaster Relief Fund under an adjustment to the discretionary spending limits is not shown in this table entry, but is reflected in Figure 1.

[e] $6,713 million in proposed FY2016 funding for disaster relief costs provided through FEMA's Disaster Relief Fund under an adjustment to the discretionary spending limits is not shown in this table entry, but is reflected in Figure 1.

In *Figure 1*, the first column of numbers shows budget authority provided in P.L. 114-4, which included the FY2015 annual appropriations for DHS: resources available under the adjustments to the discretionary spending limits provided pursuant to the BCA are shown in black. The second column shows a similar breakdown for the FY2016 request, while the third and fourth show the Senate-reported and House-reported proposed funding levels.

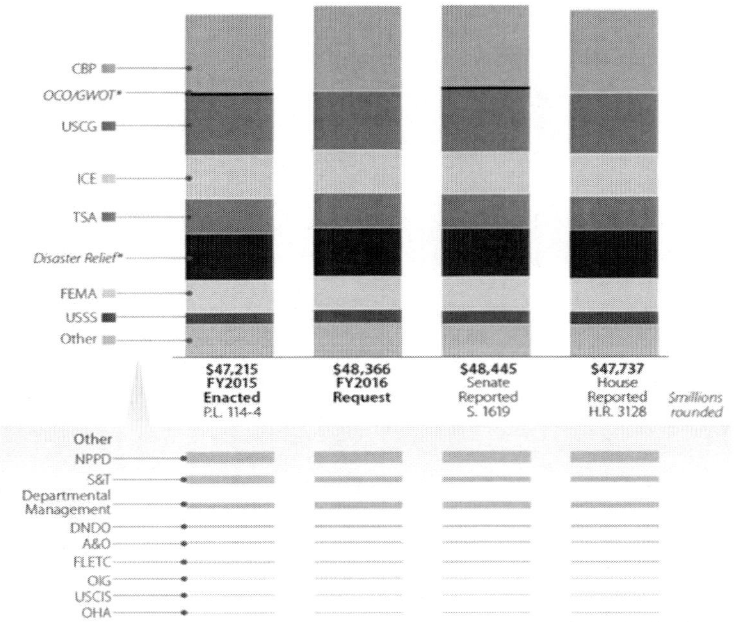

Source: CRS analysis of P.L. 114-4 and its explanatory statement as printed in the Congressional Record of January 13, 2015, pp. H275-H322, the FY2016 DHS Budget-in-Brief, S. 1619, S.Rept. 114-68, H.R. 3218 and H.Rept. 114-215.

Chart Abbreviations: CBP, Customs and Border Protection; OCO/GWOT, Overseas Contingency Operations/Global War on Terror; USCG, U.S. Coast Guard; ICE, Immigration and Customs Enforcement; TSA, Transportation Security Administration; FEMA, Federal Emergency Management Administration; USSS, U.S. Secret Service; NPPD, National Protection and Programs Directorate; S&T, Science and Technology Directorate; DNDO, Domestic Nuclear Detection Office; A&O, Analysis and Operations; FLETC, Federal Law Enforcement Training Center; OIG, Office of the Inspector General; USCIS, U.S. Citizenship and Immigration Services; OHA, Office of Health Affairs.

Note: For underlying data and notes on data, see Table 1.

* Covered by an adjustment under the Budget Control Act (P.L. 112-25).

Figure 1. Department of Homeland Security Appropriations by Component, FY2015 and FY2016.

End Note

[1] P.L. 112-25.

INDEX

B

C

D

E

F

G

H

I

J

K

L

M

N

Q

R

S

T

U

V

W

Y